3,285 BIBLE QUESTIONS & ANSWERS

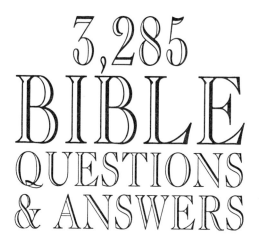

To
Jane Hudson
a dear friend, loving critic,
prejudiced supporter, and
prayerful partner.

∽

To my mother Annie,
My sister Adele Flood,
My brothers Eugene and Clarence,
their families,
and my aunt, Ella Cathey,
Who have all loved me
and given me many happy memories,
I dedicate this book.

∽

To
Ethel Knight—
a dear friend
who has rejoiced
in my accomplishments and
supported my writing endeavors.

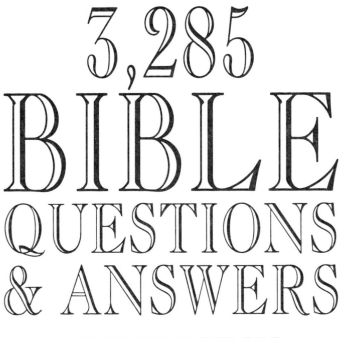

3,285 BIBLE QUESTIONS & ANSWERS

BY EMILY FILIPI

Originally published in three
separate volumes under the titles:

100 Word Puzzles on the Bible
101 Word Puzzles on the Bible
102 Word Puzzles on the Bible

WINGS BOOKS
New York • Avenel, New Jersey

This omnibus was originally published in separate volumes under the titles:
100 Word Puzzles on the Bible, copyright © 1982 by Broadman Press
101 Word Puzzles on the Bible, copyright © 1985 by Broadman Press
102 Word Puzzles on the Bible, copyright © 1988 by Broadman Press

This edition contains the complete and unabridged texts of the original editions. They have been completely reset for this volume.

This 1994 edition is published by Wings Books,
distributed by Random House Value Publishing, Inc.,
40 Engelhard Avenue, Avenel, New Jersey 07001,
by arrangement with The Sunday School Board of the
Southern Baptist Convention d/b/a Broadman Press.

Random House
New York • Toronto • London • Sydney • Auckland

Printed and bound in the United States of America

Library of Congress Cataloging-in-Publication Data

Filipi, Emily, 1932-
    3,285 Bible questions and answers / by Emily Filipi.
        p. cm.
    ISBN 0-517-02748-8
    1. Bible—Miscellanea. I. Title. II. Title: Three thousand
    two hundred eighty-five Bible questions and answers.
    BS612.F48   1990
    220—dc20   90-35302
                                                              CIP

10 9 8 7 6 5 4

QUESTIONS

1
Alike

The following people shared something alike. Match the persons with the thing they had alike.

1. Nebuchadnezzar and Aaron
   Daniel 3:1; Exodus 32:4
2. Jesus and Jonah
   Matthew 8:26; Jonah 1:15
3. Miriam and Naaman
   Numbers 12:10; 2 Kings 5:27
4. Daniel and Joseph
   Daniel 2:25 *ff.*; Genesis 41:25 *ff.*
5. Joseph and Zechariah
   Matthew 1:20; Luke 1:13
6. John the Baptist and Paul
   Mark 6:18; Acts 25:26
7. Jesus and Joseph
   Matthew 27:9; Genesis 37:28
8. Naboth and Jesus
   1 Kings 21:9-10; Mark 14:56
9. Judas and Joab
   Mark 14:44-45; 2 Samuel 20:9-10
10. Jesus and Micaiah
    Matthew 26:67; 1 Kings 22:24
11. Joseph and prodigal son
    Genesis 44:27-28; Luke 15:20

a. witnessed to kings
b. longed for by father
c. received a slap
d. built golden images
e. had leprosy
f. gave death kiss
g. stopped a storm
h. angels told of birth of a son
i. interpreted dreams
j. accused by false witnesses
k. sold for silver

2
Animals

Animals play an important role in the life of humanity. Match each statement with the correct animal.

1. Egypt was plagued with this amphibian
2. Spoke to its rider
3. Carried away sins on Day of Atonement
4. Licked the sores of Lazarus
5. Samson killed one with his hands
6. A pharaoh dreamed of fourteen
7. Transported Isaac's bride
8. Sacrificed as an offering by Abraham
9. Cannot change its spots
10. Tended by David for his father

a. kine, Genesis 41:18
b. sheep, 1 Samuel 17:34
c. ram, Genesis 22:13
d. lion, Judges 14:5-6
e. camel, Genesis 24:64
f. dogs, Luke 16:21
g. leopard, Jeremiah 13:23
h. frog, Exodus 8:6
i. goat, Leviticus 16:21
j. ass, Numbers 22:30

3
Assassinations

Each of these people were assassinated. Match the killer(s) with the victim.

1. Joab, 2 Samuel 18:14
2. Cain, Genesis 4:8
3. Herod, Matthew 14:6-10
4. Jehu, 2 Kings 9:30-33
5. Jael, Judges 4:21-22
6. Pekah, 2 Kings 15:23-25
7. Jehoiada, 2 Kings 11:15-16
8. Jozacar and Jehozabad, 2 Kings 12:20-21
9. Menahem, 2 Kings 15:14

a. John the Baptist
b. Abel
c. Pekahiah
d. Jezebel
e. Absalom
f. Sisera
g. Shallum
h. Athaliah
i. Joash

4
Associations

Match the person with the item associated with him or her.

1. Pottage
2. Plumbline
3. Harp
4. Ark
5. Axe head
6. Burning bush
7. Rib
8. Salt
9. Big fish
10. Frogs
11. Crumbs

a. Elisha, 2 Kings 6:1-6
b. Lazarus, Luke 16:20-21
c. Lot's wife, Genesis 19:26
d. Esau, Genesis 25:30
e. Moses, Exodus 3:3-4
f. Pharaoh, Exodus 8:2,6
g. Amos, Amos 7:7-8
h. Noah, Genesis 6:14
i. David, 1 Samuel 16:23
j. Jonah, Jonah 1:17
k. Eve, Genesis 2:21-22

5
Belongings

Match each of the following people with his or her belonging.

1. Joseph, Genesis 44:2
2. Jesus, John 19:23
3. Mary, John 12:3
4. Abraham, Genesis 22:6
5. Prodigal son, Luke 15:22
6. Solomon, 1 Kings 10:21
7. Jonathan, 1 Samuel 18:4
8. David, 1 Samuel 21:8-9
9. Paul, 2 Timothy 4:13
10. Dorcas, Acts 9:39

a. Spikenard
b. Silver cup
c. Seamless coat
d. Ring
e. Knife
f. Gold drinking vessel
g. Handmade coats
h. Cloak, books, and parchments
i. Sword, bow, and girdle
j. Goliath's sword

6
The Birth of Jesus

Each of the following people or groups had something to do with the story of the birth of Jesus. Match the people with the statement concerning them.

1. Caesar Augustus, Luke 2:1
2. Joseph, Luke 2:4
3. Mary, Luke 2:5
4. Angel, Luke 2:8-11
5. Shepherds, Luke 2:17
6. Those who heard, Luke 2:18
7. Herod, Matthew 2:7-8
8. Heavenly host, Luke 2:13-14
9. Wise Men, Matthew 2:11
10. God, Matthew 2:12

a. went to see Jesus, then told others about him
b. announced Jesus' birth to shepherds
c. issued a decree
d. went with her husband to Bethlehem
e. went to Bethlehem to be taxed
f. wondered at what they were told
g. said ''glory to God in the highest''
h. presented gifts of gold, frankincense, and myrrh
i. warned the Wise Men of Herod's evil plan
j. pretended to want to worship Jesus

7
Bodies of Water

Water is a major source of recreation for many people today. It is also necessary for human beings to live. Match the bodies of water with the proper statement about water:

1. A blind man washed in this pool and received sight, John 9:6-7.
2. Naaman "dipped" in this river and was healed of leprosy, 2 Kings 5:14.
3. Daniel saw a vision of a ram in this river, Daniel 8:2-3.
4. Ezekiel saw visions of God here, Ezekiel 1:3.
5. Elijah slew the prophets of Baal near this brook, 1 Kings 18:40.
6. Moses led the Israelites through dry land at this sea, Exodus 14:16.
7. Another name for the Sea of Galilee, John 6:1.
8. A river which flows out of Eden, Genesis 2:10-11.
9. The water at this place was bitter, Exodus 15:23.
10. Seraiah was commanded to read a book and cast it into this river, Jeremiah 51:60-63.
11. Jesus taught in a ship in this body of water, Luke 5:1-3.

a. Marah

b. Gennesaret

c. Kishon

d. Tiberias

e. Euphrates

f. Pison

g. Red

h. Siloam

i. Chebar

j. Jordan

k. Ulai

8
Bows and Arrows

Fill in each blank with the person associated with bows and arrows.

1. _____ was an archer, Genesis 16:15; 21:20.
2. _____ was wounded by archers, and he asked his armour-bearer to kill him with a sword, 1 Samuel 31:3-4.
3. _____ shot an arrow to warn David to flee from Saul, 1 Samuel 20:33-42.
4. _____ was hit by an arrow shot at random, and the king died, 1 Kings 22:34.
5. _____ was hit by archers and died in Jerusalem, 2 Chronicles 35:23-24.
6. _____ likened his condition to being compassed round about by archers, Job 16:13.
7. _____ was angry when Joash struck the ground only three times with an arrow, 2 Kings 13:17-19.
8. _____ prophecied that the king of Assyria would not shoot an arrow in Jerusalem, Isaiah 37:33.
9. _____ lamented over Saul and Jonathan and taught the children of Judah to use the bow, 2 Samuel 1:17-18.
10. _____ sent his son with his bow to get venison, Genesis 27:1-3.
11. _____ reminded the people assembled at Shechem that hornets, not bows, had defeated their enemies, Joshua 24:2,12.

9
Chariots

Chariots were often used in biblical days. Fill in each blank with the proper words which refer to each chariot experience.

1. The Ethiopian eunuch was reading _____ as he traveled between Jerusalem and Gaza, Acts 8:27-28.
2. Pharaoh used all the chariots of Egypt to chase the _____, Exodus 14:6-8.
3. _____ saw a chariot of fire before being taken to heaven by a whirlwind, 2 Kings 2:11.
4. God commanded _____ to cripple the horses and burn the chariots of King Jabin of Hazor, Joshua 11:1,6.
5. Pharaoh gave his ring to _____ and made him ride in Pharaoh's second chariot, Genesis 41:41-43.
6. In a war with Israel, the _____ had thirty thousand chariots and six thousand horsemen, 1 Samuel 13:5.
7. When he saw the sword of Barak, _____ got out of his chariot and fled on foot, Judges 4:14-15.
8. Elah, king of Judah, was killed by _____, the captain of half of the king's chariots, 1 Kings 16:8-10.
9. Isaiah rebuked _____ for taking pride in the multitude of his chariots, Isaiah 37:21-24.
10. After he was healed, _____ got out of his chariot when he saw Elisha's servant following him, 2 Kings 5:21.
11. _____ told Solomon that God said to use gold for the pattern of the chariot of the cherubims that spread their wings over the ark of the covenant, 1 Chronicles 28:18-19.

10
Children

Match each child with something connected to his childhood.

1. Moses, Exodus 2:3   a. sacrifice

2. Jesus, Luke 2:7   b. seven sneezes

3. Jacob, Genesis 25:26   c. red hair

4. David, 1 Samuel 17:39-40   d. not a family name

5. Joseph, Genesis 37:3   e. ark (basket)

6. Samuel, 1 Samuel 2:18   f. heel

7. Isaac, Genesis 22:6-13   g. coat of many colors

8. Shunammite's son, 2   h. linen ephod
   Kings 4:35-36
9. John (the Baptist), Luke   i. sling shot
   1:60-61
10. Esau, Genesis 25:25   j. manger

11
Christian Missions

Some of the most thrilling reading for the Christian is the story of the spread of the early church. Fill in each blank with the person or persons responsible for the mission effort.

1. _____ prayed with John that the Samaritans would receive the Holy Spirit, Acts 8:14-15.
2. _____ was sent by God to restore Saul's eye sight, Acts 9:10-12.
3. _____ witnessed to a eunuch in a chariot, Acts 8:26-27.
4. _____ sent Peter to Samaria to check on Philip's work, Acts 8:14.
5. _____ was stoned to death for his faith in Jesus, Acts 7:59.
6. _____ was the prophet the Ethiopian eunuch was reading, Acts 8:30.
7. _____ interceded in behalf of Saul after his conversion, Acts 9:27.
8. _____ caught Philip up, and the eunuch saw him no more, Acts 8:39.
9. _____ was blinded by a light on his way to persecute the Christians, Acts 9:1-3.
10. _____ wanted to buy the power of the Holy Spirit, Acts 8:18-19.

12
The Christmas Story

Fill in each blank with the correct answer about the Christmas story.

1. _____ was the home of Mary and Joseph, Luke 2:4.
2. _____ announced Jesus' birth to Mary, Luke 1:26-27.
3. _____ was the town where Jesus was born, Luke 2:4-7.
4. _____ was where Jesus was laid, Luke 2:7.
5. _____ in a manger was the sign the shepherds were to look for to find Jesus, Luke 2:12.
6. _____ kept the sayings of the shepherds in her heart, Luke 2:19.
7. _____ guided the Wise Men to Jesus, Matthew 2:2.
8. _____ was where the Wise Men found Jesus, Matthew 2:11.
9. _____ warned the Wise Men of Herod's trick, Matthew 2:12.
10. _____ told Joseph to flee with Jesus to Egypt, Matthew 2:13.

13
Creatures

The creatures God made were often used to teach important lessons. Fill in the blanks with the name of the proper creature.

1. Jesus cautioned people not to "cast ye your pearls before _____, lest they trample them under their feet," Matthew 7:6.
2. The writer of Proverbs tells us, "Go to the _____, thou sluggard; consider her ways, and be wise," Proverbs 6:6.
3. God used the foolishness of an _____ which lays her eggs on the earth where they may be stepped on to convince Job of God's mighty works, Job 39:13-17.
4. Jesus illustrated God's care for mankind by these words, "Are not two _____ sold for a farthing? and one of them shall not fall on the ground without your Father," Matthew 10:29.
5. Jesus likened his love for Jerusalem to a _____ which gathered her little ones under her wing, Matthew 23:37.
6. Isaiah likened the person who waited upon the Lord to _____ which soar above the earth, Isaiah 40:31.
7. The psalmist used the "_____ upon a thousand hills" to show God's ownership of everything, Psalm 50:10.
8. The psalmist advised, "Be ye not as the _____, . . . which have no understanding: whose mouth must be held in with bit," Psalm 32:9.
9. Luke described Jesus as being "led as a _____ to the slaughter," Acts 8:32.
10. Solomon said, "The righteous are bold as a _____," Proverbs 28:1.

14
Denials

The following people each denied something. Match the person with what he or she denied.

1. Abraham, Genesis 20:2
2. Peter, Matthew 26:69-70
3. Jonathan, 1 Samuel 20:9
4. Adam, Genesis 3:12
5. Job, Job 13:14-18
6. Sarah, Genesis 18:15
7. The crowd around Jesus, Luke 8:45
8. Barnabas, Acts 14:12-15
9. Pilate, Luke 23:4
10. Chief priests, John 19:21
11. Eliphaz, Job 4:1,7

a. That the innocent perish
b. That he was a god
c. That Jesus was guilty
d. That Jesus was the King of the Jews
e. That he would not tell David of his father's intentions
f. That his wife was his wife
g. That he was being punished for sin
h. That she laughed at an angel's message
i. That he was responsible for eating the forbidden fruit
j. That anyone had touched Jesus
k. That he knew Jesus

15
Depression

Fill in the blanks with the names of the people who experienced depression.

_____ 1. "If thou deal thus with me, kill me, I pray thee, out of hand, if I have found favour in thy sight; and let me not see my retchedness."

_____ 2. "Therefore now, O Lord, take, I beseech thee, my life from me; for it is better for me to die than to live."

_____ 3. "But he himself went a day's journey into the wilderness, and came and sat down under a juniper tree: and he requested for himself that he might die; and said, It is enough; now, O Lord, take away my life; for I am not better than my fathers."

_____ 4. "Then said I, Woe is me! for I am undone; because I am a man of unclean lips, and I dwell in the midst of a people of unclean lips: for mine eyes have seen the King, Lord of hosts."

_____ 5. "I am sore distressed· for the Philistines make war against me, and God is departed from me, and answereth me no more, neither by prophets, nor by dreams."

_____ 6. "When (he) perceived all that was done, (he) rent his clothes, and put on sackcloth with ashes, and went out into the midst of the city, and cried with a loud and bitter cry."

_____ 7. "They say unto her, Woman, why weepest thou? She saith unto them, Because they have taken away my Lord, and I know not where they have laid him."

In most of these cases of depression, and others in the Bible, the depression was overcome by service to God. For example, Jeremiah felt he had been deceived by God and vowed never to speak God's name again (Jer. 20:7-9). But in verses 12 and 13, Jeremiah spoke of his problem to the Lord and continued to serve the Lord.

16
Desires

Every individual has desires he would like to see fulfilled. Match the person with his desire:

1. Certain Greeks, John 12:21
2. Bartimaeus, Mark 10:46,51
3. Paul, Romans 10:1
4. Mother of John and James, Matthew 20:21
5. Pilate, Matthew 27:24
6. Hannah, 1 Samuel 1:9-11
7. Lazarus, Luke 16:21
8. Solomon, 2 Chronicles 1:7-12
9. Esther, Esther 7:3
10. Daniel, Daniel 1:8
11. Eunuch, Acts 8:30-31

a. to understand the Scriptures
b. Crumbs from a table
c. save her people
d. sight
e. see Jesus
f. wisdom and knowledge
g. salvation of Israel
h. to eat food of his choosing
i. innocence of Jesus' blood
j. right and left seats for sons
k. a child

17
The Disciples

Fill in each blank with the name of one of the twelve disciples whom Jesus chose to help him in his ministry.

1. _____ and _____ were good friends, John 1:45.
2. _____ was a tax collector before becoming a disciple, Matthew 9:9.
3. _____, _____, _____, and _____ left their jobs as fishermen to become disciples, Matthew 4:18-21.
4. _____ betrayed Jesus, Matthew 27:3.
5. The son of Alphaeus was _____, Matthew 10:3.
6. The disciple Lebbaeus was also known as _____, Matthew 10:3.
7. _____ wanted to see the nail prints in the hands of Jesus, John 20:24-25.
8. The name used to differentiate between Simon Peter and the other Simon was _____, Mark 3:18.
9. _____ took the place of Judas after Jesus ascended into heaven, Acts 1:26.

18
Doves

Answer each of the following questions concerning doves.

_____ 1. Who sent a dove to see if the water had dried off the earth, Genesis 8:6-8?

_____ 2. What did the dove return with the second time it was sent out, Genesis 8:11?

_____ 3. The third time the dove was sent out, what happened, Genesis 8:12?

_____ 4. Why did the psalmist want wings like a dove, Psalm 55:6?

_____ 5. Who said he mourned like a dove and his eyes failed with looking upward, Isaiah 38:9-14?

_____ 6. Whom did Jeremiah tell to dwell in the rocks and be like the dove, Jeremiah 48:28?

_____ 7. Who said that the Israelites who escaped would be like doves, mourning for their iniquities, Ezekiel 7:16?

_____ 8. Whom did Hosea say was like a silly dove, Hosea 7:11?

_____ 9. At his baptism, who saw the Spirit of God descending like a dove, Matthew 3:16?

_____10. Whom did Jesus tell to go out as harmless as doves, Matthew 10:5,16?

19
Early Church Workers

Many people in the New Testament were known for something they did for or to the early church. Match the person with what he or she did.

1. Peter, Acts 2:14-41

2. Timothy, Acts 16:3

3. Rhoda, Acts 12:12-13

4. Dorcas, Acts 9:39

5. Lydia, Acts 16:13-14

6. Sapphira, Acts 5:1,8-9

7. Matthias, Acts 1:26

8. Stephen, Acts 7:59

9. Paul, Acts 13:2-3

10. Ananias, Acts 9:17-18

a. Prayed with a group of women
b. Served as a missionary
c. Was chosen to replace Judas
d. Paul's helper
e. Lied to the church
f. Preached and about three thousand came to know Jesus
g. Recognized Peter's voice and forgot to open the gate
h. Restored Paul's sight
i. Died for his faithfulness
j. Made clothes for needy people

20
Fathers

The most influential people in the family lives of the Israelites were fathers. Match each statement with the proper father.

1. Told to sacrifice his son, Genesis 22:1-2
2. Father who walked with God, Genesis 5:21
3. Blessed the wrong son, Genesis 27:22-23
4. Betrayed by his son, 2 Samuel 15:12-31
5. Lost all his children tragically, Job 1:13-15
6. Jesus raised his daughter, Mark 5:22,42
7. Father of twelve tribes, Genesis 49:28
8. Son baptized Jesus, Luke 1:13; Mark 1:9
9. Fled to Egypt with his family, Matthew 2:13
10. Son was the first king of Israel, 1 Samuel 9:3
11. First father on Earth, Genesis 4:1

a. Job
b. Joseph
c. Adam
d. Jairus
e. Isaac
f. Enoch
g. David
h. Jacob
i. Kish
j. Zechariah
k. Abraham

21
Feed Me

Almost everyone enjoys eating. Fill in the blanks with the correct food.

1. Daniel asked to be fed _____ and _____, Daniel 1:12.
2. John the Beptist fed on _____ and _____, Matthew 3:4.
3. Hiram traded Solomon cedar and fir trees in return for _____ and _____, 1 Kings 5:11.
4. The Israelites were fed _____ from heaven, Exodus 16:35.
5. Elijah was fed _____ and _____ by a raven, 1 Kings 17:6.
6. Jesus fed a multitude of people with five _____ and two _____, Mark 6:38.
7. Lazarus wanted to be fed _____ from the rich man's table, Luke 16:21.
8. The prodigal son would have fed himself the _____, Luke 15:16.
9. Joseph sold his brothers _____ during a famine so that they might be fed, Genesis 42:25.
10. Elijah assured the widow that she and her son would not run out of _____ and _____, 1 Kings 17:14.

22
Fishermen

In Bible times, people often fished for a living. Name the person in each statement.

1. The fisherman who brought a lad with five loaves and two fish to Jesus was _____, John 6:8-9.
2. A fisherman who, with his brother John, followed Jesus was _____, Matthew 4:21.
3. The fisherman who was told by Jesus to catch a fish with money in its mouth was _____, Matthew 17:26-27.
4. The man who promised to make his followers "fishers of men" was _____, Matthew 4:19.
5. The man who was blessed by God: "And the fear of you shall be . . . upon all the fishes of the seas" was _____, Genesis 9:1-2.
6. The fisherman whose two sons became disciples was _____, Matthew 4:2.
7. Two disciples who are named among those who went fishing with Peter but didn't catch anything all night were _____ and _____, John 21:2.

23
Foods

Match the food with the consumer.

1. Samson found this in a carcase, Judges 14:8
2. Gideon brought to an angel, Judges 6:19-20
3. Jesus ate after he arose, Luke 24:42
4. Esau sold birthright for, Genesis 25:34
5. The Israelites remembered, Numbers 11:5
6. Pharaoh's baker dreamed he carried in a basket, Genesis 40:17
7. David gave an Egyptian, 1 Samuel 30:11-12
8. Abraham brought to heavenly visitors, Genesis 18:8
9. Jael brought to the enemy, Judges 4:18-19
10. Fruit brought out of the land of Canaan, Numbers 13:23

a. Raisins

b. Butter

c. Honey

d. Pottage

e. Milk

f. Bakemeats

g. Broth

h. Grapes

i. Fish

j. Melons

24
Friends of Jesus

Fill in the blanks with the names of some of Jesus' friends.

1. _____, _____, and _____ were the only witnesses at both the transfiguration, Matthew 17:1-13, and the prayer at Gethsemane, Matthew 26:36-46.
2. _____ sat at Jesus' feet and listened to him, Luke 10:39.
3. Jesus raised _____ from the dead, John 11:41-44.
4. _____ expressed her belief in Jesus, John 11:24-27.
5. _____ helped bury Jesus, John 19:39-40.
6. The tomb Jesus was buried in belonged to _____, Matthew 27:57-60.
7. _____ pointed his followers to Jesus, John 3:25-36.
8. Jesus befriended _____, Luke 19:5.
9. _____ spoke to Jesus in the garden, thinking him to be the gardener, John 20:15.
10. Jesus shared a meal with friends at the home of _____, Matthew 26:6.

25
Fruits and Vegetables

Match the fruits and vegetables with the statements about them.

1. Pomegranate, 1 Kings 7:18-21
2. Lentils, Genesis 25:34
3. Wild grapes, Isaiah 5:1-2,7
4. Hyssop, Psalm 51:7
5. Fig, Luke 13:6-7
6. Cucumbers, Numbers 11:5
7. Olive oil, Exodus 30:24-25
8. Mustard seed, Luke 17:6
9. Mandrakes, Genesis 30:14-16
10. Sycomore fruit, Amos 7:14

a. Used as an antiseptic
b. Jesus used to teach that God is merciful in giving many opportunities to show our faith by our deeds
c. Jesus used to teach about faith
d. Used to make a holy ointment
e. Decorated pillars in Temple
f. Compared to the house of Israel
g. Jacob used in his stew
h. Vegetable Hebrews longed for in the wilderness
i. Amos gathered this fruit
j. Rachel bargained with Leah to have them

26
Furnishings

Houses in biblical times had few pieces of furniture. Fill in the blanks with the furniture mentioned.

1. A man on a _____ was let down through a roof to see Jesus, Luke 5:19.
2. A beggar desired to eat crumbs which fell from a rich man's _____, Luke 16:21.
3. Jehoiada made a bank from a _____ to hold the offerings, 2 Kings 12:9.
4. A great woman of Shunem and her husband prepared a room with a _____, _____, and _____ for Elisha to use, 2 Kings 4:8-10.
5. Jesus told a man sick with palsy to take up his _____ and walk, Matthew 9:6.
6. God said the Egyptians would have frogs everywhere, even in their _____, Exodus 8:3.
7. Solomon said the virtuous woman "layeth her hands to the _____," Proverbs 31:19.
8. To protect David, Michal placed an image in a _____ and said David was sick, 1 Samuel 19:13.
9. Seven men were chosen to work at _____ to free the disciples to study and preach, Acts 6:2-3.
10. No one would put a _____ under a bushel, Matthew 5:15.

27
God Called

When God calls people, they are usually at work. Match each person with what he was doing when God called him.

1. Samuel, 1 Samuel 3:10
2. David, 1 Samuel 16:11-13
3. Paul, Acts 9:2-6
4. Amos, Amos 7:14-15
5. King Saul, 1 Samuel 9:17-20
6. Matthew, Matthew 9:9
7. James and John, Matthew 4:21
8. Nehemiah, Nehemiah 1:1; 2:1
9. Peter and Andrew, Matthew 4:18
10. Elisha, 1 Kings 19:19

a. Mending nets
b. Serving the king
c. Searching for lost animals
d. Caring for sheep
e. Herdsman and gatherer of sycomore fruit
f. Journeying to persecute Christians
g. Plowing oxen
h. Collecting taxes
i. Being a priest's helper
j. Fishing

28
God Commanded

Often God's will is not easy to obey. These people experienced some of the hard-to-obey commands of God. Match the person with what God told him to do.

1. Abram (Abraham), Genesis 12:1

2. Jonah, Jonah 1:1-3

3. Hosea, Hosea 1:2

4. Moses, Exodus 14:14-16

5. Joseph, Matthew 2:13

6. Zechariah, Luke 1:13,18

7. Ananias, Acts 9:10-15

8. Peter, Acts 10:19-20

9. Noah, Genesis 6:13-14

10. Samuel, 1 Samuel 16:1-2

a. to name his unborn son "John"
b. to anoint someone else king while Saul lived
c. to enter a Gentile's home and preach
d. to cross a sea on foot
e. leave his father's house and move to a new land
f. to take a harlot for a wife
g. to preach to his enemy
h. to help a man who killed Christians
i. to build a boat on dry land
j. to take his wife and infant son to Egypt

29
Grievers

Grief is a normal emotion in life. Match the person with the cause of his grief.

1. Job, Job 30:25
2. Jesus, Isaiah 53:4
3. Mary and Martha, John 11:19
4. Mary Magdalene, John 20:15
5. Men on Emmaus road, Luke 24:17,21
6. Jonah, Jonah 4:1-3
7. David, 2 Samuel 12:16
8. Hannah, 1 Samuel 1:5-8
9. Jonathan, 1 Samuel 20:34
10. Esther, Esther 4:4-7
11. Daniel, Daniel 7:15

a. a loved one's body
b. childless state
c. visions uninterpreted
d. the poor
e. humanity
f. repentance of enemies
g. loss of a leader
h. mistreatment of a friend
i. plot to destroy the Jews
j. death of a brother
k. a sick child

30
Headlines

Read each headline below, and match it to the person most likely referred to.

1. Young Boy Slays Giant with Slingshot
2. Rejoicing Women Led by Prophetess
3. Man Survives Lions' Den
4. King Has Church Leader Killed
5. Runaway Slave Returns to Master
6. Persecutor of Christians Converted
7. Red Sea Parts for Man and Followers
8. Successor Chosen for Moses
9. Two Cities Destroyed; One Family Survives
10. Man Hung by His Own Hair
11. Woman Reports Resurrection

a. James, Acts 12:1-2

b. Moses, Exodus 14:22

c. Joshua, Joshua 1:1-6

d. Paul, Acts 9:6

e. Miriam, Genesis 15:20-21

f. Absalom, 2 Samuel 18:10

g. Daniel, Daniel 6:12-16

h. David, 1 Samuel 17:24,50

i. Mary Magdalene, John 20:18

j. Onesimus, Philemon 10-12

k. Lot, Genesis 19:16-25

31
Jesus Asked

Jesus asked many pointed questions. List the person to whom he asked each question.

_____ 1. "If I have told you earthly things, and ye believe not, how shall ye believe, if I tell you of heavenly things?" John 3:12.

_____ 2. "Whence shall we buy bread that these may eat?" John 6:5.

_____ 3. "Lovest thou me?" John 21:15.

_____ 4. "But whom say ye that I am?" Matthew 16:15.

_____ 5. "Whom seek ye?" John 18:3-5.

_____ 6. "If I have spoken evil, bear witness of the evil: but if well, why smitest thou me?" John 18:22-23.

_____ 7. "But if ye love them which love you, what reward have ye?" Matthew 5:46.

_____ 8. "What wilt thou that I should do unto thee?" Mark 10:46-51.

_____ 9. "Wherefore think ye evil in your hearts?" Matthew 9:4.

_____10. "Believe ye that I am able to do this?" Matthew 9:28.

_____11. "Wilt thou be made whole?" John 5:6-7

32
Jesus' Miracles

Match each miracle Jesus performed with the person for whom the miracle was performed.

1. A nobleman, John 4:46-53
2. A multitude of people, Matthew 15:34-36
3. Jairus, Mark 5:22-41
4. Bartimaeus, Mark 10:46-52
5. High priest's servant, Luke 22:50-51
6. Peter, Matthew 14:29
7. Widow of Nain, Luke 7:11-16
8. Mary and Martha, John 11:39-44
9. A bridegroom, John 2:1-10
10. Peter's mother-in-law, Mark 1:30-31

a. son raised from the dead
b. water became wine
c. son healed
d. brother raised from dead
e. fed with seven loaves and a few fish
f. received sight
g. fever healed
h. walked on water
i. daughter raised from dead
j. ear restored

33
Jesus' Return

One of the most speculated about events today is Jesus' return. Fill in each blank with the proper answer about the second coming of Jesus.

_____ 1. The second coming of Christ is compared to what weather condition, Matthew 24:27?

_____ 2. The second coming is compared to what night visitor, 1 Thessalonians 5:2?

_____ 3. What virtue is encouraged as we wait for the second coming, James 5:8?

_____ 4. What did Paul tell Timothy to keep until Jesus returns, 1 Timothy 6:11-12,14?

_____ 5. Whose work did Paul say would be done before Jesus' return, 2 Thessalonians 2:9?

_____ 6. Who will meet the Lord first when he returns, 1 Thessalonians 4:16?

_____ 7. What will be changed when Jesus returns, Philippians 3:21?

_____ 8. What will God do to all believers when Jesus returns, 2 Corinthians 5:10?

_____ 9. What is the last enemy to be destroyed at Jesus' return, 1 Corinthians 15:26?

_____10. What did Jesus say he was going to prepare for us, John 14:2?

_____11. In what will Jesus return, Luke 21:27?

_____12. What occupation did Jesus liken the judgment to, Matthew 25:32?

_____13. Who is the only person who knows when Jesus' return is, Matthew 24:36?

34
Jesus Taught the Disciples

Jesus spent much time instructing his disciples so that they could take over when he left the earth. Answer these questions about what Jesus taught the disciples.

1. What was the only thing Jesus told his disciples to take on mission trips, Mark 6:8? _____

2. What were the disciples to do if they were not welcome in a place, Mark 6:11? _____

3. What were the disciples to do on their mission, Luke 9:2? ____
   _____

4. What do we call the prayer Jesus taught his disciples, Matthew 6:9-13? _____

5. How did Jesus tell his disciples to treat others, Matthew 7:12?
   _____

6. To what two things did Jesus compare the disciples, Matthew 5:13-16? _____

7. To what did Jesus compare his relationship with his disciples, John 15:5? _____

8. What did Jesus use to teach his disciples humility, Matthew 18:1-2? _____

9. What did Jesus say he was leaving with the disciples, John 14:27? _____

10. What did Jesus tell his disciples to use as a remembrance of his body, Luke 22:19? _____

11. What did Jesus tell the disciples to do if they loved him, John 14:15? _____

35
Joseph

One of the first Bible people that children learn about is Joseph.
Match the following facts about Joseph found in Genesis.

1. Home country
2. Father
3. Master
4. Oldest brother
5. New country
6. Purchasers
7. Mother
8. Grandfather
9. Temptress
10. Interpreted dreams
11. His hostage

a. Jacob, 30:25
b. Reuben, 35:23
c. Simeon, 42:24
d. Potiphar's wife, 39:7
e. Canaan, 33:18
f. Egypt, 37:36
g. Rachel, 30:22-24
h. Ishmeelites, 37:28
i. Pharaoh, 41:25
j. Laban, 29:5-7
k. Potiphar, 37:36

36
Kind Deeds

The Bible has many examples of kindness. Fill in each blank with the deed of kindness shown.

1. Abraham let Lot have first choice of _____, Genesis 13:8-12.
2. Jesus was presented _____, _____, and _____ by the Wise Men, Matthew 2:1,11.
3. The good Samaritan helped a man who was robbed by _____ up his wounds, Luke 10:30-37.
4. Jesus praised a widow because she gave _____, Luke 21:1-4.
5. Simon, a Cyrenian, carried Jesus' _____, Luke 23:26.
6. Mary anointed Jesus' feet with _____, John 12:3.
7. Boaz rewarded Ruth because of her kindness to her _____, Ruth 2:5-11.
8. David allowed Mephibosheth to _____ for Jonathan's sake, 2 Samuel 9:6-7.
9. Rahab aided the spies by letting them down _____ through a window, Joshua 2:1,15.
10. Jonathan gave David a _____, _____, _____, and _____, 1 Samuel 18:4.
11. Dorcas made _____ and _____ for widows, Acts 9:39.

37
Kings

Kings are influential in shaping the history of their nations. Match each king with the proper statement about him.

1. Built an altar, asking that a plague end
2. Carried Judah and Jerusalem into Exile
3. Built the Temple
4. Reigned three months
5. Had fifteen years added to his life
6. His hand "dried up"
7. Made a covenant before the Lord
8. Had youngest children of Bethlehem slain
9. Fell through his upper chamber
10. Gave decree to rebuild Temple
11. Threw a javelin at David

a. Jeroboam, 1 Kings 13:4
b. Ahaziah, 2 Kings 1:2
c. Solomon, 2 Chronicles 7:11
d. Darius, Ezra 6:1,8
e. David, 2 Samuel 24:25
f. Hezekiah, 2 Kings 20:5-6
g. Josiah, 2 Chronicles 34:31
h. Saul, 1 Samuel 18:10-11
i. Nebuchadnezzar, 1 Chronicles 6:15
j. Jehoiachin, 2 Kings 24:8
k. Herod, Matthew 2:16

38
Leaders

Match the leader with the activity.

1. Peter, Acts 2:1,14

2. Aaron, Exodus 32:2-4

3. Aquila and Priscilla, Acts 18:24-27

4. God, Exodus 13:21

5. Jonah, Jonah 3:4-5

6. Absalom, 2 Samuel 15:4

7. Saul, 1 Samuel 10:24

8. Paul, Acts 17:22,34

9. Joseph, Genesis 41:45-48

10. Caiaphas, John 18:14

11. Joshua, Joshua 6:2,6-7

a. Led by a cloud
b. Led the Ninevah revival
c. Preached at Pentecost
d. Led the battle of Jericho
e. Taught Apollos the things of the Lord
f. Led a conspiracy against his father
g. Led in the storing of grain for a worldwide famine
h. Led the construction of a golden calf
i. Led Jews to plot against Jesus
j. Led as first king of Israel
k. Led some Athenians to believe in Christ

39
Listeners

Match the listener and the speaker.

1. Felix, Acts 24:24
2. Eunuch, Acts 8:30-32
3. Naaman, 2 Kings 5:1-4
4. Moses, Exodus 18:17-24
5. Barak, Judges 4:6
6. Elisha, 1 Kings 19:20
7. Samson, Judges 16:16-18
8. Eve, Genesis 3:4-6
9. Ahab, 1 Kings 21:7
10. Peter, John 1:41-42
11. Zedekiah, Jeremiah 38:19-20

a. Delilah
b. Andrew
c. Jethro
d. Paul
e. Jezebel
f. Jeremiah
g. Philip
h. Elijah
i. a slave girl
j. Deborah
k. Satan

40
Loves

Match the person with the object of his or her love.

1. Christ, Ephesians 5:25
2. Father, Luke 15:20
3. God, John 3:16
4. Isaac, Genesis 27:1-4
5. Amnon, 2 Samuel 13:4
6. Young ruler, Matthew 19:22
7. Uzziah, 2 Chronicles 26:1,10
8. Jacob, Genesis 29:18
9. Scribes, Mark 13:38
10. Hosea, Hosea 3:1

a. Husbandry
b. An adulteress
c. Salutations
d. Tamar
e. World
f. Rachel
g. Savory meat
h. Prodigal son
i. Church
j. Possessions

41
Makers

Have you ever made something you were proud of? Match the following people with the things they made.

1. Ark, Genesis 6:13-14
2. House on a rock, Matthew 7:24
3. Barns, Luke 12:16-18
4. Temple, 1 Kings 6:14-17
5. Tower, Genesis 11:4-9
6. Gates, Nehemiah 3:1
7. Wells, Genesis 26:18
8. Sacrifice altar, Genesis 22:9
9. Gallows, Esther 5:14
10. Idol in a grove, 1 Kings 15:13
11. A coat, 1 Samuel 2:19

a. Maachah
b. Abraham
c. Eliashib
d. Solomon
e. Wise man
f. Noah
g. A fool
h. People of Babel
i. Isaac
j. Haman
k. Hannah

42
Medicine

God uses many methods of healing. Match the method with the person healed.

1. Jesus' fingers in ears and spit
2. Lump of figs
3. Dip in Jordan River
4. Touch by Jesus
5. Look at brass serpent
6. Spoken word of Jesus
7. Touch of Jesus' garment
8. Dip in troubled waters of pool of Bethesda
9. Prayer and laying on of hands
10. Faith of his friends

a. Centurion's servant, Matthew 8:13
b. Publius' father, Acts 28:8
c. Man with palsy, Matthew 9:2
d. Israelites' snake bites, Numbers 21:9
e. Deaf man with speech impediment, Mark 7:33
f. Peter's mother-in-law, Mark 1:30-31
g. Naaman, 2 Kings 5:14
h. Woman sick for twelve years, Mark 5:25-29
i. People around pool, John 5:4
j. Hezekiah's boils, Isaiah 38:21

43
Messianic Prophecies

The prophets wrote and spoke of the coming Messiah. Tell which prophet made the following prophecies.

1. _____ said the Messiah would be born in Bethlehem.
2. _____ said the Messiah would be born of a virgin.
3. _____ said the Messiah would be taken out of Egypt.
4. _____ said the Messiah would be a mighty prophet in word and deed.
5. _____ said the Messiah would have his hands and feet pierced.
6. _____ said the Messiah would be despised and rejected.
7. _____ said the Messiah would make a triumphal entry into Jerusalem.
8. _____ said the Messiah would be made an offering for sin.
9. _____ said soldiers would cast lots for the Messiah's garments.
10. _____ said the Messiah would be betrayed and sold for thirty pieces of silver.
11. _____ said that Jesus would suffer in silence.

44
Milestones of Jesus

Each of the following places meant something special in Jesus' life. Match the place with what happened there.

1. Bethlehem, Matthew 2:1
2. Nazareth, Matthew 2:23
3. Jerusalem, Luke 2:42
4. Jordan River, Matthew 3:13
5. Sea of Galilee, Luke 8:23-25
6. Calvary, Luke 23:33
7. Capernaum, Matthew 4:13
8. Gethsemane, Mark 14:32
9. Cana, John 2:1
10. Bethesda, John 5:2-9
11. Bethany, Luke 24:50-51

a. Attended a wedding; first miracle
b. Ascended from here
c. Center of ministry
d. Stilled a storm
e. Celebrated Passover at age twelve
f. Birthplace
g. Home
h. Baptized
i. Crucified
j. Prayed
k. Healed a man

45
Miracles

Match the miracle with the person.

1. Devils were cast out of him
2. Survived a snake bite
3. Walked on water
4. Increased the widow's oil
5. Saw a burning bush
6. Had a vision of an angel measuring Jerusalem
7. Journeyed to heaven on a whirlwind
8. Wrote about a vision of heaven
9. Turned water into wine
10. Survived a flood on a boat he built

a. Elisha, 2 Kings 4:2-6
b. John, Revelation 1:9-11
c. Noah, Genesis 8:18
d. Legion, Luke 8:30-33
e. Zechariah, Zechariah 2:1-2
f. Moses, Exodus 3:3-4
g. Paul, Acts 28:3-5
h. Peter, Matthew 14:28-29
i. Elijah, 2 Kings 1,11
j. Jesus, John 2:9

46
Mothers

Mothers have always played an important role in shaping the characters of their children. Match each mother with the proper statement.

1. Mother of all living
2. Helped son deceive his father
3. Was paid to care for her son
4. Was commended by Paul
5. Sought best for her sons
6. Wept for her children
7. Became mother to a daughter-in-law
8. Caused death of John the Baptist
9. Killed her grandsons
10. Gave her son to ministry
11. Highly favored by God

a. Rachel, Jeremiah 31:15
b. Mary, Luke 1:30
c. Eve, Genesis 3:20
d. Hannah, 1 Samuel 1:11; 2:11
e. Rebekah, Genesis 27:6-10
f. Athaliah, 2 Kings 11:1
g. Jochebed, Exodus 2:8-10; 6:20
h. Herodias, Mark 6:22-25
i. Eunice, 2 Timothy 1:5
j. Naomi, Ruth 1:16
k. Salome, Matthew 20:20; Mark 16:1

47
Murders

The people in the left column were responsible for the deaths of the people in the middle column. Match the murderer with the murdered and then, the reason for the murder.

1. Cain, Genesis 4:4-8
2. David, 2 Samuel 11:3-12
3. Joab, 2 Samuel 3:30
4. Benaiah, 1 Kings 2:29,34
5. Absalom, 2 Samuel 13:22,28-29
6. Pekah, 2 Kings 15:23-25
7. Herod, Acts 12:1-2
8. Ahimelech, 1 Samuel 22:16,18
9. Jehoiakim, Jeremiah 26:20-23
10. Jael, Judges 4:18-22

A. Amnon
B. Urijah
C. Abel
D. Uriah
E. Joab
F. James
G. Doeg
H. Pekahiah
I. Abner
J. Sisera

a. Offering
b. Revenge
c. Throne
d. Prophesy
e. Persecution
f. Solomon's instructions
g. Hatred
h. Bathsheba
i. Saul's instructions
j. Enemy

48
Natural Calamities

Regardless of where we may live, all of us are subject to natural calamities of one sort or another. Match the person with the calamity he experienced.

1. A flood
2. Drought
3. Tempest (storm)
4. Lightnings
5. Hail
6. Earthquake
7. Whirlwind
8. Black clouds and wind
9. Thunder

a. Pharaoh, Exodus 9:28
b. Elijah, 2 Kings 2:1,11
c. Samuel, 1 Samuel 7:10
d. Ahab, 1 Kings 18:45
e. Jonathan, 1 Samuel 14:13-15
f. Noah, Genesis 6:17
g. Jonah, Jonah 1:4
h. Jacob, Gen. 41:57
i. Moses, Exodus 19:16

49
Occupations

When God called the following people, they were busy working at something. Match the person with what he or she did for a living.

1. Moses, Exodus 3:1
2. Gideon, Judges 6:11
3. Elisha, 1 Kings 19:16-19
4. Lydia, Acts 16:14
5. Priscilla and Aquila, Acts 18:3
6. Zacchaeus, Luke 19
7. Luke, Colossians 4:14
8. Baruch, Jeremiah 36:4
9. Deborah, Judges 4:4
10. Esther, Esther 2:17

a. Farmer
b. Seller of purple cloth
c. Shepherd
d. Judge
e. Thresher
f. Scribe
g. Queen
h. Tentmakers
i. Tax collector
j. Doctor

50
Oil

Answer each question with the person involved with oil.

_____ 1. Who asked the wise virgins for oil for their lamps, Matthew 25:7-8?

_____ 2. Who used oil on the wounds of a man beaten by robbers, Luke 10:33-34?

_____ 3. Who multiplied the oil of a widow so she could pay her debts, 2 Kings 4:2-7?

_____ 4. What tribe received this blessing: "Let him be acceptable to his brethren, and let him dip his foot in oil," Deuteronomy 33:24?

_____ 5. To whom did Jesus say, "My head with oil thou didst not anoint: but this woman hath anointed my feet with ointment," Luke 7:43,46?

_____ 6. Who poured oil on a pillar of stone and named the place Bethel, Genesis 35:14-15?

_____ 7. Who asked a woman to pretend to be a mourner and not anoint herself with oil, 2 Samuel 14:2?

_____ 8. Who was anointed with oil by Zadok, 1 Kings 1:39?

_____ 9. To whom did Solomon give twenty thousand measures of pure oil in exchange for cedar trees, 1 Kings 5:11?

_____10. Who told a woman to make him a cake of her last meal and oil and her supply of oil and meal would not run out, 1 Kings 17:12-16?

51
Organizers

People who get things done are usually good organizers. In the Bible there are examples of people who organized. Match the person with what he organized.

1. Jethro, Exodus 18:9-24

2. The twelve, Acts 6:1-7

3. Jesus, Luke 10:1

4. Jacob, Genesis 33:1-4

5. Joshua, Joshua 6:1-7

6. David, 2 Samuel 24:1-2

7. Moses, Exodus 13:17-20

8. Gideon, Judges 7:4-7

9. Nehemiah, Nehemiah 2:17-18

10. Paul, Acts 15:40

a. suggested Moses organize judges to help him

b. organized his family when he went to meet his brother

c. organized a census of the children of Israel

d. organized seventy followers in pairs

e. organized deacons to assist them

f. organized for the defeat of Jericho

g. organized soldiers for battle by using water

h. organized a mission trip

i. organized the Israelites for a trip into the wilderness

j. organized the rebuilding of the Jerusalem wall

52
Paul's Associates

The following people were associated with Paul. Match the proper statement with the person.

1. Asked, "What must I do to be saved?" Acts 16:25-30
2. Said, "Almost thou persuadest me to be a Christian," Acts 26:28
3. Led the silversmiths in protest against Paul, Acts 19:24-25
4. Left Paul in prison in an effort to gain favor with the Jews, Acts 24:26-27
5. Sent Paul to Caesar, Acts 25:12
6. Sent with Paul to settle a dispute in Jerusalem, Acts 15:2
7. Arrested for harboring Paul, Acts 17:5
8. Guarded Paul on trip to Jerusalem for trial, Acts 27:1
9. Told Paul of a plot to kill him, Acts 23:16
10. Paul healed him of a fever, Acts 28:8
11. An orator who accused Paul before Felix, Acts 24:1-3

a. Felix
b. Julius
c. Barnabas
d. Tertullus
e. a nephew
f. jailer
g. Publius's father
h. Demetrius
i. Festus
j. Jason
k. Agrippa

53
People Jesus Helped

Everywhere Jesus went he found people with needs, and he responded in a helping way. Match the need with the appropriate scripture reference.

1. The hungry		a. John 11:43-44
2. The thirsty		b. John 3:1-3
3. The naked		c. Mark 1:34
4. The sick		d. Mark 10:51-52
5. The prisoner		e. Luke 9:13-17
6. The blind		f. Luke 8:27,35
7. The thief		g. John 11:21-27
8. The dead		h. Luke 23:39-43
9. The bereaved		i. John 4:10
10. The lost		j. Matthew 11:2-4

54
Places

Where are the following biblical places located today? Use a world atlas and Bible maps to match the biblical place in the left column with the modern location in the right column.

1.	Antioch of Pisidia	a.	Asia
2.	Bethlehem	b.	Turkey
3.	Rome	c.	Syria
4.	Damascus	d.	Jordan
5.	Jerusalem	e.	Greece
6.	Macedonia	f.	Yugoslavia and Greece
7.	Ur	g.	Israel and Jordan
8.	Thessalonica	h.	Iraq
9.	Goshen	i.	Italy
10.	Ephesus	j.	Egypt

55
Prayer Places

Wherever people are, they may call to God in prayer. Match each person with the place where he or she prayed.

1. Jesus, John 11:38-41
2. Peter and John, Acts 3:1
3. Paul and Silas, Acts 16:23-25
4. A group of women, Acts 16:13
5. Jesus, Peter, James, and John, Luke 9:28
6. Jonah, Jonah 2:1
7. Habakkuk, Habakkuk 2:1
8. David, Psalm 63:6
9. Daniel, Daniel 6:10-11
10. Hypocrites, Matthew 6:5
11. Hezekiah, 2 Kings 20:1-7

a. In a tower
b. On a mountain
c. On sick bed
d. At a grave
e. In a fish
f. In bed
g. In jail
h. At a river
i. At a window
j. In the Temple
k. On street corners

56
Prophecies Fulfilled

Using a concordance, find the prophecy that was fulfilled.

_____ 1. Paul wrote of the fulfillment of the prophecy that Jesus would be born of the "seed" of "woman," Galatians 4:4.

_____ 2. Luke wrote of the fulfillment of the prophecy that Jesus was to be from Abraham, Acts 3:25.

_____ 3. Matthew wrote of the fulfillment of the prophecy of the flight into Egypt, Matthew 2:14-15.

_____ 4. John wrote of the fulfillment of the prophecy about the rejection of Jesus, John 1:11.

_____ 5. Matthew wrote of the fulfillment of the prophecy of Jesus suffering for us, Matthew 8:17.

_____ 6. John wrote of the fulfillment of the prophecy of Jesus' bones not being broken, John 19:33.

_____ 7. The writer of Hebrews wrote of the fulfillment of the prophecy of a new covenant, Hebrews 8:8-12.

_____ 8. Paul wrote of the fulfillment of the prophecy of those God called "not my people" becoming children of God, Romans 9:26.

_____ 9. Matthew wrote of the fulfillment of the prophecy of the "stone rejected by the builders," Matthew 21:42.

_____10. Luke wrote of the fulfillment of the prophecy about kings and rulers gathering against Christ, Acts 4:25-26.

57
Praise

Many people express their joy, excitement, and sorrow by praising the Lord. Match the person with his or her statement of praise.

1. Mary, Luke 1:49

2. David, Psalm 136:1

3. Paul, 1 Corinthians 15:57

4. Daniel, Daniel 2:20

5. Jesus, Matthew 11:25

6. Nebuchadnezzar, Daniel 4:34

7. Simeon, Luke 2:25-29

8. Peter, 1 Peter 1:3

9. Jude, Jude 25

10. John, Revelation 1:6

a. "Blessed be the name of God for ever and ever: for wisdom and might are his."
b. "I blessed the most High, and I praised and honoured him that liveth for ever."
c. "Blessed be the God and Father of our Lord Jesus Christ, which according to his abundant mercy hath begotten us again unto a lively hope by the resurrection of Jesus Christ from the dead."
d. "Lord, now lettest thou thy servant depart in peace, according to thy word. For mine eyes have seen thy salvation."
e. "To the only wise God our Saviour, be glory and majesty, dominion and power, both now and ever."
f. "I thank thee, O Father . . . because thou hast hid these things from the wise and prudent, and hast revealed them unto babes."
g. "But thanks be to God, which giveth us the victory through our Lord Jesus Christ."
h. "And hath made us kings and priests unto God and his Father; to him be glory and dominion for ever and ever."
i. "For he that is mighty hath done to me great things; and holy is his name."
j. "O give thanks unto the Lord; for he is good: for his mercy endureth for ever."

58
Proverbs

Match the beginning and the ending of the Proverbs below.

1. The fear of the Lord is

2. He that hath no rule over his own spirit is

3. But the path of the just is

4. The mouth of a righteous man is

5. The law of the wise is

6. He that is slow to wrath is

7. In the fear of the Lord is

8. The highway of the upright is to

9. The name of the Lord is

10. Bread of deceit is

11. A word fitly spoken is like

a. strong confidence, 14:26.
b. a strong tower, 18:10.
c. apples of gold in pictures of silver, 25:11.
d. a fountain of life, 13:14.
e. as the shining light, that shineth more and more unto the perfect day, 4:18.
f. depart from evil, 16:17.
g. the beginning of knowledge, 1:7.
h. sweet to a man, 20:17.
i. like a city that is broken down and without walls, 25:28.
j. of great understanding, 14:29.
k. a well of life, 10:11.

59
Rebels

Each of the following people rebelled against someone. Match the rebel and the other person.

1. Cain, Genesis 4:5-9
2. Korah, Numbers 16:1-3
3. Absalom, 2 Samuel 15:14
4. Jehoiakim, 2 Kings 24:1
5. Hezekiah, 2 Kings 19:10-19
6. Saul, 1 Samuel 20:32-33
7. Esau, Genesis 27:41
8. Pharaoh, Exodus 8:19
9. Lot, Genesis 13:5-8
10. Joseph, Genesis 39:1,7-8
11. Sarai (Sarah), Genesis 16:8

a. his father, David
b. king of Assyria
c. Abram (Abraham)
d. David
e. Hagar
f. Abel
g. God
h. Potiphar's wife
i. Jacob
j. Nebuchadnezzar
k. Moses

60
Recipients

Match the person with what he received.

1. Jesus, Luke 2:25-32
2. Elisha, 2 Kings 2:13
3. Timothy, 2 Timothy 1:5
4. Solomon, 1 Chronicles 28:11 *ff.*
5. Hezekiah, 2 Kings 19:14-16
6. Bartimaeus, Mark 10:46-52
7. Judas Iscariot, Mark 14:10-11
8. Isaac, Gen. 27:9,25
9. The prodigal son, Luke 15:22
10. Joseph, Genesis 37:3
11. Solomon, 2 Chronicles 9:9

a. Received Temple plans from David
b. Received a coat from his father
c. Received sight from Jesus
d. Received silver from the priests
e. Received a letter from Shennacherib
f. Received goat meat disguised as venison from Jacob
g. Received a blessing from Simeon
h. Received spices from the queen of Sheba
i. Received a mantle from Elijah
j. Received a robe from his father
k. Received a spiritual heritage from mother and grandmother

61
Sacrifices

Sacrifices are often mentioned in the Old Testament. God commanded that sacrifices be offered on certain occasions. Match the person with the sacrifice.

1. Abel, Genesis 4:3-4

2. Noah, Genesis 8:20

3. Abraham, Genesis 22:1-19

4. Aaron, Exodus 29:38

5. Solomon, 1 Kings 12-13,62

6. David, 2 Samuel 6:12-13

7. Jesus, Hebrews 9:23-28

8. Christians, Romans 12:1

9. Jacob, Genesis 31:49-55

10. Samuel, 1 Samuel 16:2-5

a. Offer bodies as living sacrifices to God

b. offered sacrifices in the Temple

c. offered sacrifice before anointing David as king

d. offered his life as a sacrifice

e. offered the first of his flock

f. offered sacrifices daily as God instructed

g. offered sacrifice before leaving his father-in-law

h. offered sacrifice for safety of his family after the flood

i. went to offer his son for a sacrifice

j. offered sacrifice for safe return of the ark of covenant

62
Saul

Saul was the first king of Israel. Match the following facts about his life as found in 1 Samuel.

1. Anointed by
2. Played for Saul
3. Frightened by
4. Father
5. Son
6. Daughter
7. Home
8. Proclaimed king in
9. Wife
10. Place of death

a. Ahinoam, 14:50
b. David, 16:23
c. Gibeah, 10:26
d. Gilboa, 31:1,6
e. Goliath, 17:4,11
f. Gilgal, 11:15
g. Jonathan, 13:16
h. Kish, 9:3
i. Michal, 14:49
j. Samuel, 10:1

63
Says Who?

Sometimes people make statements which are long remembered by others. Fill in the blanks with the name of the person who made the statement.

_____ 1. "The Lord is my shepherd."

_____ 2. "Here am I, send me."

_____ 3. "Except a man be born again, he cannot see the kingdom of God."

_____ 4. "Believe on the Lord Jesus Christ, and thou shalt be saved."

_____ 5. "But the greatest of these is [love]."

_____ 6. "Let not your heart be troubled: ye believe in God, believe also in me."

_____ 7. "Create in me a clean heart, O God."

_____ 8. "As for me and my house, we will serve the Lord."

_____ 9. "Behold the Lamb of God, which taketh away the sin of the world."

_____10. "Silver and gold have I none, but such as I have give I thee."

64
Seafarers

Sailing was one of the main modes of transportation in Bible days. Fill in each blank with the person who sailed.

1. During a storm, _____ predicted that no life would be lost but the ship would be destroyed, Acts 27:22-26.
2. _____ took a ship to Tarshish to flee from God, Jonah 1:3.
3. Jesus found _____ and _____ with their father in a ship mending nets, Matthew 4:21.
4. Jesus was in a ship asleep when _____ awoke him because of a storm, Matthew 8:24-25.
5. _____ left a ship to walk on the water to Jesus, Matthew 14:24-29.
6. _____, _____, _____, _____, _____, and two other disciples fished all night but caught no fish, John 21:2-5.
7. _____ was instructed by God to build a ship to save him and his family from a flood, Genesis 6:13-14.
8. _____ was shipwrecked three times, 2 Corinthians 11:25.
9. _____ sent ships to Tarshish to bring back gold, silver, ivory, apes, and peacocks, 2 Chronicles 9:21.

65
Select a Person

From the answers given, select the correct person.

1. The father of John the Baptist was, Luke 1:13:
   a. Zechariah, b. Zacchaeus, c. Zephaniah.
2. Moses' sister was, Numbers 26:59:
   a. Mary, b. Miriam, c. Milcah.
3. Jesus' mother was, Luke 2:4-5:
   a. Elisabeth, b. Joanna, c. Mary.
4. The woman who was eaten by dogs was, 2 Kings 9:36-37:
   a. Jochebed, b. Jezebel, c. Joanna.
5. A woman who served as a judge was, Judges 4:4:
   a. Delilah, b. Deborah, c. Dinah.
6. A woman who lied to the church was, Acts 5:1-3,9:
   a. Sapphira, b. Salome, c. Serah.
7. A man who had a vineyard Ahab wanted was, 1 Kings 21:1:
   A. Noah, b. Naboth, c. Nicodemus.
8. A woman who left her family to live with her mother-in-law was, Ruth 1:16:
   a. Rachel, b. Rebekah, c. Ruth.
9. A young man who had a great Christian heritage was, 2 Timothy 1:5:
   a. Titus, b. Troas, c. Timothy.
10. The family of this priest was rejected by God, 1 Samuel 3:14:
    a. Elimelech, b. Eli, c. Eliphaz.

66
Seven

Seven means "complete" in biblical terms. Match each statement about seven with the proper person.

1. Had seven locks of hair
2. Labored seven years for a wife
3. Judged Israel for seven years
4. Ate grass seven times
5. Possessed seven devils
6. Dreamed of seven fat and seven lean cows
7. Built the Temple in seven years
8. Was condemned by seven princes
9. Women said her daughter-in-law was better than seven sons
10. Became king at age seven

a. Solomon, 1 Kings 6:38
b. Naomi, Ruth 4:15
c. Mary Magdalene, Mark 16:9
d. Samson, Judges 16:13
e. Pharaoh, Genesis 41:2-3
f. Ibzan, Judges 12:8-9
g. Nebuchadnezzar, Daniel 4:25,33
h. Vashti, Esther 1:14-15,19
i. Jehoash, 2 Kings 11:21
j. Jacob, Genesis 29:20

67
Sheep

One of the animals mentioned most in the Bible is sheep. Fill in the blanks with the person associated with sheep.

1. _____ was a famous shepherd boy who became a king, 1 Samuel 16:1,13.
2. _____ said that God would feed his flock like a shepherd, Isaiah 40:11.
3. _____ is the good shepherd who knows his sheep, John 10:14.
4. _____ told the shepherds about the birth of Jesus, Luke 2:8-9.
5. _____ was a shepherd while his brother was a farmer, Genesis 4:2.
6. _____ included in his daily supplies one hundred sheep, 1 Kings 4:22-23.
7. _____ led the Israelites in an offering of seven thousand sheep, 2 Chronicles 15:8-11.
8. _____ took brown sheep for his own, Genesis 30:33.
9. _____ received the first fleece of a sheep, Deuteronomy 18:4.
10. _____ gave the king of Israel many sheep as tribute, 2 Kings 3:4.

68
Sight

Sometimes we forget how very important our sight is. Fill in the blanks with the name of the person who saw something.

1. _____ saw a man in a chariot on a desert road, Acts 8:26-27.
2. _____ saw a bright light on the Damascus road, Acts 9:1-3; 26:13.
3. _____ saw a vessel descending with four-footed beasts, creeping things, and fowl, Acts 10:9-12.
4. _____ saw the Lord "high and lifted up," Isaiah 6:1.
5. _____ was old when he saw "the Lord's Christ," Luke 2:25-26.
6. _____ when he was being stoned to death, saw Jesus in the heavens, Acts 7:55,59.
7. _____ saw a woman bathing and later sinned because of it, 2 Samuel 11:2-4.
8. _____ saw Elijah go up in a chariot of fire, 2 Kings 2:11-12.
9. _____ saw an angel in a vision who told him to send to Joppa for Peter, Acts 10:3-5.
10. _____ saw the fingers of a man's hand write on the wall, Daniel 5:15.

69
Sins

Sometimes a person is known for one sin he or she committed. Match each person with the sin he or she committed.

1. Peter

2. Diotrephes

3. Saul

4. Saul (Paul)

5. Cain

6. Ananias

7. David

8. Noah

9. Abram (Abraham)

10. Woman and her husband (Adam and Eve)

a. Took another man's wife, 2 Samuel 12:9.

b. Lied about his wife, Genesis 12:18-19

c. Persecuted Christians, Acts 9:1

d. Ate forbidden fruit, Genesis 3:6

e. Denied Jesus, Luke 22:55-60

f. Murdered his brother, Genesis 4:8

g. Had too much pride, 3 John 9-10

h. Lied to the Holy Spirit, Acts 5:3

i. Took spoils, 1 Samuel 15:9

j. Got drunk, Genesis 9:20-21

70
Slaves

Slaves were common in Bible days. Name the person involved.

_____ 1. Who was the slave Paul wrote his friend Philemon about, Philemon 10?

_____ 2. Who was told of a way to be cured from leprosy by a slave girl, 2 Kings 5:1-3?

_____ 3. Who made slaves of the Israelites, Exodus 1:7-11?

_____ 4. Who was sold into slavery by his brothers, Genesis 37:26-28?

_____ 5. Who killed an Egyptian for hitting a Hebrew slave and then had to run to save his life, Exodus 2:11-13?

_____ 6. Who sent a slave to find his son a wife, Genesis 24:1-4?

_____ 7. Who was the slave who told David where Jonathan's son was, 2 Samuel 9:1-3?

_____ 8. Who was Elisha's slave, 2 Kings 4:12?

_____ 9. Who cut off the ear of a slave, John 18:10-11?

_____10. Which prophet left his slave and went a day's journey, sat under a juniper tree, and wished to die because Jezebel was trying to kill him, 1 Kings 19:1-4?

_____11. Who had a slave inform him that his sons and daughters had all been killed by a great wind, Job 1:18-20?

71
Soldiers

Soldiers are mentioned frequently in the Bible. Match the soldier with the correct event.

1. Centurion of an Italian cohort
2. Had eyes put out by Philistines
3. Had an army of a million men
4. Had bodyguards who could throw and shoot with either hand
5. Waged war with Ahab against Syria
6. The Syrians fled before him
7. Prayed and an angel destroyed the Assyrian army
8. Caught his head on a tree
9. Was defeated by the Chaldeans
10. Centurion assigned to guard Paul

a. Jehoshaphat, 2 Chronicles 18:1,30
b. Hezekiah, 2 Chronicles 32:20-21
c. Joab, 1 Chronicles 19:14
d. Absalom, 2 Samuel 18:9-10
e. Samson, Judges 16:20-21
f. Julius, Acts 27:1
g. Zedekiah, Jeremiah 39:5
h. Zerah, 2 Chronicles 14:9
i. Cornelius, Acts 10:1
j. David, 1 Chronicles 11:1-2

72
Statements

Match what was said with the person about whom it was said.

1. Enoch, Genesis 5:24
2. Noah, Genesis 6:8
3. King Solomon, 1 Kings 11:1
4. John the Baptist, Luke 1:17; John 1:23
5. Abraham, James 2:23
6. Demas, 2 Timothy 4:10
7. Peter, John 1:42
8. Mary, Luke 1:30
9. Job, Job 2:3
10. A rich, young man, Luke 18:23
11. Mary, Luke 10:42
12. Judas Iscariot, Matthew 26:24

a. There is none like him in the earth
b. In love with this world
c. Walked with God
d. Cephas, a stone
e. Found grace with God
f. Voice of one crying in the wilderness
g. He went away sorrowful
h. Chose the good part
i. Friend of God
j. Loved many strange women
k. Found favor with God
l. Would have been good if he had not been born

73
Sportsmen

Sports occupy much of our attention and time today. Many activities we call sports were necessary to life in Bible times. Match the person with an activity.

1. Samson	a. Runner, 2 Samuel 18:19
2. Paul	b. Hunter, Genesis 10:9
3. Ishmael	c. Fighter, 1 Samuel 29:5
4. David	d. Archer, Genesis 17:20; 21:20
5. Ahimaaz	e. Weight lifter, Judges 16:29
6. Benhadad	f. Dart thrower, 2 Samuel 18:14
7. Jehu	g. Swimmer, Acts 27:43-44
8. Nimrod	h. Horseman, 1 Kings 20:20
9. Joab	i. Racer, 2 Kings 9:20

74
They Cried Out

People often "cry out" to someone about something. Match the persons who cried out with what they cried out about.

1. The people when Jesus entered Jerusalem, John 12:13
2. The Israelites before the golden calf was made, Exodus 32:1
3. The crowd at Jesus' trial, Mark 15:13
4. The sons of the prophets to Elisha, 2 Kings 4:40
5. The disciples as Jesus walked on water, Matthew 14:26
6. The people at Jerusalem when Paul gave his testimony, Acts 22:22
7. A man with an unclean spirit, Mark 1:23-24
8. Two blind men, Matthew 20:30
9. Stephen as he was stoned, Acts 7:60
10. David upon hearing tragic news, 2 Samuel 18:33
11. Jesus on the cross, Matthew 27:46

a. "O thou man of God, there is death in the pot."
b. "My God, my God, why hast thou forsaken me?"
c. "Let us alone; what have we to do with thee, thou Jesus of Nazareth?"
d. "Up, make us gods, which shall go before us."
e. "Away with such a fellow from the earth: for it is not fit that he should live."
f. "Have mercy on us, O Lord, thou son of David."
g. "Hosanna: Blessed is the King of Israel."
h. "Lord, lay not this sin to their charge."
i. "It is a spirit."
j. "O my son Absalom, my son, my son Absalom!"
k. "Crucify him."

75
Thieves

Match the thief with the object stolen and from whom it was stolen.

1. Ahab, 1 Kings 21:14-15
2. Jacob, Genesis 25:27-34
3. Achan, Joshua 7:20-21
4. Absalom, 2 Samuel 15:6
5. Jehosheba, 2 Kings 11:2
6. Rachel, Genesis 31:19
7. Shishak, 2 Chronicles 12:9
8. Micah, Judges 17:1-2
9. Nebuchadnezzar, 2 Kings 25:1,13

A. Joash
B. images
C. birthright
D. brass pillars
E. silver
F. vineyard
G. treasures
H. hearts
I. spoils

a. Jerusalem Temple
b. the king's house
c. Mother
d. Naboth
e. Esau
f. Athaliah
g. Jericho
h. David
i. Laban

76
Titles

If we gave titles to biblical characters, the following could be supported by the facts in the Bible about them. Match titles and people.

1. The Fallen Angel
2. The Mother of All Living
3. The Wise King
4. Father of Many Nations
5. Prophet of Love
6. The Doubter
7. The Beloved Disciple
8. The Betrayer
9. The Weeping Prophet
10. The Lamb of God
11. Man Who Walked with God

a. Thomas, John 20:27
b. Enoch, Genesis 5:22
c. Jeremiah, Lamentations 1:16
d. Lucifer, Isaiah 14:12
e. Abram (Abraham) Genesis 17:4
f. John, John 13:23
g. Jesus, John 1:29
h. Eve, Genesis 3:20
i. Judas, Iscariot Matthew 10:4
j. Solomon, 1 Kings 4:29
k. Hosea, Hosea 3:1-5

77
To Whom Said?

Many times Jesus spoke to individuals rather than to the disciples or a crowd. Match what Jesus said with the person to whom it was said.

1. "Because thou has seen me, thou hast believed: blessed are they that have not seen, and yet have believed," John 20:29

2. "Lovest thou me more than these?" John 21:15.

3. "Touch me not; for I am not yet ascended to my Father: but go to my brethren, and say unto them, I ascend unto my Father," John 20:17.

4. "For the poor always ye have with you; but me ye have not always," John 12:8.

5. "I am the resurrection, and the life: he that believeth in me, though he were dead, yet shall he live," John 11:25.

6. "Go and sell that thou hast, and give to the poor, and thou shalt have treasure in heaven," Matthew 19:21.

7. "See thou tell no man; but go thy way, shew thyself to the priest, and offer . . . a testimony unto them," Matthew 8:3.

8. "Verily I say unto you, I have not found so great faith, no, not in Israel," Matthew 8:8-10.

9. "Neither do I condemn thee; go, and sin no more," John 8:11.

10. "Rise, take up thy bed, and walk," John 5:7-11.

11. "Go thy way; thy son liveth," John 4:49-50.

a. Judas Iscariot

b. Centurion

c. Rich young ruler

d. A nobleman

e. Martha

f. Thomas

g. Mary Magdalene

h. Adulterous woman

i Simon Peter

j. Sick man

k. A leper

78
True-False Christmas Quiz

Some statements about the Christmas story are told so frequently that we assume they are correct. Answer *true* or *false* to each of the following statements. Check the references before you check your answers.

_____ 1. Mary and Joseph traveled by donkey to Bethlehem, Luke 2:3-5.

_____ 2. Jesus was laid in a manger, Luke 2:7.

_____ 3. The cattle kept Joseph and Mary company in the stable, Luke 2:7.

_____ 4. The shepherds were told to follow a star, Luke 2:11-12.

_____ 5. Angels told the shepherds of Jesus' birth, Luke 2:11.

_____ 6. Three Wise Men visited Jesus, Matthew 2:1.

_____ 7. The Wise Men found Jesus in a house, Matthew 2:11.

_____ 8. The angels sang, "Glory to God in the Highest," Luke 2:13-14.

_____ 9. The Wise Men were kings who rode on camels, Matthew 2:1-2.

_____10. Herod wanted to find Jesus to worship him, Matthew 2:8,12.

_____11. The Wise Men presented gifts of gold, frankincense, and myrrh, Matthew 2:11.

79
Trees

Trees always play an important role in history. Match these trees with the incidents below.

1. Cedar, 1 Kings 6:2,9

2. Oak, 2 Samuel 18:9

3. Fir, Psalm 104:17

4. Sycomore, Luke 19:1-4

5. Bay, Psalm 37:35

6. Mustard, Mark 4:30-32

7. Elms, Hosea 4:13

8. Juniper, 1 Kings 19:2-4

9. Fig, Matthew 24:32

a. Used to illustrate rapid growth

b. Good shade like oak and poplar

c. Jesus used to teach a lesson

d. Elijah sat under when he fled from Jezebel

e. Used in building the Temple

f. Jesus used to illustrate growth of his kingdom

g. Absalom caught his head in one

h. Storks built nests in

i. Zacchaeus climbed to see Jesus

80
Two of a Kind

Often two people will agree on something while the rest of the crowd disagree. The two people listed in the right-hand column were alike on one thing. Match the two with how they were alike.

1. Walked on water

2. Dogs licked their blood

3. Slew a lion

4. Fell from a window

5. Appeared at transfiguration

6. Were first two disciples

7. Were Lazarus' kin

8. Became friends at Jesus' trial

9. Were let down over a wall

10. Gave good reports of the Promised Land

a. David and Paul, 1 Samuel 19:12; Acts 9:25

b. Mary and Martha, John 11:19

c. Jesus and Peter, Matthew 14:29

d. Joshua and Caleb, Numbers 14:6-8

e. Ahaziah and Eutychus, 2 Kings 1:2; Acts 20:9

f. Benaiah and Samson, 2 Samuel 23:20; Judges 14:5-6

g. Ahab and Jezebel, 1 Kings 22:37-38; 2 Kings 9:33-36

h. Moses and Elias (Elijah), Matthew 17:2-3

i. Peter and Andrew, Matthew 4:18-20

j. Herod and Pilate, Luke 23:12

81
Unique Items

Sometimes a possession makes a person stand out. Match the unique item with the person who owned it.

1. A hole in the ear, Exodus 21:6
2. A crippled limb, Genesis 32:24-25
3. A thorn in the flesh, 2 Corinthians 12:7
4. Empty lamps, Matthew 25:3
5. A colorful coat, Genesis 37:3
6. A seamless robe, John 19:23-24
7. Long-lasting shoes, Deuteronomy 29:5
8. Sightless eyes, Judges 16:21-22
9. Seven hundred wives, 1 Kings 11:3
10. Five husbands, but not one, John 4:18
11. A harlot wife, Hosea 1:2
12. A withered hand, 1 Kings 13:4

a. Paul
b. Jesus
c. A lifetime slave
d. Solomon
e. Jeroboam
f. Hebrews
g. Joseph
h. Jacob
i. Hosea
j. Samson
k. Foolish virgins
l. Samaritan woman

82
Unusual Experiences

Some people experience the unusual. Match the person with his experience.

1. Moses

2. Paul

3. Jacob

4. Stephen

5. Joshua

6. Balaam

7. Elisha

8. Hebrews

9. Naaman

10. Hezekiah

11. Gideon

a. Stoning mob, Acts 7:59
b. Parting sea, Exodus 14:21
c. Wet and dry fleece, Judges 6:36-40
d. Talking donkey, Numbers 2:27-28
e. Burning bush, Exodus 3:2
f. Reversing sundial, 2 Kings 20:10-11
g. Dipping in muddy water, 2 Kings 5:11-14
h. Blinding light, Acts 9:3
i. Fighting angel, Genesis 32:24
j. Sun standing still, Joshua 10:12-13
k. Swimming axe head, 2 Kings 6:1-6

83
Uses of Oil

There were many uses for oil in the Bible. Match the use and user.

1. Wise virgins

2. Jacob

3. Solomon

4. Elijah

5. Samaritan man

6. Samuel

7. Huram

8. A widow

9. Moses

10. Israelites

11. Issachar

a. Anointing a king, 1 Samuel 16:1

b. Bathing, 2 Chronicles 2:10-11

c. Celebrating joy, 1 Chronicles 12:39-40

d. Consecrating a place, Genesis 35:14

e. Cooking, 1 Kings 17:12-16

f. Doctoring, Luke 10:34

g. Blessing a tribe, Deuteronomy 33:24

h. Exchanging for cedar, 1 Kings 5:10-11

i. Lighting lamps, Matthew 25:7-8

j. Paying debts, 2 Kings 4:2-7

k. Offering, Numbers 15:10

84
Valentines

If you were asked to pick out people who might have sent valentines during biblical days, who would you pick? Match the person with his or her likely valentine.

1. Jacob, Genesis 29:18
2. Ruth, Ruth 4:13
3. Zipporah, Exodus 2:21
4. Bathsheba, 2 Samuel 12:24
5. Rebekah, Genesis 24:67
6. Samson, Judges 16:4
7. Elkanah, 1 Samuel 1:8
8. Abraham, Genesis 17:15
9. Elimelech, Ruth 1:2
10. Joseph, Matthew 1:24-25

a. Isaac
b. Sarah
c. Rachel
d. Mary
e. Boaz
f. Delilah
g. Naomi
h. Hannah
i. Moses
j. David

85
Wash

One of the necessary activities of human beings is washing. Match the person with the kind of washing he or she did.

1. Mary, John 12:3

2. Pilate, Matthew 27:4

3. A blind man, John 9:7

4. Job, Job 9:30-31

5. David, Psalm 51:7

6. Jeremiah, Jeremiah 4:14

7. Jesus, John 13:5

8. Peter, John 13:9

9. Pharaoh's daughter, Exodus 2:5-6

10. Elders, Deuteronomy 21:6-7

a. wanted Jesus to wash his whole body

b. told the Israelites they could be saved by washing their hearts from wickedness

c. washed Jesus' feet with ointment

d. found a baby when she came to wash in a river

e. washed in the pool of Siloam

f. prayed, "Wash me, and I shall be whiter than snow."

g. washed the disciples' feet

h. said washing in snow water could not make him clean

i. washed his hands to rid himself of guilt

j. washed their hands to show innocence

86
Water

Without water no living thing can exist. Answer each statement with the name of the person involved with water.

1. _____ and _____ turned water to blood, Exodus 7:20.
2. _____ baptized with water, Matthew 3:11.
3. _____ moved upon the face of the waters, Genesis 1:2.
4. _____ said to "let judgment run down as waters," Amos 5:24.
5. _____ commanded his chariot to stop so he could be baptized in water, Acts 8:36.
6. _____ said one had to be born of water and the Spirit to enter the kingdom of God, John 3:5.
7. _____ drew water from a rock, Exodus 17:5-6.
8. _____ lay beside a pool waiting for the moving of the water, John 5:7.
9. _____ had water poured over his sacrifice until it filled the trench around the altar, 1 Kings 18:30,35.
10. _____ lived on a boat many months because of a flood, Genesis 7:1,24.

87
Wells

Wells were a major source of water in biblical times. Match the person with the proper statement about wells.

1. Herdsmen of Gerar, Genesis 26:20
2. Isaac, Genesis 26:18

3. Jesus, John 4:6-14

4. Uzziah, 2 Chronicles 26:9-10
5. Isaiah, Isaiah 12:3

6. Abraham's servant, Genesis 24:10-13
7. Joseph, Genesis 49:22

8. Moses, Numbers 21:16

9. David, 2 Samuel 23:15-17

10. Marah, Exodus 15:23

a. Produced bitter water
b. Was given water at the well in Beer
c. Fought over a well
d. Witnessed to a woman at a well
e. Built towers and wells in the desert
f. Waited at a well to find Isaac a wife
g. Refused to drink water because three men risked their lives getting it for him
h. Was blest as "a fruitful bough by a well"
i. Prophesied that people would "draw water out of the wells of salvation"
j. Dug again the wells of his father

88
What Shall I Do?

Often in desperation, people cry, What shall I do? Match the person with the question.

1. Jailer, Acts 16:30

2. Rich young ruler, Matthew 19:16
3. Pilate, Matthew 27:22

4. Rich man, Luke 12:17

5. Lord of the vineyard, Luke 20:13
6. Paul, Acts 9:6

7. Isaac, Genesis 27:37

8. Moses, Exodus 17:4

9. Job, Job 31:14

10. Rebekah, Genesis 27:46

a. "What shall I do then with Jesus?"
b. "What shall I do? I will send my beloved son: it may be they will reverence him."
c. "What shall I do now unto thee my son?"
d. "What then shall I do when God riseth up? . . . what shall I answer him?"
e. "If Jacob take a wife of . . . the daughters of the land, what good shall my life do me?"
f. "What shall I do unto this people?"
g. "Lord, what wilt thou have me to do?"
h. "What shall I do, because I have no room where to bestow my fruits?"
i. "Good Master, what good thing shall I do, that I may have eternal life?"
j. "Sirs, what must I do to be saved?"

89
What's In a Name?

Biblical names usually have a significance. Match each name with its meaning.

1. Ishmael, Genesis 16:11

2. Eve, Genesis 3:20

3. Jesus, Matthew 1:21

4. Cain, Genesis 4:1

5. Noah, Genesis 5:29

6. Sarah, Genesis 17:16

7. Mara, Ruth 1:20

8. Reuben, Genesis 29:32

9. Loammi, Hosea 1:9

10. Emmanuel, Matthew 1:23

a. "The Almighty hath dealt very bitterly with me"

b. "I have gotten a man from the Lord"

c. "God with us"

d. "This same shall comfort us concerning our work and toil"

e. "Because the Lord hath heard thy affliction"

f. "Surely the Lord hath looked upon my affliction"

g. "For he shall save his people from their sins"

h. "She shall be a mother of nations"

i. "Because she was the mother of all living"

j. "For ye are not my people, and I will not be your God"

90
Wheels

Wheels are important to society. Identify the people involved in each of these questions.

_____ 1. Whose chariots lost their wheels because God would not let them follow his people?

_____ 2. Who was the mother who asked why her son's chariot wheels tarried?

_____ 3. Who saw a wheel in a wheel in the sky?

_____ 4. Who had a dream about burning wheels?

_____ 5. Who did the psalmist want God to make like a wheel?

_____ 6. Who used the potter and his wheel to illustrate how God wants to mold his people?

_____ 7. Who built a house with ten bases of brass and each base had four brasen wheels?

_____ 8. Who had a vision of a man removing fire from a wheel?

_____ 9. Who did Ezekiel say God would send to punish Tyrus and cause the walls to shake at the noise of wheels?

_____10. Who did Nahum say God would punish because of their wickedness by letting "the noise of the rattling of the wheels" bring destruction?

91
Where in the Bible?

It is important to know where certain passages are located in the Bible. See how many of these passages you can locate.

_____ 1. In what books of the Bible are the Ten Commandments found?

_____ 2. In what book of the Bible are 150 songs to be sung with stringed instruments?

_____ 3. In what book of the Bible do we find many wise sayings of Solomon?

_____ 4. In what book of the Bible do we find the story of how God sent Jonah to preach in Nineveh?

_____ 5. In what book of the Bible do we find the history of the first churches after Jesus' ascension?

_____ 6. In what book of the Bible do we find the battle of Jericho?

_____ 7. In what book of the Bible do we find the story of a queen who saved her people?

_____ 8. In what book of the Bible do we find the story of a man in a lion's den?

_____ 9. In what book of the Bible do we find Jesus' Sermon on the Mount?

_____10. In what book of the Bible do we find the creation story?

_____11. In what book of the Bible do we find the story of a runaway slave who returned to his master?

92
Where Jesus Prayed

Jesus prayed before each major task he faced. List the places or circumstances when Jesus prayed.

1. On a _____, Jesus prayed all night before he chose the twelve disciples, Luke 6:12-13.
2. At _____, Jesus prayed that God would remove the "cup" from him if it were possible, Mark 14:32-36.
3. In a _____, Jesus prayed before he fed five thousand people, Matthew 14:13-21.
4. Jesus prayed at a _____, John 11:40-44.
5. When he was _____, Jesus prayed, Luke 3:21.
6. At _____, Jesus prayed for forgiveness for those who crucified him, Luke 23:33-34.
7. When he was _____, Jesus prayed the Model Prayer Matthew 5:1; 6:9.
8. In a _____, Jesus thanked God for the food, and two traveling companions suddenly recognized him, Luke 24:28-31.
9. In the _____, Jesus took bread and blessed it, thereby instituting the Lord's Supper, Luke 22:16-20.
10. On the coasts of _____, children were brought to Jesus for him to pray for them, Matthew 19:1-14.

93
Who Did It?

Human beings are busy creatures. Match each person with what he did.

1. Named all the animals, Genesis 2:20
2. Built an ark, Genesis 6:13-14,22
3. Prepared a meal for Jesus, Luke 10:40
4. Introduced Paul to the Jerusalem church, Acts 9:27
5. Was in business with her husband, Acts 18:2-3
6. Stilled a storm, Mark 4:39
7. Walked on water, Matthew 14:29
8. Received a beautiful coat, Genesis 37:3
9. Killed a giant, 1 Samuel 17:42-43
10. Found a baby in a basket, Exodus 2:5
11. Burned Jeremiah's scroll, Jeremiah 36:20

a. Barnabas

b. Jesus

c. David

d. Adam

e. Jehoiakim

f. Joseph

g. Pharaoh's daughter

h. Noah

i. Peter

j. Priscilla

k. Martha

94
Who Said It?

We are often known by something that we say. Fill in the blanks with the person who made the statement.

_____ 1. "I indeed baptize you with water unto repentance: but he that cometh after me is mightier than I, whose shoes I am not worthy to bear," Matthew 3:11.

_____ 2. "How is it that ye sought me? wist ye not that I must be about my Father's business?" Luke 2:49.

_____ 3. "Choose you this day whom ye will serve . . . but as for me and my house, we will serve the Lord," Joshua 24:15.

_____ 4. "For I know that my redeemer liveth, and that he shall stand at the latter day upon the earth," Job 19:25.

_____ 5. "Give me now wisdom and knowledge, that I may go out and come in before this people," 2 Chronicles 1:10.

_____ 6. "Thou art the Christ, the Son of the living God," Matthew 16:16.

_____ 7. "And if I perish, I perish," Esther 4:16.

_____ 8. "Behold, to obey is better than sacrifice, and to harken than the fat of rams," 2 Samuel 15:22.

_____ 9. "Come, see a man, which told me all things that ever I did: is not this the Christ?" John 4:29.

_____10. "I believe that thou art the Christ, the Son of God, which should come into the world," John 11:27.

95
Widows

Widows in the Bible often had great difficulty managing. Answer each question about a widow.

_____ 1. Which widow took off her widow's garment, veiled her face, and her father-in-law thought she was a harlot, Genesis 38:13-15?

_____ 2. Which widow had two widowed daughters-in-law, Ruth 1:3-5?

_____ 3. Which widow had a son who witnessed the prediction of the division of Solomon's kingdom, 1 Kings 11:26-31?

_____ 4. Which widow praised God when she saw the infant Jesus, Luke 2:36-38?

_____ 5. Why did Jesus say a widow had given more than anyone else, Mark 12:42-44?

_____ 6. Which widow made a living for herself and her widowed mother-in-law, Ruth 2:2?

_____ 7. What did Jesus do for a weeping widow in a funeral procession, Luke 7:12-15?

_____ 8. Who pretended to be a widow and spoke to the king in behalf of Joab, 2 Samuel 14:2,5?

_____ 9. What happened when some people in the early church complained that widows were being neglected, Acts 6:1-3?

_____10. Which widow left her mother-in-law and went back to her family, Ruth 1:4?

96
Witnesses

A witness is one who testifies to what he knows. Answer each question by telling who the witness was.

_____ 1. Who witnessed to a man in a chariot, Acts 8:31?

_____ 2. Who sang in jail and witnessed to a jailer, Acts 16:29-31?

_____ 3. Who was stoned to death as a result of his witnessing, Acts 7:56-60?

_____ 4. Who witnessed to a king named Agrippa, Acts 26:1-7?

_____ 5. Who witnessed in a lion's den, Daniel 6:22?

_____ 6. Who witnessed of God's love by sewing for needy people, Acts 9:36?

_____ 7. Who witnessed to his brother saying, "We have found . . . the Christ," John 1:40-41?

_____ 8. Who witnessed in the wilderness, crying, "Repent," Matthew 3:1-2?

_____ 9. Who were the two men who had witnessed Jesus' resurrection, one of whom took the place of Judas Iscariot, Acts 1:22-23?

_____ 10. Who described himself as "a witness of the sufferings of Christ," 1 Peter 5:1?

_____ 11. Who witnessed to his friend saying, "We have found him, of whom Moses in the law, and the prophets, did write," John 1:45?

_____ 12. Who were two men who were called gods and used the occasion to witness of the living God, Acts 14:12-15?

_____ 13. Who witnessed to Apollos showing "him the ways of God more perfectly," Acts 18:24-26?

97
Women

Fill in the blanks with the correct name of the woman.

1. After _____ husband died, she became David's wife, 1 Samuel 25:39-42.
2. Abraham told people _____ was his sister, Genesis 12:11-13.
3. Jacob had twelve sons and a daughter named _____, Genesis 34:1.
4. Among other believers, Paul saluted _____ in his letter to the Roman Christians, Romans 16:15.
5. The _____ visited Solomon, 1 Kings 10:1-2.
6. _____ spoke the word of God to Hilkiah the priest, 2 Kings 22:14-15.
7. _____ instructed her daughter to ask for John the Baptist's head, Matthew 14:6-8.
8. Jesus said to _____: "Woman, behold thy son," John 19:26.
9. Mary's cousin, _____, conceived a son in her old age, Luke 1:36.
10. _____ faith kept her from perishing with unbelievers, Hebrews 11:31.
11. _____ saved her people from extinction, Esther 8:7.

98
Women in the Headlines

The women listed below might have made the headlines in the local paper of Bible times (if there had been one). Match the headline with the woman.

1. Woman Kills Man with Nail
2. Woman Healed by Prayer
3. Virgin Has a Son
4. Woman Predicts Man's Death
5. Woman Returns to Bethlehem with daughter-in-law
6. Woman Gleans Corn in Relative's field
7. Mother Helps Son Deceive Father
8. Son Given to Temple Service by Mother
9. Woman Slays Prophets
10. Woman Among First to Acclaim Christ

a. Anna, Luke 2:36-38
b. Rebekah, Genesis 27:6-30
c. Ruth, Ruth 2:2-3
d. Jael, Judges 4:21
e. Mary, Luke 1:26-31; 2:4-7
f. Miriam, Numbers 12:10-15
g. Hannah, 1 Samuel 1:20-28
h. Jezebel, 1 Kings 18:4,13
i. Naomi, Ruth 1:19
j. Deborah, Judges 4:49

99
Wood

The kind of wood used in building is very important. Different woods have qualities which make them more suitable to certain construction. Name the wood used in building in each case.

1. The ark of the covenant was built of _____ wood, Deuteronomy 10:1-3.
2. King David's house was built of _____ wood, 2 Samuel 7:2.
3. Solomon's Temple was built of _____ wood, 1 Kings 6:15.
4. The cherubim, posts, and doors of the Temple were built of _____, 1 Kings 6:23,31-33.
5. The floors of the Temple were made from _____ wood, 1 Kings 6:15.
6. Ships were made from _____ wood with masts of_____, Ezekiel 27:5.
7. Ship oars were made from _____, Ezekiel 27:6.
8. Musical instruments were made from _____ wood, 2 Samuel 6:5.
9. Booths for the Feast of Tabernacles were made from _____, _____,_____,and_____wood, Nehemiah 8:15.
10. The altar in the tabernacle was made of _____ wood, Exodus 27:1.
11. Noah's ark was built with _____ wood, Genesis 6:14.
12. Solomon's house was built of _____ wood, 1 Kings 7:1-3.

100
Years

One way to measure time is in years. Answer the questions with the number of years.

_____ 1. How many years did it take Solomon to build the Temple, 1 Kings 6:38?

_____ 2. How many years old was Jesus when he attended the Passover feast, Luke 2:42?

_____ 3. How many years did the Israelites wander in the wilderness, Numbers 14:33?

_____ 4. How many years did Methuselah live, Genesis 5:27?

_____ 5. How many years did Abraham live before Isaac was born, Genesis 21:5?

_____ 6. How many years did the woman whom Jesus healed have a crooked back, Luke 13:11?

_____ 7. How many years had Sarah lived when Isaac was born, Genesis 17:17?

_____ 8. How many years had the woman with "an issue of blood" been sick, Matthew 9:20?

_____ 9. How many years had Mahlon and Chilion lived in Moab, Ruth 1:1,4-5?

_____10. How many years did Eli judge Israel, 1 Samuel 4:16-18?

_____11. How many years did it not rain on the Israelites when Elijah asked God to withold the rain, Luke 4:25?

_____12. How many years was Paul a house prisoner, Acts 28:30?

_____13. How many years had Noah lived when Shem, Ham, and Japheth were born, Genesis 5:32?

101
Abraham

The faith of Abraham has been preached about for years. Match these facts about the life of this man of faith.

1. Native place
2. Father
3. Nephew
4. Wife #1
5. Maid
6. Maid's son
7. King of Gerar
8. Sacrificial place
9. Burial place
10. Daughter-in-law
11. Grandson
12. Wife #2

a. Rebekah (Gen. 24:67)
b. Keturah (Gen. 25:1)
c. Machpelah (Gen. 23:17-20)
d. Jacob (Gen. 25:26)
e. Ur of the Chaldees (Gen. 11:28)
f. Lot (Gen. 11:31)
g. Hagar (Gen. 16:1)
h. Terah (Gen. 11:27)
i. Ishmael (Gen. 16:11)
j. Abimelech (Gen. 20:2)
k. Sarah (Gen. 11:31)
l. Jehovah-jireh (Gen. 22:14)

102
Actions

Everything in the world has a function. Match each action with the correct object.

1. The earth	a. "is an unruly evil" (Jas. 3:8).
2. The heavens	b. "consumeth the chaff" (Isa. 5:24).
3. The firmament	c. "is a wellspring of life" (Prov. 16:22).
4. The Lord	d. "is the Lord's" (Ps. 24:1).
5. The lilies	e. "declare the glory of God" (Ps. 19:1).
6. The ravens	f. "sheweth his handiwork" (Ps. 19:1).
7. The ant	g. "boasteth of his heart's desire" (Ps. 10:3).
8. The wicked	h. "provideth her meat in the summer" (Prov. 6:8).
9. The eye	i. "is my light" (Ps. 27:1).
10. The tongue	j. "neither sow nor reap" (Luke 12:24).
11. The fire	k. "[is] the light of the body" (Matt. 6:22).
12. Understanding	l. "toil not, neither . . . spin" (Matt. 6:28).

103
Anger

Anger is a normal human emotion. What people do with anger is the proof of character. Name the angry persons below.

1. _____ anger was stirred over a revival of his enemies (Jonah 4:1).

2. _____ anger was stirred at the sight of a golden calf (Ex. 32:19).

3. _____ anger rose over a rejected offering which led to murder (Gen. 24:5,8).

4. _____ anger was kindled because his wife said, "Give me children, or else I die" (Gen. 30:1-2).

5. _____ anger flared when a donkey saw an angel and fell down (Num. 22:27).

6. _____ anger grew because he had asked for his enemies to be cursed, and they were blessed instead (Num. 24:10).

7. _____ anger was provoked by the words of John the Baptist (Matt. 14:3).

8. _____ anger was kindled when his wife revealed the answer to his riddle (Judg. 14:17-19).

9. _____ anger was kindled when he heard the conditions for a covenant made by Nahash and he cut a yoke of oxen in pieces and sent them throughout the coasts of Israel (1 Sam. 11:1-7).

10. _____ anger was provoked over a story Nathan told him about a rich man and a poor man (2 Sam. 12:1-5).

11. _____ anger was stirred when she heard Elijah had slain all the prophets with the sword (1 Kings 19:1-2).

104
Anointed

Anointing in the Bible was a common practice. Oil was poured upon the head. Christians receive an anointing with the Holy Spirit. Fill in the blanks about anointing.

1. Aaron and his sons were anointed for work in ministering as _____ (Ex. 28:41).

2. After a sacrifice, the altar was anointed to _____ it to the Lord (Ex. 29:36).

3. The tabernacle was anointed after it was set up to make it _____ (Ex. 40:9).

4. Ruth anointed herself and went to meet _____ (Ruth 3:1-5).

5. Samuel anointed Saul to be _____ of Israel (1 Sam. 15:1).

6. Jesus told his disciples to anoint themselves when they _____ (Matt. 6:17).

7. A woman anointed Jesus' body _____ (Mark 14:8).

8. Three women came to anoint Jesus' body after His _____ (Mark 16:1).

9. An angel told the church in Philadelphia to anoint their eyes that they may _____ (Rev. 3:18).

10. God anointed Jesus with the _____ (Acts 10:38).

11. James told the early Christians to anoint the sick and pray for _____ (Jas. 5:14).

105
Authority

Authority was ordained by God to help people live together harmoniously. Fill in the blanks with the proper persons related to authority.

1. Daniel said _____ had power to remove kings (Dan. 2:21).

2. Daniel said God gave authority to _____ (Dan. 2:37).

3. Daniel said _____ would set up a kingdom "which shall never be destroyed . . . and shall stand for ever" (Dan. 2:44).

4. _____ dreamed a dream which warned him that his kingdom would be taken from him (Dan. 4:24-25).

5. The church's authority comes from _____ (Eph. 5:24).

6. _____ are to accept authority from their husbands (1 Pet. 3:1).

7. The Christian's authority is from _____ (Jas. 4:7).

8. We are to obey _____ (Titus 3:1).

9. Peter said _____ are to be under the authority of their masters (1 Pet. 2:18).

10. Peter also said _____ were to be under the authority of the elder people (1 Pet. 5:5).

11. _____ should submit to the authority of their parents (1 Tim. 3:4).

12. Christians are to submit themselves to every _____ for the Lord's sake (1 Pet. 2:13).

106
Behold

The word *behold* was often used in the Bible to call attention to what was to follow, or to say, "Look." Match the persons with their "behold."

1. "Behold, the Lamb of God"
2. "Behold, the handmaid of the Lord"
3. ". . . Behold thy son"
4. "Behold, I shew you a mystery"
5. "Behold, I am with thee"
6. "Behold the place where they laid him"
7. "Behold, a virgin shall conceive"
8. "Behold, I bring him forth to you"
9. "Behold, thy King cometh unto thee"
10. "Behold the blood of the covenant"
11. "Behold, I was shapen in iniquity"

a. Moses (Ex. 24:8)
b. Pilate (John 19:4)
c. God (Gen. 28:15)
d. Isaiah (Isa. 7:14)
e. John the Baptist (John 1:29)
f. Jesus (John 19:26)
g. Zechariah (Zech. 9:9)
h. a young man (Mark 16:6)
i. David (Ps. 51:5)
j. Paul (1 Cor. 15:51)
k. Mary (Luke 1:38)

107
Biblical Alphabet

Fill in each blank with a name that begins with the letter listed.

A _____ caught his hair in an oak tree (2 Sam. 18:9).
B _____ was the second husband of Ruth (Ruth 4:13).
C _____ was a centurion who believed in Jesus (Acts 10:48).
D _____ was a woman who betrayed Samson (Judg. 16:10-20).
E _____ was a priest with whom Samuel worked (1 Sam. 1:25).
F _____ trembled at Paul's preaching (Acts 24:25).
G _____ the man who appeared to Daniel in a vision (Dan. 9:21).
H _____ was the mother of Samuel (1 Sam. 1:20).
I _____ is another name for Judas (Matt. 10:4).
J _____ was sold as a slave by his brothers (Gen. 37:28).
K _____ was the father of Saul (1 Sam. 9:1).
L _____ was the brother of Mary and Martha (John 12:1).
M _____ replaced Judas as treasurer (Acts 1:23,26).
N _____ showed David his sin (2 Sam. 12:1).
O _____ was a converted slave of Philemon (Philem. 10)
P _____ denied Jesus three times (Matt. 26:69-75).
Q _____ was a man Paul called brother (Rom. 16:23).
R _____ was a harlot who hid Israel's spies (Josh. 6:22).
S _____ was known for his strength (Judg. 14:5-6).
T _____ was a young companion to Paul (Acts 16:1).
U _____ was Bathsheba's first husband (2 Sam. 11:3).
V _____ was a beautiful queen replaced by Esther (Esther 1:9).
W _____ came from the East seeking a newborn king (Matt. 2:1-2).
Y _____ directed Saul to Samuel (1 Sam. 9:11).
Z _____ was the man who climbed a tree to see Jesus (Luke 19:2).

108
Birds

At least fifteen different birds are named in the Bible. Fill in each blank with the proper bird.

1. Jesus said one _____ shall not fall on the ground without our Father's knowledge (Matt. 10:29).

2. The psalmist said he was like a _____ in the wilderness (Ps. 102:6).

3. Isaiah said that people who wait upon the Lord shall renew their strength as _____ (Isa. 40:31).

4. Jesus likened His feelings for Jerusalem to a _____ who gathers her young under her wings (Matt. 23:37).

5. The navy of Tarshish came every three years bringing _____ and other gifts to Solomon (1 Kings 10:22).

6. God gave _____ and manna to the Israelites for food (Ex. 16:13).

7. Job asked if God gave wings and feathers unto the _____ (Job 39:13).

8. Micah said that he would mourn like an _____ (Mic. 1:8).

9. The psalmist said that the _____ has her house in the fir trees (Ps. 104:17).

10. Job asked if the _____ flies by God's wisdom (Job 39:26).

11. When a male child was born, an offering of two _____ or two young _____ was required (Luke 2:23-24).

12. Noah sent out a _____ to see if the flood waters had receded (Gen. 8:7).

13. The psalmist said the _____ had found a place to lay her young in the altar of the Lord (Ps. 84:3).

109
Blindness

Draw a line under the proper person connected with blindness.

1. (Barnabas, Bartimaeus, Barsabas) was blind and begged for a living (Mark 10:46).

2. (David, Elijah, Elisha) prayed for people to be made blind (2 Kings 6:18).

3. (Two angels, Gabriel, Michael) smote men at Lot's door with blindness (Gen. 19:11).

4. (Saul, Elymas, Naboth) was made blind because he tried to turn Serguis Paulus from faith (Acts 13:7-10).

5. (David, Eliphaz, Job) said he was eyes to the blind (Job 29:15).

6. (Moses, Aaron, Eli) said the man who led the blind in the wrong way would be cursed (Deut. 27:18).

7. (Mark, Jesus, Peter) was followed by two blind men (Matt. 9:27).

8. (Jesus, James, John) likened some people to the blind leading the blind (Matt. 15:14).

9. (Sadducees, Herodians, Pharisees) were called blind guides by Jesus (Matt. 23:16).

10. (Samson, Adoniram, Jonah) was blinded by his enemies who put out his eyes (Judg. 16:21).

11. (Peter, James, Saul) was blinded by a great light on his way to persecute Christians (Acts 9:5-8).

110
Boys

Match each boy with the correct statement.

1. Jesus (Luke 2:47)
2. David (1 Sam. 16:19)
3. Joseph (Gen. 37:3)
4. Isaac (Gen. 22:12)
5. Moses (Ex. 2:10)
6. Samuel (1 Sam. 3:1)
7. Josiah (2 Kings 22:1)
8. Ishmael (Gen. 21:12-16)
9. Jacob (Gen. 25:28)
10. Esau (Gen. 25:25)
11. Cain (Gen. 4:1)

a. became a king at eight years of age
b. almost became a sacrifice
c. covered with red hair
d. astounded Temple leaders
e. driven from home by his father
f. given a beautiful coat
g. grew up as a princess' son
h. first boy on the earth
i. loved by his mother
j. a shepherd boy
k. lived in the Tabernacle (Temple, KJV)

111
Brides

Match each bride with her groom.

1. Rebekah (Gen. 24:63-67).	a.	Zacharias
2. Leah (Gen. 29:23-25)	b.	Othniel
3. Deborah (Judg. 4:4)	c.	Heber
4. Eve (Gen. 2:21-23)	d.	Ahab
5. Hannah (1 Sam. 1:1-2)	e.	Isaac
6. Jael (Judg. 4:17)	f.	Lapidoth
7. Abigail (1 Sam. 25:42)	g.	Boaz
8. Jezebel (1 Kings 21:25)	h.	David
9. Asenath (Gen. 41:45)	i.	Joseph
10. Elisabeth (Luke 1:5)	j.	Jacob
11. Mary (Matt. 1:20)	k.	Elkanah
12. Ruth (Ruth 4:10)	l.	Adam
13. Achsah (Josh. 15:17)	m.	Joseph

112
Burning Objects

Fire is often mentioned in the Bible. Match each biblical character with the correct burning object.

1. Moses (Ex. 3:2)
2. Isaiah (Isa. 6:6-7)
3. Apostles (Acts 2:3)
4. Israelites (Deut. 4:11)
5. David (2 Sam. 5:21)
6. Josiah (2 Kings 23:6)
7. Amaziah (2 Chron. 25:14)
8. Jehoiakim (Jer. 36:30)
9. Wise virgins (Luke 12:35)
10. Shadrach (Dan. 3:20)
11. Samson (Judg. 15:14)

a. burning incense
b. burning flax
c. burning mountain
d. burning lamps
e. burning furnace
f. burning bush
g. burning coal
h. burning roll
i. burning tongues
j. burning images
k. burning grove

113
Characteristic Qualities

The word *spirit* may refer to a characteristic quality of a person: broken, dumb, faithful, foul, good, humble, meek, ministering, new, perverse, quiet, unclean, and wounded. Fill in each blank with one of these kinds of spirits.

1. "Are they not all _____ spirits, sent forth to minister for them who shall be heirs of salvation?" (Heb. 1:14).

2. "But let it be the hidden man of the heart, in that which is not corruptible, even the ornament of a _____ and _____ spirit, which is in the sight of God of great price" (1 Pet. 3:4).

3. "Master, I have brought unto thee my son, which hath a _____ spirit" (Mark 9:17).

4. "A talebearer revealeth secrets: but he that is of a _____ spirit concealeth the matter" (Prov. 11:13).

5. "When Jesus saw that the people came running together, he rebuked the _____ spirit, saying unto him, . . . I charge thee, come out of him" (Mark 9:25).

6. "Thou gavest also thy _____ spirit to instruct them, and withheldest not thy manna from their mouth, and gavest them water for their thirst" (Neh. 9:20).

7. "Better it is to be of an _____ spirit with the lowly, than to divide the spoil with the proud" (Prov. 16:19).

8. "And I will give them one heart, and I will put a _____ spirit within you" (Ezek. 11:19).

9. "The Lord hath mingled a _____ spirit in the midst thereof: and they have caused Egypt to err in every work thereof" (Isa. 19:14).

114
Church

Fill in each blank with something associated with church.

1. Ezra stood at a _____ made of wood to read the law of God to the people (Neh. 8:4).

2. The Levites served as _____ to praise God (2 Chron. 7:6).

3. The disciples sang a _____ after the Last Supper and went out into the Mount of Olives (Matt. 26:30).

4. Jesus said that when we bring our gifts to the _____ and remember that a brother has something against us, we are to leave the gift and go right the wrong (Matt. 5:24).

5. When Peter was in prison, " _____ was made without ceasing . . . unto God for him" (Acts 12:5).

6. " The _____ is quick, and powerful, and sharper than any two-edged sword" according to the writer of Hebrews (Heb. 4:12).

7. Paul asked, "And how shall they hear without a _____ ?" (Rom. 10:14).

8. David said, "Give unto the Lord glory due unto his name: bring an _____ , and come before him" (1 Chron. 16:29).

9. The psalmist said, "O come, let us _____ and bow down" (Ps. 95:6).

10. Heman, Asaph, and Ethan were _____ who "were appointed to sound with cymbals of brass" (1 Chron. 15:19).

11. John said the _____ he declared is "that God is light" (1 John 1:5).

115
Church Members

No church can function without members. Match the church member below with his or her church.

1. Phebe
2. Ananias and Sapphira
3. Epaphroditus
4. Epaphras
5. Barnabas
6. Sergius Paulus
7. Epaenetus
8. Manaen
9. Aquila and Priscilla
10. Gaius and Aristarchus
11. Philip
12. Aristobulus
13. The eunuch

a. Paphos (Acts 13:6-12)
b. Corinth (Acts 18:1-2)
c. Achaia (Rom. 16:5)
d. Antioch (Acts 13:1)
e. Caesarea (Acts 21:8)
f. Colosse (Col. 4:12)
g. Ethiopia (Acts 8:27-38)
h. Macedonia (Acts 19:29)
i. Jerusalem (Acts 5:1)
j. Philippi (Phil. 4:18)
k. Rome (Rom. 1:7; 16:10)
l. Antioch (Acts 13:1)
m. Cenchrea (Rom. 16:1)

116
Clothes

Fill in each blank with the person associated with the clothing mentioned:

1. Jacob said of his son _____ "he washed his garments in wine, and his clothes in the blood of grapes" (Gen. 49:11).

2. The _____ bound up their kneadingtroughs in their clothes as Moses commanded (Ex. 12:34).

3. A sick woman said, "If I but may touch his [_____] clothes, I shall be whole" (Mark 5:28).

4. For forty years the _____ wore the same clothes which did not wear out (Deut. 29:5).

5. _____ wrapped her baby in swaddling clothes and laid Him in a manger (Luke 2:7).

6. Jesus found _____ wearing no clothes in a graveyard (Luke 8:27-28).

7. As _____ entered Jerusalem riding a colt, people spread their clothes in His path (Luke 19:36).

8. _____ was bound with graveclothes and Jesus said, "Loose him, and let him go" (John 11:44).

9. Friends took the body of _____ and wound it in linen clothes (John 19:40).

10. At the stoning of Stephen, witnesses laid down their clothes at the feet of a young man named _____ (Acts 7:58).

11. _____ rent his clothes in mourning over the king's decree against his people, the Jews (Esther 4:1).

117
Clothing

Match each piece of clothing with the person who wore it.

1. Paul (2 Tim. 4:13)   a. apron
2. Jesus (John 19:2)   b. camel's hair
3. Adam (Gen. 3:7)   c. colorful coat
4. Job (Job 16:15)   d. fisherman's coat
5. John the Baptist (Matt. 3:4)   e. needlework girdle
6. Boaz (Ruth 3:9)   f. royal robe
7. Peter (John 21:7)   g. purple robe
8. Joseph (Gen. 37:3)   h. sackcloth
9. Jonathan (1 Sam. 18:4)   i. a linen cloth
10. Aaron (Ex. 28:38-39)   j. skirt
11. a young man (Mark 14:51-52)   k. cloak

118
Co-laborers

Match the two people below who worked together in an endeavor.

1.	Aquila	a.	Sapphira (Acts 5:1-10)
2.	Barnabas	b.	God (2 Cor. 6:1)
3.	Moses	c.	Herod (Matt. 14:6-10)
4.	Christians	d.	Priscilla (Acts 18:26)
5.	Rebekah	e.	John (Matt. 4:21)
6.	Abraham	f.	Paul (Acts 9:26-31)
7.	Ananias	g.	Eli (1 Sam. 2:11)
8.	Joshua	h.	Lot (Gen. 13:1-5)
9.	Samuel	i.	Caleb (Num. 14:30)
10.	Herodias	j.	Jacob (Gen. 27:6-10)
11.	James	k.	Aaron (Ex. 5:20)

119
Colorful Things

Imagine what the world would be without the beauty of colors. Match the item with its color in each of the following examples.

1. Jesus' robe (Matt. 27:28)
2. Lydia sold (Acts 16:14)
3. Mordacai's robe (Esther 8:15)
4. Daniel's robe given him by Belshazzar (Dan. 5:29)
5. Withs which bound Samson (Judg. 16:7)
6. Hair of a leper (Lev. 13:30)
7. Jacob's sorrowing hair (Gen. 42:36-38)
8. Laban's cattle (Gen. 30:32)
9. Harvest fields (John 4:35)
10. Gates of Jerusalem (Jer. 14:2)
11. Joseph's cup (Gen. 44:2)

a. black
b. brown
c. green
d. blue-and-white
e. purple
f. silver
g. white
h. scarlet
i. scarlet
j. yellow
k. gray

120
Commands

Commands are a part of living. Match each command with the person to whom it was given.

1. "Come forth."
2. "Get thee out of thy country."
3. "Get thee behind me."
4. "Of the fruit of the tree . . . ye shall not eat."
5. "Put off thy shoes"
6. "Feed my sheep."
7. "Go and sell that thou hast."

8. "Arise, go to Nineveh."
9. "Go and wash in Jordan seven times."
10. "Come over into Macedonia, and help us."
11. "Take now . . . thine only son . . . and offer him"

a. Naaman (2 Kings 5:9-10)
b. Moses (Ex. 3:5)
c. Lazarus (John 11:43)
d. Jonah (Jonah 1:1-2)

e. Paul (Acts 16:9)
f. Abram (Gen. 12:1)
g. rich young ruler (Matt. 19:21-22)

h. Abraham (Gen. 22:1-2)
i. Satan (Matt. 16:23)

j. Eve (Gen. 3:3)

k. Simon Peter (John 21:16)

121
Creation

Fill the blanks under each day with the creation of God on that day. Use the words in the second column.

1. First day (Gen. 1:3)
   _____

2. Second day (Gen. 1:7)
   _____

3. Third day (Gen. 1:10-13)
   _____
   _____
   _____

4. Fourth day (Gen. 1:14-19)
   _____
   _____
   _____

5. Fifth day (Gen. 1:20-23)
   _____
   _____

6. Sixth day (Gen. 1:25-27)
   _____
   _____
   _____
   _____

7. Seventh day (Gen. 2:3)
   _____

beast
cattle
creeping things
earth
firmament
fish
fowl
fruit tree
grass
light
male and female
moon
God rested
seas
sun
stars
whales

122
Crucifixion of Jesus

Match the correct person with the fact about the crucifixion.

1. Judas (John 18:2)
2. Peter (John 18:27)
3. Caiaphas (John 18:14)
4. Barabbas (John 18:40)

5. Pilate (John 19:6)
6. Soldiers (John 19:23-24)
7. Chief priests (Matt. 27:6-8)
8. Simon (Mark 15:21)
9. Herod (Luke 23:8)
10. Mary and Mary Magdalene (Matt. 27:55-56)
11. Joseph (Luke 23:51-52)

a. carried the cross
b. stood at the cross
c. betrayed Jesus
d. wanted to see Jesus do a miracle
e. buried Jesus
f. denied knowing Jesus
g. cast lots for Jesus' coat
h. released instead of Jesus
i. found no fault in Jesus
j. bought the potter's field called "The field of blood"
k. counseled the people to kill Jesus

123
David

The life of David is one of the most illustrous in the Bible. Match these facts about David's life.

1. father
2. native town
3. anointed by
4. champion he slew
5. became an enemy
6. gave him shewbread
7. cave where he hid
8. lame boy he helped
9. had him killed in battle
10. wife
11. prophet who rebuked him
12. rebellious son
13. escorted him over Jordan
14. successor

a. Nathan (2 Sam. 12:1-14)
b. Mephibosheth (2 Sam. 9:7-8)
c. Barzillai (2 Sam. 19:31-32)
d. Jesse (1 Sam. 16:11)
e. Samuel (1 Sam. 16:13)
f. Uriah (2 Sam. 11:17)
g. Solomon (1 Chr. 23:1)
h. Absalom (2 Sam. 15:1-6)
i. Bethlehem (1 Sam. 16:1)
j. Ahimelech (1 Sam. 21:16)
k. Saul (1 Sam. 18:29)
l. Goliath (1 Sam. 17:1)
m. Adullam (1 Sam. 22:1)
n. Bathsheba (2 Sam. 11:26-27)

124
Deceivers

One of Satan's greatest tricks is the use of deceit. Fill in each blank with the proper deceiver.

1. Joab warned King David that _____ sought to deceive the king (2 Sam. 3:25-26).

2. _____ deceived Jacob by withholding part of his wages (Gen. 31:7).

3. _____ and his wife sought to deceive the church by holding back part of the price of land they sold (Acts 5:1-2).

4. _____ attempted to deceive the Wise Men by pretending to want to worship the baby Jesus (Matt. 2:7-8).

5. _____ deceived her father Saul by sending his enemy David away (1 Sam. 19:17).

6. _____ deceived a witch by disguising himself (1 Sam. 28:8,12).

7. _____ accused Job of deceit by hiding his sin (Job 15:1-31).

8. Jesus warned His followers of people who deceived by saying, "I am _____ " (Luke 21:8).

9. The sons of Jacob deceived _____ , son of Hamor, because of the defilement of Dinah (Gen. 34:13).

10. _____ deceived the Israelites into believing that he would let them leave Egypt (Ex. 8:29).

11. _____ deceived his father by pretending to be Esau (Gen. 27:12).

125
Descriptions

Descriptions without colors are incomplete. Match each of the following colored objects with the person who mentioned it.

1. The psalmist (Ps. 71:18)	a. yellow feathers
2. Jeremiah (Jer. 22:14)	b. black heaven
3. Mathew (Matt. 16:2)	c. brown sheep
4. Jacob (Gen. 30:35)	d. green tree
5. Elijah (1 Kings 18:41-45)	e. blue robe
6. Joshua (Josh. 2:18)	f. grey hair
7. Psalmist (Ps. 68:13)	g. red sky
8. Aaron (Ex. 28:31)	h. purple raiment
9. Luke (Luke 23:31)	i. scarlet thread
10. John (Rev. 7:9)	j. vermillion houses
11. Kings of Midian (Judg. 8:26)	k. white robes

126
Disciples

Match each disciple with the statement which most nearly fits him.

1. sat under a fig tree (John 1:48)
2. walked on water (Matt. 14:29)
3. Disciple of love (1 John 4:7)
4. tax collector (Luke 5:27-28)
5. brought Nathanael to Jesus (John 1:45)
6. Doubter (John 20:24-25)
7. called Lebbaeus (Matt. 10:3)
8. betrayed Jesus (Matt. 26:14-16)
9. first to die (Acts 12:2)
10. Peter's brother (Mark 1:16)
11. The Zealot (Acts 1:13)

a. James
b. Philip
c. Peter
d. Simon
e. Thomas

f. Thaddaeus
g. Nathanael
h. Matthew (Levi)
i. Andrew
j. Judas Iscariot
k. John

127
Disobedience

Match each person with his act of disobedience.

1. Abraham (Gen. 16:1-3)

2. Jacob (Gen. 27:6-29)
3. Joseph's brothers
   (Gen. 37:28)

4. Moses (Ex. 2:11-15)
5. Children of Israel
   (Num. 14:1-10)
6. Jonah (Jonah 1:1-3)
7. Saul (1 Sam. 15:20-21)

8. David (2 Sam. 11:3-21)

9. Peter (John 18:25)

10. Uzziah (2 Chron. 26:16)

11. Solomon (Neh. 13:25-27)

a. tried to deliver Israel by his own power
b. sold brother into slavery
c. refused to enter the Promised Land according to God's schedule
d. took spoils of battle
e. gained first place in family by deceit
f. married strange wives
g. lied about being Jesus' disciple
h. killed a man whose wife he coveted
i. failed to believe God for promised descendants
j. fled to keep from preaching to Nineveh
k. burned incense upon the altar in the Temple

128
Divination

The use of divination is strongly forbidden in the Bible. Fill in each blank with the name of the person involved with divination.

1. God told _____ that the prophets prophesied false visions to him (Jer. 14:14).

2. A _____ possessed with a spirit of divination which brought her masters much gain by soothsaying was cleansed of the evil spirit (Acts 16:16-19).

3. _____ , a sorcerer, tried to give the apostles money for the Holy Spirit's power (Acts 8:9,18).

4. _____ , a sorcerer, sought to turn away a deputy of Paphos from hearing the word of God (Acts 13:6-8).

5. _____ called in sorcerers who cast down their rods which became serpents like Moses' and Aaron's did (Ex. 7:11-12).

6. _____ called in sorcerers to explain his dream (Dan. 2:2).

7. _____ used divination and consulted images (Ezek. 21:21).

8. _____ warned the Israelites to stay away from divination, observers of times, enchanters, charmers, consulters with familiar spirits, wizards, and necromancers (Deut. 18:10-12).

9. _____ sought advice from a woman with a familiar spirit (1 Sam. 28:7).

10. _____ consulted astrologers to interpret the handwriting on the wall (Dan. 5:16).

11. _____ used enchantments, witchcraft, familiar spirits, wizards, and observers of times when he ruled (2 Chron. 33:1-6).

129
Dogs

Dogs have not always been looked upon as favored pets. Fill in each blank with the proper person connected with the statement about dogs.

1. God told _____ to pick soldiers from the men who lapped water like dogs (Judg. 7:5).

2. The dogs licked the sores of _____ (Luke 16:20-21).

3. The Lord said the dogs would eat _____ by the wall of Jezreel (1 Kings 21:23).

4. A woman said unto _____ , ". . . the dogs under the table eat of the children's crumbs" (Mark 7:28).

5. _____ was slain in battle and the dogs licked up his blood (1 Kings 22:38).

6. _____ cautioned his followers not to give holy things to the dogs (Matt. 7:6).

7. _____ told Moses that no dog would move his tongue against the Israelites in order that they could understand that they were different from the Egyptians (Ex. 11:7).

8. _____ said to David, "Am I a dog that you come to me with staves?" when David came to defeat him with stones (1 Sam. 17:4,43).

9. _____ angered Abner who asked, "Am I a dog's head?" because of Abner's alliance with Saul against David (2 Sam. 3:8).

10. _____ asked David who befriended him for his father's sake, "What is thy servant, that thou shouldest look upon such a dead dog as I am?" (2 Sam. 9:6-8).

11. _____ asked Elisha, ". . . is thy servant a dog, that he should do this great thing?" as he tried to conceal from Elisha a plan to kill Ben-hadad and become king (2 Kings 8:13-15).

130
Drunkenness

Alcoholic beverages have always created problems for people. Fill in each blank with the person associated with drunkenness.

1. _____ planted a vineyard, got drunk, and lay uncovered in his tent (Gen. 9:21).

2. _____ saw his father's drunken state and told his brothers (Gen. 9:22-26).

3. _____ and Japheth covered their father's drunken nakedness (Gen. 9:23).

4. _____ was made drunk by his two daughters so that they could bear his children (Gen. 19:31-34).

5. _____ made Uriah drunk in order to cover his sin with Uriah's wife (2 Sam. 11:13).

6. _____ and the other disciples were accused of being drunk on the Day of Pentecost (Acts 2:14-15).

7. _____ , king of Israel, was drunk when he was killed by his servant Zimri in a conspiracy (1 Kings 16:9-10).

8. _____ was grieved over her barrenness and Eli accused her of being drunk (1 Sam. 1:13-14).

9. _____ was drunk when his wife tried to talk to him; but when she did, he "became as a stone" (1 Sam. 25:36-37).

10. _____ rebuked the Corinthians for their drunkenness at church suppers (1 Cor. 11:21).

11. _____ warned the Israelites that God will not spare the man who boasts that he can have peace though he added drunkenness to thirst (Deut. 29:19).

131
Easter

The first day of Jesus' resurrection was a busy one. Fill in the blanks about the first Easter with the proper persons.

1. _____ , _____ , and _____ were the first people to visit the tomb on Easter Sunday (Mark 16:1).

2. _____ rolled back the stone and sat on it (Matt. 28:2).

3. _____ told the two Marys to tell the disciples to go to Galilee and there they would see Jesus (Matt. 28:9).

4. _____ were given money to say that the disciples had stolen Jesus' body (Matt. 28:12-13).

5. Jesus found _____ in the garden crying (Mark 16:9).

6. _____ ran to the sepulcher to see if the women had spoken the truth about Jesus being alive (Luke 24:12).

7. _____ outran Peter to the sepulcher (John 20:4).

8. _____ mistook Jesus for the gardener (John 20:15).

9. _____ and another person walked with Jesus and did not know Him (Luke 24:18).

10. Jesus found the frightened _____ in an upper room (John 20:19).

11. _____ said unless he could see and touch Jesus, he would not believe the news of His resurrection (John 20:25).

132
Elijah Fill-in

"The fiery prophet" Elijah was a unique person. Fill in the blanks with the proper fact about Elijah's life.

1. God sent _____ to care for Elijah by the brook (1 Kings 17:4).

2. In the town of Zarephath _____ gave Elijah food to eat (1 Kings 17:9).

3. God gave the woman _____ until it started raining again (1 Kings 17:14).

4. Israel had been without rain _____ years when Elijah went back to see Ahab (1 Kings 18:1).

5. Elijah used _____ stones for the altar he built (1 Kings 18:31).

6. Elijah told the people to fill the barrels with water _____ times (1 Kings 18:34).

7. Elijah _____ when the altar was ready (1 Kings 18:36-37).

8. After Elijah sat down under the juniper tree, he asked the Lord to _____ (1 Kings 19:4).

9. God spoke to Elijah on Mount Horeb by _____ (1 Kings 19:12).

10. Elijah called _____ from God to kill 102 men (2 Kings 1:9-12).

11. Elijah parted water with his _____ (2 Kings 2:6-8).

12. Elijah fled to the _____ to escape Queen Jezebel (1 Kings 19:34).

13. Elijah was taken up to heaven in a _____ (2 Kings 2:11).

14. Elijah sat under a juniper tree and prayed; an angel told him to _____ (1 Kings 19:4-8).

15. God told Elijah _____ people had not bowed to Baal (1 Kings 19:18).

133
Elijah Match

Match the names in the first column with the fact in Elijah's life associated with the name.

1. Ahab
2. Baal
3. Naboth
4. Hazael
5. Elisha
6. Jezebel
7. Cherith
8. Gilead
9. Zarephath
10. Obadiah
11. Ahaziah

a. brook where Elijah hid (1 Kings 17:3).
b. governor who hid prophets from Jezebel (1 Kings 18:4).
c. Elijah told him he would not recover from a fall (2 Kings 1:1-4).
d. Elijah told him no rain would fall (1 Kings 17:1).
e. Elijah anointed him king of Syria (1 Kings 19:15).
f. widow who fed Elijah lived here (1 Kings 17:9).
g. false God challenged by Elijah (1 Kings 16:32).
h. successor to Elijah (1 Kings 19:16).
i. home of Elijah (1 Kings 17:1).
j. queen who threatened Elijah (1 Kings 19:2).
k. Elijah reprimanded Ahab for killing this man (1 Kings 21:17-24).

134
Elisha Fill-In

Elisha was a faithful follower of Elijah. Fill in the blanks with the proper facts about Elisha.

1. Elisha healed the waters of Jericho by putting _____ into the spring (2 Kings 2:21).

2. The sons of the prophets of Jericho declared about Elisha: "The spirit of _____ doth rest upon Elisha" (2 Kings 2:15).

3. Elisha helped the widow of Shunem by _____ her son from the dead (2 Kings 4:18-37).

4. Elisha's servant was _____ (2 Kings 4:12).

5. _____ heard about Elisha through a slave girl (2 Kings 5:1-14).

6. Elisha caused an _____ to float on water (2 Kings 6:5-6).

7. _____ brought good tidings to the famished city of Samaria (2 Kings 7:3-11).

8. At Elisha's death, Joash said, "O my father, my father; the _____ of Israel and the horsemen thereof" (2 Kings 13:14).

9. Elisha used a _____ and _____ to predict the destruction of Syria (2 Kings 13:15).

10. When Elisha prayed, God opened the eyes of his servant, and he saw a mountain full of _____ and chariots (2 Kings 6:17).

11. Elisha told Naaman to _____ in Jordan seven times and leprosy would leave him (2 Kings 5:10).

12. Elisha helped a widow save her two sons by _____ (2 Kings 4:1-7).

13. Elisha prayed for a _____ to relieve the drought (2 Kings 3:9-16).

135
Eyes

Many people say they would rather lose their ears than their eyes. Fill in each blank with the proper set of eyes.

1. _____ wanted Jabesh-gilead to pay with their right eyes for a covenant of protection (1 Sam. 11:1-2).

2. _____ ate honey in unknown defiance of his father's oath and his eyes were "enlightened" (1 Sam. 14:27).

3. _____ , a blind prophet was told by the Lord that Jeroboam's wife was coming in disguise to ask a favor of him (1 Kings 14:4-5).

4. _____ the prophet stretched across a dead child's body and the child opened his eyes (2 Kings 4:32-35).

5. _____ saw his sons killed by the Chaldees who put his eyes out and carried him captive to Babylon (2 Kings 25:5-7).

6. _____ healed a blind man who said he saw men walking like trees (Mark 8:23-24).

7. _____ had a vision of a goat with a horn between his eyes (Dan. 8:5).

8. _____ , fastening his eyes upon a lame man at the Beautiful Gate, told him, "Look on us" (Acts 3:2-3).

9. _____ was on the Damascus road when a light appeared and his eyes were opened but he could see no one (Acts 9:8).

10. _____ commanded the Israelites to wear the words of the Lord as frontlets between their eyes (Deut. 11:18).

11. _____ asked God to strike the Syrians blind and then prayed for their eyes to be opened (2 Kings 6:18-20).

136
Families

Fill in each blank with the proper biblical family member.

1. A boy _____ , his mother, _____ and his grandmother _____ were friends of Paul (2 Tim. 1:1-5).

2. Two sisters _____ and _____ and a brother _____ were friends of Jesus (John 11:1).

3. The first family were: father _____ , mother _____ and two sons _____ and _____ (Gen. 4:1-2).

4. A brother, _____ , told about his dream, and his brothers sold him into slavery (Gen. 37:3-28).

5. Twin brothers _____ and _____ , father _____ and mother _____ were an early family (Gen. 25:21-26).

6. A young boy _____ and a priest _____ lived together in the tabernacle (1 Sam. 2:11).

7. Jesus' parents were: mother _____ and earthly father _____ (Matt. 1:18).

8. Brothers who followed Jesus were: _____ and _____ and their father was _____ (Matt. 4:21).

9. A sister _____ , who watched over a baby brother named _____ , had another brother _____ who became famous (Ex. 2:1-3; 4:14).

10. A wilderness prophet was _____ ; his father, _____ ; and his mother, _____ (Luke 1:5, 60).

11. A prophet _____ , his wayward wife _____ , two sons _____ and _____ , and a daughter _____ lived in Old Testament days (Hos. 1:2-9).

137
Fasting

Before many miraculous acts from God people fasted and prayed. Match the person who fasted with the event which took place.

1. Moses (Ex. 34:28)
2. Ahab (1 Kings 21:29)
3. Daniel (Dan. 10:3ff)

4. Peter (Acts 10:11-15, 34)
5. Jesus (Luke 4:2)
6. Ezra (Ezra 10:1-6).
7. Nehemiah (Neh. 1-6)
8. Jehoshaphat
   (2 Chron. 20:3-22)
9. Paul and friends
   (Acts 27:33-44)
10. Nineveh (Jonah 3:5-10)
11. Antioch church
    (Acts 13:1-3)

a. revival came to wicked people
b. missionaries sent out
c. enemy defeated with songs that praised God
d. lives spared though shipwrecked
e. marriages purified
f. walls rebuilt in Jerusalem
g. prejudices removed
h. evil withheld in his day

i. was tempted by Satan

j. visions revealed
k. Ten Commandments received

138
Fathers

Fill in each blank with the name of the correct father.

1. _____ was a priest whose two sons went bad (1 Sam. 2:12,17).

2. _____ was the father of Samuel (1 Sam. 1:1-2).

3. _____ sacrificed his daughter (Judg. 11:34-40).

4. _____ took Isaac to a mountain to sacrifice him as God had commanded (Gen. 22:1-2).

5. _____ was the father of twins (Gen. 25:20,24).

6. _____ lamented over a wayward son who tried to steal the kingdom (2 Sam. 18:33).

7. _____ acted as a father to his cousin who become queen (Esther 2:11).

8. _____ was Saul's father (1 Sam. 9:3).

9. _____ lost all his children in a wind storm (Job 1:19).

10. _____ was the father of an apostle named James (Matt. 10:3).

11. _____ was ordered to take his sons and daughters into an ark for safety (Gen. 7:7).

12. _____ was the father of Methuselah (Gen. 5:22).

139
Firsts

Many statements in the Bible contain the word *first*. Answer each question with the correct first.

1. What is the First Commandment? (Ex. 20:3)
2. Who did John say first loved us? (1 John 4:19)
3. What first thing were the Israelites to bring to the house of the Lord? (Ex. 23:19).
4. Who asked Job if he were the first man who ever lived? (Job 15:7).
5. Who made Daniel first over the three presidents? (Dan. 6:1-2).
6. Who said, "I will . . . return to my first husband"? (Hos. 2:7).
7. What are Christians to seek first? (Matt. 6:33).
8. What did Jesus tell us to do first, then we could remove the mote from someone else's eye? (Luke 6:42).
9. What did the young man say he had to do first and then he could follow Jesus? (Matt. 8:21).
10. What first did Jesus tell Peter to get tax money from? (Matt. 17:27).
11. To whom did Jesus appear first after His resurrection? (Mark 16:9).
12. Who did Andrew first find to tell him about Jesus? (John 1:4).
13. Who wrapped her firstborn son in swaddling clothes and laid Him in a manger? (Luke 2:7).

140
Followers

Each of the following people followed something. Match the person with what he followed:

1. Wise Men (Matt. 2:2).
2. Peter (Acts 12:8)
3. Moses (Num. 10:33-34)
4. Ananias (Acts 5:3)
5. Samson (Judg. 14:3)
6. David (2 Sam. 11:2-4)
7. Timothy (1 Cor. 16:10)
8. Pharaoh (Ex. 8:19)
9. Paul (Acts 16:9)
10. Saul (1 Sam. 28:7-8)
11. Joseph (Gen. 37:5,9-10)

a. an evil woman
b. his dream
c. a missionary
d. a heavenly vision
e. a star
f. a soothsayer
g. a hardened heart
h. an angel
i. lust
j. a pillar of cloud and fire
k. greed

141
Fools

A fool is a person who acts unwisely. Match the "foolish" statement with the foolish person.

1. He died as a fool
2. spoke as a fool
3. "I have played the fool, and have erred exceedingly."
4. "There is no God"
5. "So he that getteth riches, and not by right . . . shall be a fool."
6. "Whosoever shall say, Thou fool, shall be in danger of hell fire."
7. "Thou fool, this night thy soul shall be required of thee."
8. "Let him become a fool, that he may be wise."
9. "Thou speakest as one of the foolish . . . shall we receive good at the hand of God and shall we not receive evil."
10. Called fools because they were unprepared
11. Told to avoid foolish questions

a. Rich farmer (Luke 12:20)
b. Jeremiah (Jer. 17:11)
c. Anyone who seems to be wise (1 Cor. 3:18)
d. Timothy (2 Tim. 2:23)
e. the fool (Ps. 14:1)

f. Job (Job 2:10)

g. Abner (2 Sam. 3:33)

h. Jesus (Matt. 5:22)

i. Saul (1 Sam. 26:21)

j. Five virgins (Matt. 25:1-12)

k. Paul (2 Cor. 11:23)

142
Friends

Pick out the two friends in each set of names. In the blanks, write the names of the persons who were not friends.

_____ 1. a-David, b-Judah, c-Jonathan (1 Sam. 18:1).
_____ 2. a-Jonah, b-Pharaoh, c-Joseph (Gen. 41:42)
_____ 3. a-Shadrach, b-Darius, c-Meshach (Dan. 3:14)
_____ 4. a-Abel, b-Joshua, c-Caleb (Num. 14:30)
_____ 5. a-Barnabas, b-Paul, c-Caesar (Acts 12:25)
_____ 6. a-Elijah, b-Elisha, c-Shem (2 Kings 2:8-9)
_____ 7. a-Noah, b-Samuel, c-Eli (1 Sam. 3:4-5)
_____ 8. a-Elias, b-Silas, c-Paul (Acts 15:40)
_____ 9. a-Job, 2-Issachar, c-Eliphaz (Job 4:1)
_____ 10. a-Bartholomew, b-Agrippa, c-Philip (Matt. 10:3)
_____ 11. a-Peter, b-James, c-Joseph (Acts 1:13)

143
The Good Shepherd

The story of the Good Shepherd has been a favorite of Christians for many years. Fill in each blank with the proper person according to John 10.

1. The _____ enters the sheepfold by the door (v. 2).
2. A _____ enters the sheepfold by another way (v. 1).
3. The _____ opens the door for the shepherd (v. 3).
4. The _____ calls the sheep by their names (v. 3).
5. The sheep will flee from a _____ (v. 5).
6. _____ is the door of the sheep (v. 7).
7. _____ and _____ came before Jesus (v. 8).
8. If any _____ enters the fold, he shall be saved (v. 9).
9. The _____ comes to steal, kill, and destroy (v. 10).
10. The good _____ gives his life for the sheep (v. 11).
11. The _____ flees when trouble comes (vv. 12-13).
12. The good _____ knows his sheep (v. 14).
13. Jesus said He must bring in the _____ which are not of this fold (v. 16).

144
Go

God's will for His people often requires that they "go" to another place. Match each person with the place he was to go.

1. Moses (Ex. 19:20)
2. Joshua and Caleb (Deut. 1:35-38)
3. Jacob (Gen. 35:1)
4. David (1 Sam. 23:4)
5. Jeremiah (Jer. 18:2)
6. Samuel (1 Sam. 16:4)
7. Disciples (Matt. 28:19)
8. Abraham (Gen. 22:2)
9. Elijah (1 Kings 17:9)
10. Jonah (Jonah 1:2)
11. Philip (Acts 8:26)

a. all nations
b. Bethel
c. Bethlehem
d. Gaza
e. Mount Sinai
f. Promised Land
g. Moriah
h. Zarephath
i. the potter's house
j. Keilah
k. Nineveh

145
Hunger

Fill each blank with the person who was hungry.

1. _____ sold his birthright because he was hungry (Gen. 25:30-34).

2. _____ , after forty days of fasting, was hungry and was tempted by Satan (Matt. 4:1-3).

3. _____ were fed bread from heaven for their hunger in the wilderness (Ex. 16:4).

4. _____ was afraid Jeremiah would die from hunger in a dungeon (Jer. 38:9).

5. _____ came to himself and said, "How many hired servants of my father have bread enough and to spare, and I perish with hunger!" (Luke 15:17).

6. "If thine _____ hunger, feed him" (Rom. 12:20).

7. The _____ scolded Jesus and His disciples for plucking corn on the sabbath when they were hungry (Matt. 12:1).

8. _____ cursed a barren fig tree when He was hungry (Matt. 21:18-19).

9. _____ ate shewbread when he was hungry (1 Sam. 21:6).

10. _____ became very hungry and fell into a trance in which he saw a sheet filled with "fourfooted beasts" (Acts 10:10-13).

11. _____ said that when we fail to feed the hungry, we fail to feed Him (Matt. 25:44-45).

146
If

God waits upon people to fulfill his conditions. Match each "if" with the way it is fulfilled according to God.

1. "If ye know these things, (John 13:17)

2. "If I wash thee not, (John 13:8)

3. "If ye love me, (John 14:15)

4. "If ye had known me, (John 14:7)

5. "If ye shall ask any thing in my name, (John 14:14)

6. "If ye keep my commandments, (John 15:10)

7. "For if I go not away (John 16:7)

8. "But if ye believe not his writings, (John 5:47)

9. "If any man will do his will, (John 7:17)

10. "If any man thirst, (John 7:37)

11. "If this man were not of God (John 9:33)

12. "If I do not the works of my Father, (John 10:37)

13. "If I will that he tarry till I come, (John 21:22)

a. I will do it."

b. he shall know of the doctrine."

c. he could do nothing."

d. believe me not."

e. happy are ye if ye do them."

f. how shall ye believe my words?"

g. keep my commandments."

h. let him come unto me."

i. the Comforter will not come unto you."

j. ye should have known my Father also."

k. ye shall abide in my love."

l. what is that to thee? follow thou me."

m. thou hast no part of me."

147
In-Laws

Match each in-law.

1. Sarah	a. Caiaphas (John 18:13)
2. Moses	b. David (2 Sam. 11:3)
3. Jacob	c. Potipherah (Gen. 41:45)
4. Ruth	d. Jethro (Ex. 3:1)
5. Joseph	e. Laban (Gen. 29:13)
6. David	f. Shechaniah (Neh. 6:18)
7. Tobiah	g. Saul (1 Sam. 18:21)
8. Judah	h. Tamar (Gen. 38:11)
9. Annas	i. Rebekah (Gen. 25:67)
10. Orpah	j. Naomi (Ruth 1:14)
11. Eliam	k. Ruth (Ruth 1:4)

148
Intercessory Prayer

Most people pray for themselves more than they pray for other people. Match each person with the person they prayed for.

1. Abraham (Gen. 18:23-33)
2. Jesus (John 17:20-21)
3. Paul (Col. 1:3)
4. Moses (Ex. 32:30-32)
5. Rhoda (Acts 12:12)
6. Abraham (Gen. 20:6-7).
7. Isaiah (2 Chron. 32:20-22)
8. "The man of God" (1 Kings 13:6)
9. Israelites (Ezra 6:10)
10. James (Jas. 5:13)
11. Mordecai (Esther 4:1-2)

a. Hezekiah
b. Jews
c. Jeroboam
d. Lot
e. afflicted
f. king and his sons
g. followers
h. saints and faithful brethren
i. Peter
j. Israelites
k. Abimelech

149
Jacob

People are influenced by kinfolk. Match each person with his relationship to Jacob.

<table>
<tr><td>1. father-in-law (Gen. 29:25)</td><td>a. Joseph</td></tr>
<tr><td>2. first wife (Gen. 29:25)</td><td>b. Esau</td></tr>
<tr><td>3. favorite wife (Gen. 29:28)</td><td>c. Dinah</td></tr>
<tr><td>4. youngest son (Gen. 35:18)</td><td>d. Benjamin</td></tr>
<tr><td>5. favored son (Gen. 37:3)</td><td>e. Isaac</td></tr>
<tr><td>6. mother (Gen. 25:21-26)</td><td>f. Reuben</td></tr>
<tr><td>7. father (Gen. 25:21)</td><td>g. Laban</td></tr>
<tr><td>8. twin brother (Gen. 25:26)</td><td>h. Leah</td></tr>
<tr><td>9. first son (Gen. 29:32)</td><td>i. Bilhah</td></tr>
<tr><td>10. handmaid (Gen. 30:3)</td><td>j. Rebekah</td></tr>
<tr><td>11. daughter (Gen. 30:21)</td><td>k. Rachel</td></tr>
</table>

150
Jesus Loved

Love is a human emotion. Everybody loves someone. Match each person Jesus loved with the correct statement about that person.

1. Bartimaeus	a.	a despised tax collector (Luke 19:1-8)
2. Lazarus	b.	a sister of Lazarus (John 11:1)
3. Zacchaeus	c.	a blind man (Mark 10:46)
4. Mary	d.	Jesus raised his daughter (Luke 8:41-56)
5. John	e.	a disciple hard to convince (John 20:27)
6. Martha	f.	betrayed Jesus (Mark 14:10)
7. Mary Magdalene	g.	denied Jesus (Luke 22:34, 54-62)
8. Jairus	h.	a dead man (John 11:1-44)
9. Thomas	i.	the beloved disciple (John 19:26)
10. Peter	j.	his mother (Luke 2:5-7)
11. Judas Iscariot	k.	a forgiven woman (John 21:1-16)

151
Jesus' Last Week

The last week of Jesus' earthly life was a difficult experience for Him and those who loved Him. Fill in the blanks about the last week.

1. On the Sunday before His death, Jesus entered Jerusalem on a _____ (Matt. 21:5).

2. When Jesus saw the moneychangers and sellers of doves in the Temple, he _____ (Mark 11:15).

3. As Jesus watched the people giving their offerings into the treasury, He commended a widow who gave _____ (Mark 12:42).

4. The Last Supper was held in _____ (Mark 14:15).

5. The two disciples sent to prepare the Last Supper were told to follow a man carrying a _____ (Mark 14:13).

6. After the Last Supper, Jesus went to the Garden of Gethsemane to _____ (Mark 14:32).

7. Judas betrayed Jesus for _____ pieces of silver (Matt. 26:15).

8. The crowd demanded that _____ be set free and that Jesus be crucified (Mark 15:15).

9. _____ carried the cross for Jesus (Mark 15:21).

10. Jesus prayed for _____ for those who crucified Him (Luke 23:34).

11. On the cross, Jesus refused _____ (Mark 15:23).

12. "This is Jesus the _____ " was written and placed over the cross of Jesus (Matt. 27:37).

13. _____ begged for the body of Jesus and buried it (Luke 23:50-53).

152
Joseph Fill-In

Fill in the blanks with the facts about Joseph's life.

   1. Joseph had _____ brothers (Gen. 35:22).

   2. Jacob gave Joseph a _____ of many colors (Gen. 37:3).

   3. Joseph's brothers became jealous when Joseph told about his _____ (Gen. 37:8).

   4. Joseph was sold for _____ pieces of silver (Gen. 37:28).

   5. Pharaoh made Joseph a _____ over all Egypt (Gen. 41:43).

   6. Pharaoh rewarded Joseph because Joseph interpreted his _____ (Gen. 41:14-38).

   7. Ten of Joseph's brothers came to Egypt seeking _____ (Gen. 42:3).

   8. Joseph accused his brothers of _____ (Gen. 42:9).

   9. Joseph asked for _____ for his brothers to eat (Gen. 43:30-31).

   10. Joseph said God had sent him to Egypt to preserve _____ (Gen. 45:5).

   11. Joseph sent _____ to bring Jacob to Egypt (Gen. 45:27).

153
Joseph Matching

Joseph was one of the most colorful people in the Old Testament. Match the facts about Joseph's life.

1. parents
2. recommended selling Joseph
3. youngest brother
4. where his brothers settled
5. sons

6. sold to
7. interpreted a dream for
8. prison companions
9. wife
10. saved Joseph's life
11. first burial place

a. Manasseh and Ephraim (Gen. 41:51-52)
b. Egypt (Gen. 50:26)

c. Pharaoh (Gen. 41:25)
d. Asenath (Gen. 41:45)

e. Jacob and Rachel (Gen. 30:22-26)
f. Reuben (Gen. 37:22)
g. butler and baker (Gen. 40:1-4)
h. Goshen (Gen. 47:6)
i. Judah (Gen. 37:26-27)
j. Benjamin (Gen. 42:4,13)
k. Potiphar (Gen. 37:36)

154
Judges

Judges have been essential in keeping conflict down. Fill in each blank with the name of the judge involved.

1. _____ wanted to be made judge in order to take the throne from his father (2 Sam. 15:4).

2. _____ is a judge of the widows declared the psalmist (Ps. 68:5).

3. Jesus told a story about a judge and a _____ (Luke 18:2-5).

4. _____ is the Judge of the quick and the dead according to Paul (Acts 10:42).

5. _____ said he would not be the judge of words, names, and Jewish law (Acts 18:15).

6. _____ wore himself out serving as a judge for all the Israelites (Ex. 18:13-14).

7. _____ was a woman judge (Judg. 4:4).

8. Moses decreed that the _____ would serve as judge in the case of a slayer and the revenger of blood (Num. 35:24).

9. The Israelites pleaded with Moses for a _____ to judge the people (1 Sam. 8:5).

10. _____ built a porch for the throne where he could judge the people (1 Kings 7:7).

11. Pilate told the _____ to serve as their own judge of Jesus (John 18:31).

155
Laughter

Often laughter is better than medicine. Answer each question about laughter in the Bible.

1. Where did people laugh at Jesus? (Mark 5:40).

2. Who laughed when she was told she would have a child when she was past the childbearing age? (Gen. 18:11-15).

3. Who did Jesus say shall laugh? (Luke 6:21).

4. To whom did Isaiah say, "The virgin the daughter of Zion hath . . . laughed thee to scorn"? (2 Kings 19:21).

5. Who laughed at Nehemiah for rebuilding the Jerusalem wall? (Neh. 2:19).

6. Who laughed when told he would have a son when he was 100 years old? (Gen. 17:17).

7. Who said everyone who saw him laughed him to scorn? (Ps. 22:7).

8. Who did Solomon say would laugh at calamity? (Prov. 1:26).

9. Who did David say the Lord would laugh at? (Ps. 37:12-13).

10. What did the Preacher say was better than laughter? (Eccl. 7:3).

156
Law

Law is a means of helping people live peacefully together. Fill in each blank with the word which properly tells about the law involved.

1. God gave the Ten Commandments to Moses on ____ _____ (Josh. 8:32).

2. Moses said that God came with ten thousands of saints and from His right hand came a _____ law (Deut. 33:2).

3. When King Josiah heard the words of the law, he rent his _____ (2 Chron. 34:19).

4. Ezra was a _____ of the law of Moses (Ezra 7:6).

5. Jeremiah sealed the bid for the purchase of the _____ of Hanameel according to the law (Jer. 32:9-12).

6. Daniel was accused of breaking the law of the Medes and Persians by _____ three times a day (Dan. 6:13).

7. The spiritual leaders, the _____ , and the prophets had "done violence" to the law (Zeph. 3:4).

8. Jesus said He did not come to destroy the law but to _____ it (Matt. 5:17).

9. Not one _____ or tittle shall pass from the law until all be fulfilled (Matt. 5:18).

10. Jesus said the greatest commandment in the law is to _____ wholeheartedly (Matt. 22:36).

11. Paul said that the _____ of the law shall be justified, not the hearers (Rom. 2:13).

157
Leaders

Every cause has a leader. Match the leader with the event in which he led.

1. Revival in Nineveh
2. Rebuilt Jerusalem walls
3. Construction of golden calf
4. Exodus
5. First missionary journey
6. Slaughter of Hebrew children
7. Construction of Temple
8. Conquest of Jericho
9. Conspiracy against his father David
10. Three-hundred-man battle with the Midianites
11. The Flood Era

a. Aaron (Ex. 32:35)
b. Absalom (2 Sam. 15:31)
c. Noah (Gen. 6:13)
d. Solomon (1 Kings 6:1)
e. Jonah (Matt. 12:41)
f. Moses (Ex. 14:27-31)

g. Gideon (Judg. 7:7)
h. Joshua (Josh. 6:20-26)
i. Paul (Acts 13:2)

j. Nehemiah (Neh. 3:16)

k. Pharaoh (Ex. 1:22)

158
Legal Matters

Match each name with the proper legal term.

1. Moses (Gen. 49:10)	a. advisor to lawgiver
2. Deborah (Judg. 4:4)	b. deputy of Achaia
3. Jethro (Ex. 18:1-26)	c. doctor of law
4. Solomon (1 Kings 3:28)	d. freed prisoner
5. Gamaliel (Acts 5:34)	e. The condemned
6. God (Gen. 18:25)	f. lawgiver
7. Gallio (Acts 18:12)	g. lawyer
8. Paul (Acts 26:22)	h. prophetess-judge
9. Jesus (Matt. 20:18)	i. Judge of all
10. Barabbas (John 18:40)	j. wise judge
11. Zenas (Titus 3:13)	k. witness

159
Locations

Many of us can pinpoint highlights in our lives by recalling places. Match each place with the important thing that happened there.

1. Jerusalem
2. Lydda
3. Joppa
4. Caesarea
5. Samaria
6. Gaza desert
7. Damascus
8. Antioch
9. Gethsemane
10. Jerusalem
11. Athens

a. altar to an unknown god (Acts 17:23)
b. Philip preached and many turned to Jesus (Acts 8:5)
c. first Christian church (Acts 8:1)
d. Ethiopian saved (Acts 8:26-28)
e. place where Jesus prayed (Matt. 26:36)
f. Saul visited by Ananias (Acts 9:10-18)
g. Aenaeus healed (Acts 9:32-33)
h. Stephen stoned (Acts 7:58-60)
i. Tabitha raised (Acts 9:36)
j. Cornelius lived here (Acts 10:1)
k. followers called Christians first (Acts 11:26)

160
Moses Fill-In

Fill in each blank with the correct answer about Moses.

1. Moses fled from Egypt because he had _____ (Ex. 2:12-15).

2. Moses was looking at a _____ when a voice told him to take off his shoes (Ex. 3:2-5).

3. _____ plagues fell on Egypt (Ex. 7-11).

4. Moses instituted the _____ feast (Ex. 12:3-14).

5. God used _____ by day and a _____ by night to escort his people out of Egypt (Ex. 13:21).

6. God fed the Israelites with _____ in the wilderness (Ex. 16:15).

7. On Mount Sinai, Moses received two stone tablets containing the _____ (Ex. 20).

8. God told Moses to _____ to get water (Ex. 17:6).

9. Jethro told Moses how to _____ to help Moses judge the people (Ex. 18:1-21).

10. Moses was _____ years old when he died (Deut. 34:7).

11. Moses was buried by _____ (Deut. 34:6).

161
Moses Matching

Moses was known as "the lawgiver" for the Israelites. Match these facts about his life.

1. Father-in-law (Ex. 18:1)
2. wife (Ex. 18:2)
3. son (Ex. 18:3)
4. sister (Ex. 15:20)
5. brother (Ex. 4:14)
6. king (Ex. 6:11)
7. nephew (Ex. 6:25)
8. held up Moses' hands (Ex. 17:12)
9. rebelled against Moses (Num. 16:1-3)
10. successor (Deut. 31:14)
11. death place (Deut. 34:5)

a. Eleazar
b. Korah
c. Moab
d. Jethro
e. Gershom
f. Aaron
g. Joshua
h. Hur
i. Pharaoh
j. Miriam
k. Zipporah

162
Paul

One of the strongest personalities in the New Testament is Paul. Match each person associated with Paul with the proper description about the person.

1. Epaphroditus (Phil. 2:25-30)
2. Eutychus (Acts 20:9)
3. Agabus (Acts 21:10-11)
4. Demetrius (Acts 19:24)
5. Alexander (Acts 19:33-34)
6. Priscilla (Acts 18:24-26)
7. Gaius (Acts 19:29)
8. sons of Sceva (Acts 19:14)
9. Gallio (Acts 18:14-17)
10. Lydia (Acts 16:14)
11. Claudius Lysias (Acts 22:23)

a. tried to quiet the riot in Ephesus
b. predicted Paul's imprisonment
c. ordered Paul beaten
d. drove Paul's accusers from the judgment seat
e. provided help for missionaries
f. taken to theater during riot
g. opposed Paul's teachings
h. fell from window while Paul preached
i. friend who almost died
j. helped instruct Apollos in the truth
k. tried to drive evil spirits from a man in the name of Jesus

163
Persecuted

Jesus told His disciples that they would be persecuted for His cause. Match each person with his persecution.

1. Stephen (Acts 7:59)
2. Peter and John (Acts 4:1-4)
3. John the Baptist (Matt. 14:10)
4. Early Christians (Acts 8:1)
5. Paul and Barnabas (Acts 13:50)
6. Paul (2 Cor. 11:25)
7. Jason (Acts 17:5)
8. Jesus (Luke 23:36)
9. James (Acts 12:2)
10. John the apostle (Rev. 1:9)

a. assaulted his house
b. beaten
c. beheaded
d. imprisoned
e. exiled
f. mocked
g. scattered
h. stoned to death
i. expelled from coasts
j. killed with sword

164
Place Associations

Often when a place is mentioned, a certain item comes to mind. Match each place with the item most often associated with it.

1. Calvary (Luke 23:33)		a.	a light
2. Gethsemane (Matt. 26:36)		b.	the Temple
3. Golgotha (Mark 15:22)		c.	the cross
4. Jericho (Josh. 6:2ff.)		d.	falling walls
5. Red Sea (Heb. 11:29)		e.	slaves
6. Bethlehem (Matt. 2:1)		f.	a skull
7. Garden of Eden (Gen. 2:8-9)		g.	prayer
8. Jerusalem (Ps. 68:29)		h.	an altar
9. Bethel (Gen. 28:18-19)		i.	dry land
10. Egypt (Ex. 3:7)		j.	Baby Jesus
11. Damascus Road (Acts 9:1-3)		k.	tree of life

165
Plants

Our earth would be desolate without growing plants. Fill in each blank with the proper plant.

1. Jesus said we should consider the _____ ; they do not work or worry, but God clothes them more richly than Solomon (Luke 12:27).

2. _____ and _____ shall grow in Adam's garden because he listened to Eve (Gen. 3:18).

3. Isaiah cried, "All flesh is _____ " (Isa. 40:6).

4. Jesus likened the kingdom of heaven to a _____ seed (Luke 13:19).

5. Ruth gleaned _____ in Boaz's field (Ruth 2:17).

6. Jonah sat under a vine of a _____ (Jonah 4:6-10).

7. The manna of the Israelites was described as seed from a _____ plant (Ex. 16:31).

8. Rahab hid the spies under stalks of _____ (Josh. 2:6).

9. Jesus is the _____ , and His disciples are the branches (John 15:1).

10. Moses' mother made an ark of _____ to float him in water (Ex. 2:3).

11. Isaiah said the desert would blossom as a _____ (Isa. 35:1).

166
Prayer Promises

The Bible contains many prayer promises. Fill in the blanks to complete the prayer promise in each statement.

1. "If ye abide in me, and my words abide in you, ye shall ask what ye will; and it shall _____ _____ _____ _____ " (John 15:7).

2. "Delight thyself also in the Lord; and he shall give thee _____ _____ _____ _____ _____ " (Ps. 37:4).

3. "And we know that all things work together for good to them that love God, to them who are the called _____ _____ _____ _____ " (Rom. 8:28).

4. "The righteous cry, and the Lord heareth, and delivereth them _____ _____ _____ _____ _____ " (Ps. 34:17).

5. "Evening and morning, and at noon, will I pray, and cry aloud: and he shall _____ _____ _____ " (Ps. 55:17).

6. "Ask, and it shall be given you; seek, and ye shall find; knock, and it shall _____ _____ _____ _____ " (Matt. 7:7).

7. "Call unto me, and I will answer thee, and shew thee great and mighty things, which _____ _____ _____ " (Jer. 33:3).

8. "For every one that asketh receiveth; and he that seeketh findeth; and to him that knocketh it _____ _____ _____ " (Luke 11:10).

9. "He shall call upon me, and I _____ _____ _____ : I will be with him in trouble; I will deliver him, and honour him" (Ps. 91:15).

10. "And whatsoever we ask, _____ _____ _____ _____ , because we keep his commandments, and do these things that are pleasing in his sight" (1 John 3:22).

11. "And all things, whatsoever ye shall ask in prayer, _____ , _____ _____ _____ " (Matt. 21:22).

167
Prayers

Fill in the blanks with the persons mentioned with the prayer statement.

1. "Therefore the people came to _____ , and said, We have sinned, for we have spoken against the Lord, and against thee; pray unto the Lord, that he take away the serpents from us. And _____ prayed for the people." (Num. 21:7).

2. Jesus said, "I have prayed for thee [_____], that thy faith fail not" (Luke 22:32).

3. "And _____ said, Gather all Israel to Mizpeh, and I will pray for you unto the Lord" (1 Sam. 7:5).

4. " _____ therefore was kept in prison: but prayer was made without ceasing of the church unto God for him" (Acts 12:5).

5. "The Lord said to Eliphaz, . . . My wrath is kindled against thee, and against thy two friends. . . . my servant _____ shall pray for you" (Job 42:7-8).

6. _____ said, "I pray for them. I pray not for the world, but for them which thou hast given me; for they are thine" (John 17:9).

7. _____ prayed, "Let thine ear now be attentive . . . that thou mayest hear the prayer of thy servant, which I pray before thee . . . for the children of Israel . . . and confess the sins . . . which we have sinned against thee" (Neh. 1:6).

8. "I [_____] pray that your love may abound yet more and more in knowledge and in all judgment" (Phil. 1:9).

9. _____ said, "Always in every prayer of mine, I pray for you all making request with joy" (Phil. 1:4).

10. _____ instructed, "Pray ye therefore the Lord of the harvest, that he will send forth labourers into his harvest" (Matt. 9:38).

168
Quakes

Match the occasions with the person who experienced the "shaking" object.

1. Earth shook at His death
2. Felt the earth shake at Jesus' resurrection
3. Felt "the place" shake at Pentecost
4. Were released from prison by an earthquake
5. Asked if the people had come to see a "reed shaken with the wind"
6. Shook the wilderness
7. Spoke two years before the earthquake of King Uzziah's day
8. Was spoken to by God after an earthquake
9. Was promised "a visit" from God through an earthquake
10. As the earth shook, he said "Truly this was the Son of God"
11. Shook his clothing and announced, "I will go unto the Gentiles."

a. Paul and Silas (Acts 16:26)
b. The voice of the Lord (Ps. 29:8)
c. Jesus (Matt. 27:51)
d. Paul (Acts 18:6)
e. Ariel (Isa. 29:1-6)
f. keepers of Jesus' tomb (Matt. 28:1-4)
g. Elijah (1 Kings 19:11)
h. the disciples (Acts 4:31)
i. centurion (Matt. 27:54)
j. John (Luke 7:24)
k. Amos (Amos 1:1)

169
Queens

Queens, like all people, are either good or bad. Match each queen with the correct statement about her.

1. Risked her life for her people
2. Replaced by Esther
3. Inquired about Solomon's fame
4. Removed from power because of idols
5. Queen of the Ethiopians
6. Queen who made Elijah flee
7. Saul's daughter, married to David
8. King David saw her wash herself on a roof
9. Queen by marriage to Saul
10. Queen of Egypt
11. Attended the anointing of David as king of Judah with Ahinoam

a. Michal (1 Sam. 18:27)

b. Ahinoam (1 Sam. 15:50)

c. Candace (Acts 8:27)

d. Queen of Sheba (1 Kings 10:1)

e. Abigail (2 Sam. 2:2)
f. Bathsheba (2 Sam. 11:1-3)

g. Tahpenes (1 Kings 11:19)

h. Esther (Esther 5:8)

i. Jezebel (1 Kings 16:31; 19:1-2)
j. Maachah (1 Kings 15:13)
k. Vashti (Esther 1:19)

170
Rain

Rain is essential to our existence. Fill in each blank with the proper person associated with the rain mentioned.

1. _____ saw it rain for forty days and forty nights as he built the ark (Gen. 7:12).

2. _____ prayed and it rained not for three years (Jas. 5:17).

3. _____ sends rain on the just and the unjust alike (Matt. 5:45).

4. _____ told a story about two men who built houses which encountered rain (Matt. 7:25-27).

5. _____ said the people of Melita treated them kindly because of the rain and cold (Acts 28:2).

6. _____ prayed for rain for Judah because the ground was chapt (Jer. 14:4).

7. _____ promised that there would be a covert from the storm and rain for God's people (Isa. 4:6).

8. _____ sent rain upon one city and withheld it from another (Amos 4:7).

9. _____ spread his hand to the Lord and the plague of hail and rain stopped (Ex. 9:33).

10. _____ received bread rained from heaven (Ex. 16:4).

11. _____ was rained upon with fire and brimstone from heaven (Luke 17:29).

171
Redirection

Each of the following people redirected their lives. Match each person with the correct statement about his redirection.

1. Zacchaeus (Luke 19:5-8)
2. Onesimus (Philem. 11)
3. Moses (Ex. 3:9-10)
4. Joseph (Gen. 37:28; 39:4)
5. Paul (Acts 9:1-6)
6. Peter (Mark 14:71; Acts 2:14)
7. Judas ((Luke 6:16)
8. Aaron (Ex. 4:14; 7:2)

9. David (1 Sam. 16:11-13)
10. Thomas (John 20:25-27)
11. Lazarus (Luke 16:20-22)

a. from denier to preacher
b. from doubter to believer
c. from beggar to honoree
d. from fugitive to leader
e. from follower to traitor
f. from persecutor to persecuted
g. from slave to brother
h. from tax collector to benefactor
i. from slave to ruler
j. from obscurity to spokesman
k. from shepherd to king

172
Relatives

Pick out the two people in each set who are related. In each blank write the name of the person who was not related.

_____ 1. a-Andrew, b-Peter, c-Felix (John 1:40)
_____ 2. a-Leah, b-Deborah, c-Rachel (Gen. 29:17)
_____ 3. a-Levi, b-Simeon, c-Ahaz (Gen. 49:5)
_____ 4. a-Elisabeth, b-Rhoda, c-Mary (Luke 1:33-36)
_____ 5. a-James, b-Matthew, c-John (Matt. 4:21)
_____ 6. a-Noami, b-Orphah, c-Hagar (Ruth 1:4)
_____ 7. a-Benjamin, b-Naaman, c-Joseph (Gen. 45:14)
_____ 8. a-Sapphira, b-Lois, c-Eunice (2 Tim. 1:5)
_____ 9. a-Moses, b-Isaiah, c-Aaron (Ex. 7:1)
_____ 10. a-Noah, b-Cain, c-Abel (Gen. 4:8)
_____ 11. a-Abraham, b-Lot, c-Eli (Gen. 12:4)

173
Repeated Phrases

Repetition adds emphasis or calls for attention. Fill in each blank with the person who reported a phrase.

1. "My God, my God, why has thou forsaken me?" (Matt. 27: 46)._____

2. "O earth, earth, earth, hear the word of the Lord" (Jer. 22:29). _____

3. "Holy, holy, holy, is the Lord of hosts" (Isa. 6:3). _____

4. "O Jerusalem, Jerusalem, which killest the prophets" (Luke 13:34). _____

5. "Simon, Simon, behold, Satan hath desired to have you" (Luke 22:31). _____

6. "Martha, Martha, thou art careful and troubled about many things" (Luke 10:41). _____

7. "Unto thee, O, God, do we give thanks, unto thee do we give thanks" (Ps. 75:1). _____

8. "My son Absalom, my son, my son" (2 Sam. 18:33). _____

9. "And why call ye me, Lord, Lord, and do not the things which I say?" (Luke 6:46). _____

10. "Saul, Saul, why persecutest thou me?" (Acts 9:4). _____

11. "My father, my father, the chariot of Israel, and the horsemen" (2 Kings 2:12). _____

174
Romance

Most people enjoy a good romance. Match the following with their outstanding romance.

1. Jacob (Gen. 29:20)
2. Boaz (Ruth 4:3-9)
3. Hosea (Hos. 3:2)
4. Michal (1 Sam. 18:25-28)
5. Ishmael (Gen. 21:21)
6. Esther (Esther 2:7)
7. Rebekah (Gen. 24:1-67)
8. Samson (Judg. 16:17)
9. Esau (Gen. 28:8-9)
10. Ruth (Ruth 2:2)
11. Leah (Gen. 30:14-16)

a. attracted a husband by her beauty
b. bought his wife from slavery
c. proposed to by a servant
d. lost his strength because he broke his Nazarite vow for love
e. bought a night with Jacob with mandrakes
f. married two women and grieved his parents
g. met her husband in a field
h. given to David for killing two hundred Philistines
i. bought a parcel of land to get Ruth for his wife
j. served fourteen years for Rachel
k. wife was chosen by his mother

175
Scrambled Folks

Unscramble each set of letters below to form the name of a Bible character. Write the name in the blank.

1. Silo _____
2. Tol _____
3. Charle _____
4. Thru _____
5. Samhot _____
6. Beal _____
7. Kram _____
8. Ohan _____
9. Theres _____
10. Lie _____
11. Shebbatha _____

176
Scoundrels

Some people are known for their mean acts. Match the person with the "mean" act.

1. Judas (Matt. 26:47-49)
2. Demas (2 Tim. 4:10)
3. Shimei (2 Sam. 16:5-6)
4. Balaam (2 Pet. 2:15)

5. Prodigal son (Luke 15:13)

6. Ananias (Acts 5:1)
7. Jacob (Gen. 27:18-29)
8. Alexander (2 tim. 4:14)

9. Delilah (Judg. 16:18-19)
10. Athaliah (2 Kings 11:1)
11. Jezebel (1 Kings 18:13)

a. betrayed Samson
b. killed the prophets
c. stole birthright
d. wasted possessions on riotous living
e. cursed and threw stones at David
f. betrayed Jesus
g. forsook Paul
h. "loved the wages of unrighteousness"
i. lied to the Holy Spirit
j. did Paul "much evil"
k. destroyed royal descendants

177
Seasonings

Spices were used in biblical days in many different ways. Fill in each blank with the correct words about spices.

1. Myrrh, aloes, and cinnamon were used as perfume for _____ (Prov. 7:17).

2. Moses commanded the children of Israel to gather myrrh, cinnamon, calamus, and cassia to make oil for _____ (Ex. 30:23-25).

3. Cassia and calamus were sold in the _____ (Ezek. 27:19).

4. Nicodemus brought myrrh and aloes to _____ Jesus' body after death (John 19:39).

5. Mary Magdalene anointed the _____ of Jesus with an ointment of spikenard (John 12:3).

6. The _____ complained because they missed the onions and garlic they had in Egypt (Num. 11:5).

7. _____ were to salt the animals for the burnt offering (Ezek. 43:24).

8. _____ fought against the city of Gaal, defeated it, and sowed it with salt (Judg. 9:45).

9. _____ said Christians should season their speech with salt (Col. 4:6).

10. _____ asked, "If the salt have lost his savour, wherewith shall it be seasoned?" (Luke 14:34).

11. _____ sent balm, spices, and myrrh to Joseph as a present when grain was needed from Egypt (Gen. 43:11).

178
Shepherds

Shepherds have been known for their love of their sheep. Fill in each blank with the person involved with the statement about shepherds.

1. _____ told his brothers to deny to Pharaoh that they were shepherds because "every shepherd is an abomination unto the Egyptians" (Gen. 46:31-34).

2. _____ was a shepherd before he became a king (1 Sam. 16:11-13).

3. _____ taught a lesson about God by using a shepherd for an illustration (John 10:14).

4. _____ wrote about God being his shepherd (Ps. 23:1)

5. _____ wrote about the Lord feeding His flock like a shepherd (Isa. 40:11).

6. Jeremiah predicted that _____ would "array himself with the land of Egypt, as a shepherd putteth on his garment" (Jer. 43:12).

7. _____ served as a shepherd of the flock of his father-in-law (Ex. 3:1).

8. _____ told shepherds about the birth of Jesus (Luke 2:8-10).

9. _____ was the first known shepherd (Gen. 4:2).

10. _____ was a shepherdess (Gen. 29:9).

11. _____ told a story about a shepherd who left ninety-nine sheep to search for one lost sheep (Matt. 18:12).

179
Small Creatures

How many of the small creatures mentioned below can you name?

1. The _____ do not procrastinate; they prepare their meat in the summer (Prov. 30:25).

2. The _____ build their homes in the shelter of rocks (Prov. 30:26).

3. The hypocrite is likened to a _____ which cannot be trusted (Job 8:14).

4. The _____ have no king, but they organize into bands (Prov. 30:27).

5. The psalmist said the nations "compassed me about like _____ " (Ps. 118:12).

6. Isaiah said that one day God would [whistle] hiss for the _____ and the _____ in the rivers of Egypt to fill the desolate valleys (Isa. 7:18-19).

7. Jesus reprimanded the scribes and Pharisees for straining at a _____ and swallowing a camel (Matt. 23:24).

8. God promised Moses that the Hivite, the Canaanite, and the Hittite would be driven out by _____ (Ex. 23:28).

9. When he was pursued by Saul, David said, "the king of Israel is come out to seek a _____" (1 Sam. 26:20).

10. The Philistines made five golden _____ as part of a peace offering when they returned the ark to the Israelites (1 Sam. 1:18).

11. Aaron stretched forth his rod, struck the dust, and it became _____ which plagued men and beasts (Ex. 8:17).

180
Small Things

A once popular song stated, "Little things mean a lot." Match each person with the "little thing" associated with them.

1. Moses (Ex. 17:9)
2. David (1 Sam. 17:50)
3. Elijah (1 Kings 17:12-13)
4. Widow (Mark 12:42)
5. Jesus (John 2:6-7)
6. Ruth (Ruth 2:2)
7. Gideon (Judg. 7:6)
8. Esau (Gen. 25:34)
9. Naaman (2 Kings 5:14)
10. Paul (Acts 26:1-13)
11. Amos (Amos 7:7)

a. two mites
b. leftover grain
c. bowl of pottage
d. plumbline
e. muddy water
f. a rod
g. water in pots
h. bright light
i. handfuls of water
j. handful of meal
k. sling

181
Smells

Fill in each blank with the item which smelled.

1. Isaac smelled the _____ of Jacob and thought he was Esau (Gen. 27:27).

2. Daniel's friends did not even smell of _____ when they came out of the furnace (Dan. 3:27).

3. The psalmist said that God's _____ smelled of myrrh, aloes, and cassia (Ps. 45:8).

4. Job said the smell of _____ will make a dry root grow (Job 14:9).

5. Hosea said Israel would smell like the _____ of Lebanon if they would repent (Hos. 14:7).

6. Solomon said the wicked woman had made her bed smell of _____ (Prov. 7:17).

7. God told Moses to make _____ for God and anyone who made any like it to smell himself should be cut off from his people (Ex. 30:37-38).

8. Job said the horses could smell the _____ afar off (Job 39:25).

9. Mary filled the house with the sweet smell of _____ which she put on Jesus' feet (John 12:3).

10. Paul told the Philippians that their _____ were a sweet smell well pleasing to God (Phil. 4:18).

11. Solomon said the tender _____ gave a good smell (Song of Sol. 2:13).

182
Speech

Speech tells a lot about a person. Fill in each blank with the person associated with the mentioned speech.

1. "Surely thou art also one of them; for thy speech betrayeth thee" (Matt. 26:73) was said to _____ .

2. The people of Lystra saw _____ heal a cripple, and they said in the speech of Lycaonia, "The gods are come down to us in the likeness of men" (Acts 14:11).

3. When Paul preached until midnight, _____ went to sleep and fell from a window on the third loft and was taken for dead (Acts 20:7-10).

4. _____ sent to Tekoah for a wise woman and gave her a speech for the king (2 Sam. 14:19-20).

5. The speech of _____ , "Give therefore thy servant an understanding heart to judge thy people" pleased God (1 Kings 3:9-10).

6. _____ pleaded in his defense with his friends, "Hear diligently my speech, and my declaration with your ears" (Job 13:17).

7. _____ wrote, "Day unto day uttereth speech, and night unto night sheweth knowledge" (Ps. 19:2).

8. _____ said, "Excellent speech becometh not a fool; much less do lying lips a prince" (Prov. 17:7).

9. _____ healed a man with a speech impediment by putting his fingers into the man's ears, spitting, and touching the man's tongue (Mark 7:32-33).

10. _____ told the Corinthians, "I . . . came not with excellency of speech or of wisdom, declaring unto you the testimony of God" (1 Cor. 2:1).

183
Spiritual Awakenings

Spiritual awakenings may involve an individual or a nation. Match the event that inspired an awakening and the person involved.

1. Escape at the Red Sea
2. Restoring of the ark
3. Discovery of a scroll
4. Return to Jerusalem
5. Pentecost
6. Moving of the ark
7. End of suffering
8. Birth of Jesus
9. After healing
10. A birth foretold
11. Conversion of Gentiles

a. the disciples (Acts 2)
b. David (1 Chron. 16:1-4)
c. Mary (Luke 1:26-33)
d. a lame man (Acts 3:8-9)
e. Moses (Ex. 14:16-23)
f. Josiah (2 Kings 22)
g. Job (Job 42:1-6)
h. Samuel (1 Sam. 6:1-21)
i. shepherds (Luke 2:18)
j. Peter (Acts 11:15-19)
k. Nehemiah (Neh. 8:1-18)

184
Structures

Tourists travel many miles to view structures of all types. Match each of the following structures with the person or persons associated with it.

1. High priest (Matt. 26:58)
2. Babel (Gen. 11:4)
3. Amos (Amos 3:15)
4. Wife of Shallum (2 Kings 22:14)
5. Jesus (Luke 2:7)
6. Rabbah (Ezek. 25:5)
7. Rich man (Luke 12:18)
8. Levites (Num. 1:51)
9. Paul (Acts 19:29)
10. Daughter of Zion (Isa. 1:8)
11. Solomon (1 Kings 6:14)

a. college
b. cottage and lodge
c. inn
d. stable
e. summer and winter houses
f. Temple (house of God)
g. tabernacle
h. theater
i. tower
j. barns
k. palace

185
Sweet Things

Different people think of different things as "sweet." Match each person with the sweet thing.

1. The Lord (Gen. 8:21)
2. Moses (Ex. 15:25)
3 David (2 Sam. 23:1)
4. Nehemiah (Neh. 8:10)
5. Pleiades (Job 38:31)
6. The preacher (Eccl. 11:7)
7. "My beloved" (Song of Sol. 2:3)
8. Isaiah (Isa. 23:16)
9. Jesus (Mark 16:1)
10. Jeremiah (Jer. 6:20)
11. mountain (Amos 9:13)

a. sweet cane and sacrifices
b. sweet fruit
c. sweet drinks
d. sweet waters
e. sweet spices
f. sweet light
g. sweet melody

h. sweet wine
i. sweet savour
j. sweet influences
k. sweet psalmist

186
Teachers

Many people contribute their success in life to people who taught them. Fill in the blanks with the proper teacher.

1. _____ was the first person in the Bible called a teacher; he instructed workers in brass and iron (Gen. 4:22).

2. _____ told Moses "I . . . will teach you what ye shall do" (Ex. 4:15).

3. Habakkuk said the graven _____ was a teacher of lies (Hab. 2:18).

4. Nicodemus said to _____ , "Rabbi, we know that thou art a teacher come from God" (John 3:2).

5. Paul told the _____ that they were instructors of the foolish and teachers of babes (Rom. 2:20).

6. _____ and _____ were teachers in Antioch (Acts 13:1).

7. Paul admonished aged _____ to be teachers of good things (Titus 2:3).

8. _____ went about Galilee teaching in the synagogues (Matt. 4:23).

9. _____ and the other apostles were found teaching in the Temple after an angel released them from prison (Acts 5:21).

10. One of Jesus' disciples said to Jesus, "Lord, teach us to pray, as _____ also taught his disciples" (Luke 11:1).

11. Jesus promised that the _____ "shall teach you all things" (John 14:26).

187
Temple

The Temple was built as a place to worship God. Fill in the blanks with the proper words about the Temple.

1. The people charged themselves _____ for the service of the Temple (Neh. 10:32).

2. The people decided when they would bring their offerings of wood to the Temple by _____ (Neh. 10:34).

3. The wood offering was to be used in the Temple to _____ (Neh. 10:34).

4. The "first things" the Israelites were to bring included _____ and _____ (Neh. 10:35-37).

5. _____ was supposed to receive the offering at the Temple (Neh. 10:38).

6. When Nehemiah returned to Jerusalem, the Levites and the singers had _____ (Neh. 13:10).

7. Nehemiah decided that the Levites and the singers left their work because _____ (Neh. 13:10).

8. Nehemiah _____ together when he found the Temple forsaken (Neh. 13:11).

9. When Nehemiah saw people in Judah treading wine presses on the sabbath, he _____ (Neh. 13:15).

10. Nehemiah _____ on the sabbath to keep people from working on the sabbath (Neh. 13:19).

11. The bad example of _____ was used by Nehemiah when he spoke against mixed marriages (Neh. 13:26).

188
Testings

The character and faith of people are often tested by circumstances over which they have no control. Match the person tested with the item representing his circumstances.

1. Job (Job 1:8-12)   a. a woman
2. Jesus (Matt. 4:1-3)   b. tithe
3. Abraham (Gen. 22:1-2)   c. brother
4. Solomon (1 Kings 10:1)   d. spoils of war
5. Israelites (Mal. 3:10)   e. money
6. Samson (Judg. 16:9)   f. Potiphar's wife
7. Judah (Gen. 43:3-9)   g. possessions, family, and body
8. Ananias (Acts 5:1-3)   h. son
9. Joseph (Gen. 39:7)   i. bread
10. Noah (Gen. 6:13-14)   j. an ark
11. Achan (Josh. 7:20-21)   k. questions of Queen of Sheba

189
They Prayed

Sometimes when people pray, God makes miraculous things happen. Match each person with the miraculous happening because of prayer.

1. Abraham (Gen. 18:23-33).
2. Hezekiah (2 Kings 19:14-35)
3. Elijah (1 Kings 18:36-38)

4. Elisha (2 Kings 4:32-37)
5. Daniel (Dan. 2:17-19)
6. Jesus (John 11:41-44)
7. Thief on cross (Luke 23:42-43)
8. Paul and Silas (Acts 16:25-26)
9. Peter (Acts 9:40-41)

10. Moses (Num. 11:1-2)
11. Jonah (Jonah 2:1-10)

a. Dorcas was raised
b. delivered out of a fish
c. he and his friends were saved
d. fire consumed altar
e. fire quenched
f. Lazarus raised
g. jail opened by earthquake
h. Paradise assured
i. Shunammite woman's son was raised
j. Lot spared from Sodom
k. Sennacherib's army destroyed

190
They Sang

Music has been around almost as long as human beings. Answer each question with the person who sang.

1. What two men sang in prison? (Acts 16:25).

2. Who sang as they left the Last Supper and went into the Mount of Olives? (Matt. 26:30).

3. Who sang the first recorded song in the Bible? (Ex. 15:1).

4. Who sang the last recorded song in the Bible? (Rev. 15:1-3).

5. Who sang at the digging of a well? (Num. 21:17-18).

6. Who sang at the avenging of Israel? (Judg. 5:1).

7. Which two warriors did the Israelites sing about? (1 Sam. 29:5).

8. Who commanded the restoration of sacrifices causing people to sing? (2 Chron. 29:27-28).

9. Which two people wrote songs which the Israelites sang in the Temple? (2 Chron. 29:30).

10. What man sang with the singers at the dedication of the walls of Jerusalem? (Neh. 12:42).

11. Who asked Job about the morning stars singing? (Job 38:1-7).

191
Thirst

Fill in each blank with the name of the person who was thirsty.

1. _____ was cast under a shrub, because his mother could find no water for him to drink (Gen. 21:5).

2. The _____ were thirsty and blamed Moses (Ex. 17:2-3).

3. _____ were to be served in their thirst according to God's command to the Israelites (Deut. 28:48).

4. _____ said, "I thirst," and was given vinegar instead of water (John 19:28).

5. A _____ woman was given living water so that she would never thirst again (John 4:13-14).

6. _____ asked Jael for water to quench his thirst, and she gave him milk (Judg. 4:19).

7. _____ said his soul thirsted for God (Ps. 63:1).

8. _____ said his ministry brought him weariness and pain, and hunger and thirst (2 Cor. 11:23-27).

9. _____ cried for someone to dip the tip of his finger in water to relieve his torment in the flames of hell (Luke 16:24).

10. _____ servant was instructed to ask for water to drink as a sign for chosing a wife for Isaac (Gen. 24:43).

11. _____ drank water from a jawbone (Judg. 15:19).

12 _____ found an Egyptian who had drunk no water for three days and nights (1 Sam. 30:11-12).

192
Titles

Match each person with the proper title as given in Acts.

1. Annas (Acts 4:6)
2. Herod (Acts 13:1)
3. Agrippa (Acts 25:26)
4. Julius (Acts 27:1)
5. Candace (Acts 8:27)
6. Elymas (Acts 13:8)
7. Sergius Paulus (Acts 13:7)
8. Paul (Acts 14:12)
9. Lydia (Acts 16:14)
10. Crispus (Acts 18:8)
11. Demetrius (Acts 19:24)
12. Diana (Acts 19:27)
13. Tertullus (Acts 24:1)
14. Lysias (Acts 24:7)

a. chief captain
b. chief speaker
c. centurion
d. goddess
e. chief ruler of the synagogue
f. high priest
g. deputy
h. orator
i. silversmith
j. queen of Ethiopia
k. seller of purple
l. tetrarch
m. sorcerer
n. king

193
Tongue

Fill in each blank with the proper tongue from this list: backbiting, deceitful, false, froward, lying, naughty, perverse, slow, soft, stammering, and wholesome.

1. "These things doth the Lord hate . . . A proud look, a _____ tongue, and hands that shed innocent blood" (Prov. 6:16-17).

2. "A _____ tongue is a tree of life: but perverseness therein is a breach in the spirit" (Prov. 15:4).

3. "A wicked doer giveth heed to false lips; and a liar giveth ear to a _____ tongue" (Prov. 17:4).

4. "The north wind driveth away rain: so doth an angry countenance a _____ tongue" (Prov. 25:23).

5. "Thou shalt not see a fierce people, a people of a deeper speech than thou canst perceive; of a _____ tongue, that thou canst not understand" (Isa. 33:19).

6. "What shall be given thee? or what shall be done unto thee, thou _____ tongue?" (Ps. 120:3).

7. "The mouth of the just bringeth forth wisdom: but the _____ tongue shall be cut out" (Prov. 10:31).

8. "Thou lovest all devouring words, O thou _____ tongue" (Ps. 52:4).

9. "By long forbearing is a prince persuaded, and a _____ tongue breaketh the bone" (Prov. 25:15).

10. Moses told God, "I [have] a _____ tongue" (Ex. 4:10).

11. "He that hath a froward heart findeth no good: and he that hath a _____ tongue falleth into mischief" (Prov. 17:20).

194
Unwavering Faith

In spite of tremendous trials, some people do not waver in their faith. Match these unwavering Bible people with their trials.

1. Peter (Acts 12:5)
2. Daniel (Dan. 6:7)
3. Moses (Ex. 14:21)
4. John (Rev. 1:9)
5. Noah (Gen. 7:15-18)
6. Sarah (Heb. 11:11-12)
7. Abraham (Heb. 11:8-9)
8. Hosea (Hos. 1:2)
9. John the Baptist
   (Matt. 14:10)
10. Paul (Acts 21:32)
12. Joseph (Gen. 37:28)

a. King's sword
b. childless state
c. exile on Patmos
d. sold into slavery
e. sojourned in a strange country
f. beating
g. prison
h. unfaithful wife
i. flood
j. Red Sea
k. lions' den

195
Utensils

Though utensils used in biblical days may seem primitive to us, they played an important role in everyday life of the people. Fill in the blanks with the correct utensil.

1. Jesus told the Pharisees to clean the inside of the _____ and _____ (Matt. 23:25-26).

2. Gideon caught the water from the fleece in a _____ (Judg. 6:36-37).

3. Elisha told his servant to get a big _____ and make pottage for the sons of the prophets (2 Kings 4:38).

4. Jesus filled a _____ with water in order to wash his disciples' feet (John 13:5).

5. Jesus told two disciples to go to a city and follow a man carrying a _____ (Mark 14:13).

6. The children of Israel baked manna in _____ (Num. 11:8).

7. Jesus used a _____ to illustrate the magnitude of influence (Matt. 5:15).

8. A woman with a _____ of oil fed Elijah (1 Kings 17:12).

9. Samuel anointed Saul with a _____ of oil (1 Sam. 10:1).

10. As the Israelites left Egypt, they took their dough in _____ (Ex. 12:34).

11. The disciples gathered twelve _____ of leftovers after the five thousand were fed (Matt. 14:20).

12. Bezaleel made _____ of pure gold for the tabernacle (Ex. 37:16).

196
Victories

The following people each won a victory over something or some-one. Match each person with his victory.

1. Joshua
2. Paul
3. David and warriors
4. Jesus
5. Christian
6. Moses
7. David
8. Samson
9. Serpent
10. Lazarus
11. Peter

a. the world (1 John 5:4)
b. Eve (2 Cor. 11:3)
c. jail (Acts 12:6-9)
d. Goliath (1 Sam. 17:4-5)
e. the course of life (2 Tim. 4:7)
f. rich man (Luke 16:25)
g. spoils of battles (1 Chron. 26:27)
h. death (1 Cor. 15:55,57)
i. Philistines (Judg. 16:29-30)
j. Pharaoh (Ex. 15:1)
k. Battle of Jericho (Josh. 6:2)

197
Walls

In Old Testament days, walls were valuable as they served to protect people and possessions. Fill in each blank with the proper wall.

1. The walls of _____ fell by faith (Heb. 11:30).

2. Ezekiel predicted that the walls of _____ would be destroyed because the people spoke against Jerusalem (Ezek. 26:2-4).

3. The Chaldees broke down the walls of _____ (2 Kings 25:10).

4. The Israelites fled by night through a gate between two walls of _____ (2 Kings 25:4).

5. Jeremiah said the walls of _____ were torn down because of God's vengeance (Jer. 50:15).

6. When leprosy was found in the walls of a _____ , certain things had to be done to cleanse the place (Lev. 14:37-39).

7. When Sanballat and Tobiah heard that the walls of _____ were being repaired, they conspired to stop the repairs (Neh. 4:7-8).

8. Isaiah said one day God would appoint salvation for the walls of _____ (Isa. 26:1).

9. The wall of _____ allowed the Israelites to cross the Red Sea on dry ground (Ex. 14:22).

10. A _____ wall and an angel stopped Balaam's donkey (Num. 22:24).

11. The Philistines fastened Saul's body to the wall of _____ (1 Sam. 31:10).

12. The Syrians fled as the walls of _____ fell killing twenty-seven thousand men (1 Kings 20:30).

13. Dogs ate Jezebel by the wall of _____ (1 Kings 21:23).

198
What They Died For

Most people are willing to die for something important to them. Match each person with the thing for which they died.

1. Jezebel (1 Kings 21:15-19)
2. Saul (1 Chron. 10:13)
3. Absalom (2 Sam. 15:10)
4. Achan (Josh. 7:20-26)
5. Ananias (Acts 5:3)
6. Stephen (Acts 7:59)
7. Uriah (2 Sam. 11:14-15)
8. Samson (Judg. 16:28)
9. Haman (Esther 5:13)
10. John the Baptist (Mark 6:18-28)
11. Abel (Gen. 4:5-8)

a. an offering
b. witnessing
c. to avenge the Philistines
d. Naboth's vineyard
e. spoils of Jericho
f. hatred of a Jew
g. denouncing Herod
h. deceit over land
i. power
j. his transgressions
k. to cover David's sin

199
Where Found?

Each of the following people were found "under" something. Match the person with where he was found.

1. Nathanael (John 1:48)
2. Elijah (1 Kings 19:4)
3. Deborah (Judg. 4:4-5)
4. Jonah (Jonah 4:6)
5. Israelites (Ex. 6:6)
6. Moses (Ex. 18:5-7)
7. Ruth (Ruth 2:12)
8. Jews and Gentiles (Rom. 3:9)
9. Christians (Rom. 6:15)
10. Servants (1 Tim. 6:1)
11. Samson and Philistines
    (Judg. 16:29-30)

a. burdens of Egyptians
b. grace
c. God's wings
d. fig tree
e. juniper tree
f. pillars
g. sin
h. yoke
i. a tent
j. palm tree
k. gourd vine

200
Writing Materials

Creative people find materials to write on and with. Fill in each blank with the proper writing materials.

1. Jesus wrote on the _____ in defense of an adulterous woman (John 8:8).

2. Ezekiel was told by God to write on _____ (Ezek. 37:16).

3. Moses was commanded to go into Mount Sinai and God would give him two tables of _____ on which the law and Commandments were written (Ex. 24:12).

4. A hand wrote on the _____ at Belshazzar's party (Dan. 5:5).

5. God wrote with His _____ upon the stone tables (Ex. 34:28).

6. Paul said the Corinthians were his epistle written in his _____ (2 Cor. 3:2).

7. John said that the woman arrayed in purple and scarlet colors had a name written on her _____ (Rev. 17:5).

8. God commanded the Israelites to write His Commandments on the _____ and _____ of their houses (Deut. 6:9).

9. God told Isaiah to take a great _____ and write in it with a man's _____ (Isa. 8:1).

10. Moses was told by God to write Aaron's name on Levi's _____ (Num. 17:3).

11. Before John was born, mute Zacharias asked for a writing _____ and wrote "His name is John" (Luke 1:63).

201
Z

Names beginning with the letter "Z" were not uncommon in the Bible. Match each name with the proper identification.

1. Zacchaeus
2. Zachariah
3. Zadok
4. Zebedee
5. Ziba
6. Zilpah
7. Zedekiah
8. Zipporah
9. Zur
10. Zophar
11. Zibeon

a. father of fifteen sons (2 Sam. 9:10)
b. the Naamathite, friend of Job (Job 2:11)
c. daughter of Jethro (Ex. 2:21)
d. a duke of Edom (Gen. 36:29)
e. porter of the door of the tabernacle (1 Chron. 9:21)
f. a fisherman, father of James and John (Matt. 4:21)
g. prince of Midian (Num. 31:8)
h. the scribe treasurer (Neh. 13:13)
i. Leah's maid (Gen. 30:9)
j. king of Judah (2 Kings 24:17-18)
k. a short, rich publician (Luke 19:2-4)

202
Angels

Angels in the Bible were not seen only at Christmas. Match each person with his or her angel experience.

1. Jesus (Mark 1:13)
2. Assyrians (2 Kings 19:35)
3. John the Baptist (Luke 1:13)
4. Jacob (Gen. 48:16)
5. Elijah (1 Kings 19:5-6)
6. Moses (Acts 7:35)
7. Cornelius (Acts 10:5-7)
8. Peter (Acts 12:8)
9. Hagar (Gen. 16:7)
10. Balaam's donkey (Num. 22:23)
11. Philip (Acts 8:26)

a. Angel appeared to him in a bush
b. Redeemed by an angel
c. Found in the wilderness by an angel
d. Sent on a witnessing mission by an angel
e. Angel told to send for Peter
f. Angels ministered to him in the wilderness
g. Named by an angel
h. Saw an angel in a road
i. Angel told him to put on his shoes
j. An angel prepared food for him
k. Smitten by an angel

203
Altars

Altars have played important roles in worship throughout history. Match each person with the proper altar name or location.

1. Abraham (Gen. 12:6-7)
2. Jacob (Gen. 35:1)
3. Moses (Ex. 17:15)
4. Reuben and Gad (Josh. 22:34)
5. Isaac (Gen. 26:23-25)
6. Balak (Num. 23:14)
7. Joshua (Deut. 27:4-5)
8. Gideon (Judg. 6:24)
9. Samuel (1 Sam. 7:17)
10. Saul (1 Sam. 14:2,35)
11. David (2 Sam. 24:18-19)

a. Araunah's threshing floor
b. Beersheba
c. Ebal
d. Ed
e. Bethel
f. Gibeah
g. Jehovah-nissi
h. Jehovah-shalom
i. Ramah
j. Sichem
k. Pisgah

204
Ashamed

Sometimes the word *ashamed* is used in the Bible to refer to confounded. Fill in each blank with the person or persons who were ashamed.

1. _____ was ashamed to ask the king for soldiers to fight because he had rebuked the king (Ezra 8:22).
2. _____ asked Job if no man could make him ashamed (Job 11:3).
3. _____ is ashamed like a thief when he is caught (Jer. 2:26).
4. _____ of a rich man said, "I cannot dig; to beg I am ashamed" (Luke 16:3).
5. _____ asked, "What fruit had ye then in those things whereof you are now ashamed?" (Rom. 6:21).
6. _____ shall be ashamed of Chemosh, as the house of Israel was ashamed of Bethel their confidence," said Jeremiah (Jer. 48:13).
7. _____ shall remember her ways and be ashamed, according to Ezekiel (Ezek. 16:3,61).
8. _____ shall be ashamed of their visions, according to Zechariah (Zech. 13:4).
9. _____ instructed the Thessalonians to make the man ashamed who does not obey the word of his epistle (2 Thess. 3:14).
10. _____ prayed that God would make the men ashamed who hated him (Ps. 86:17).

205
Awoke

For many people, the hours immediately after awaking are not the best times to make rational decisions. Answer the following questions about what happened after awaking.

1. When Peter, James, and John awoke after Jesus talked to Moses and Elijah, what did Peter want Jesus to do (Luke 9:33)?
2. When Pharaoh awoke from his dream of seven fat kine, what did he do (Gen. 41:4-5)?
3. When Samson awoke after telling Delilah the secret of his strength, what did he fail to realize (Judg. 16:20)?
4. When Solomon awoke from his dream of God giving him understanding, what did he do (1 Kings 3:15)?
5. Why did the disciples awake Jesus when he slept in a boat (Matt. 8:25)?
6. When Gehazi laid his staff on the face of the widow's son and the child awoke not, what was wrong (2 Kings 4:31-32)?
7. When Elijah mocked the followers of Baal, how did he tell them to awaken their god (1 Kings 18:27)?
8. When Jacob awoke from his dream about a ladder, what did he do (Gen. 28:16-18)?
9. Why did the disciples try to talk Jesus out of trying to awaken Lazarus (John 11:11-13)?
10. When the keepers of the prison awoke and found Paul and Silas gone, what did he attempt to do (Acts 16:27)?

206
Bartimaeus

The story of Jesus healing Bartimaeus is a well-known story. Answer the following questions about the incident.

1. Why was Bartimaeus begging beside the road (Mark 10:46)?
2. Where was the road (Mark 10:46)?
3. Who was Bartimaeus's father (Mark 10:46)?
4. When Bartimaeus heard that Jesus was coming, what did he cry out (Mark 10:47)?
5. What did the crowd charge Bartimaeus to do (Mark 10:48)?
6. What was Bartimaeus's response to their charge (Mark 10:48)?
7. When Jesus called, what did Bartimaeus do (Mark 10:50)?
8. What did Bartimaeus ask Jesus to do for him (Mark 10:51)?
9. What did Jesus do for Bartimaeus (Mark 10:52)?
10. What did Jesus say to Bartimaeus (Mark 10:52)?
11. What did Bartimaeus do after his sight was restored (Mark 10:52)?

207
Baskets

In recent years, baskets have become a popular sales item. In biblical days, baskets had many uses. Match the person and the basket use associated with him.

1. Paul (Acts 9:24-25)
2. Moses (Ex. 2:3)
3. Baker (Gen. 40:16)
4. Priest (Ex. 29:23-24)
5. Gideon (Judg. 6:19-21)
6. Jeremiah (Jer. 24:2-3)
7. Amos (Amos 8:1-2)
8. Joseph (Gen. 40:18)
9. Israel (Jer. 6:9)
10. Disciples (Matt. 14:20)

a. Carried meat to a rock for an angel
b. Interpreted a dream of three baskets
c. Gathered twelve baskets of leftovers
d. Envisioned a basket of summer fruit
e. Future predicted by baskets of grape gatherers
f. Held bread for offering
g. Used to float in a river
h. Dreamed of three white baskets
i. Used to escape
j. Envisioned two baskets of figs

208
Blood

Without blood, there is no life. Fill in each blank with the person or persons associated with blood.

1. _____ coat was dipped in blood in an attempt to deceive his father (Gen. 37:31).
2. _____ poured river water on the ground, and it became blood (Ex. 4:9).
3. _____ prayed that God would not let his blood "fall to the earth before the face of the Lord" (1 Sam. 26:20).
4. _____ called David a bloody man (2 Sam. 16:8).
5. _____ cut themselves until blood gushed out, because their god did not answer them (1 Kings 18:25-28).
6. _____ saw the water as red as blood and assumed they had won a battle (2 Kings 3:22-23).
7. _____ said the moon will turn to blood in the day the Lord comes (Acts 2:20).
8. _____ said they could not keep the betrayal money from Judas because it was the price of blood (Matt. 27:6).
9. _____ prayed earnestly "and his sweat was as it were great drops of blood" (Luke 22:44).
10. _____ said to Peter and the other apostles "Ye have filled Jerusalem with your doctrine, and intend to bring this man's blood upon us (Acts 5:26-28).
11. _____ washed his hands and said, "I am innocent of the blood of this just person" (Matt. 27:24).

209
Books

Though books as we know them did not exist in biblical times, books are mentioned in the Bible. Fill in each blank with the person mentioned with a book.

1. _____ found the book of the law in the Temple (2 Kings 22:8).
2. _____, the scribe, read the book of the law found in the Temple (2 Kings 22:9-10).
3. _____ tore his clothing when he read the book of the law found in the Temple (2 Kings 22:1,11).
4. _____ was commanded to eat the roll of a book (Ezek. 2:8-10).
5. _____ prayed to be blotted out of God's book in exchange for forgiveness for the Israelites (Ex. 32:32).
6. _____ opened the book of the law, began to read, and the people stood up (Neh. 8:3-5).
7. _____, the king, could not sleep and called for the book of records of the chronicles where he learned of Mordecai saving the king's life (Esther 6:1-3).
8. _____ wrote a book as Jeremiah dictated it to him (Jer. 45:1).
9. _____ received a book sent to him in a hand (Ezek. 2:8-9).
10. _____ was the book given to Jesus to read in the synagogue (Luke 4:17).
11. _____ sprinkled blood on the book of law after he had told the people every precept in the book (Heb. 9:19).
12. _____ was told to write what he saw and send it to the seven churches (Rev. 1:9-11).

210
Bread

Many people cannot imagine meals without bread. Fill in each blank with the person or persons associated with the statement about bread.

1. _____ brought bread and wine and blessed Abraham (Gen. 14:18-19).
2. _____ and her son left with bread and water given to her by Abraham (Gen. 21:14).
3. _____ could not eat bread with Hebrews (Gen. 43:32).
4. _____ gave the Egyptians bread in exchange for horses (Gen. 47:17).
5. _____ rained bread from heaven for the Israelites (Ex. 16:4).
6. _____ sent a donkey loaded with bread to Saul (1 Sam. 16:20).
7. _____ ate sacred bread, because no "common" bread was available (1 Sam. 21:5-6).
8. _____ fed a hundred prophets and hid them in a cave (1 Kings 18:4).
9. _____ shared bread from a man of Baal-shalisha with the people (2 Kings 4:38-42).
10. _____ did not eat the king's bread for twelve years (Neh. 5:14).
11. _____ forgot to take bread into the ship, and Jesus used the occasion to teach them (Mark 8:14-15).
12. _____ "came neither eating nor drinking wine" (Luke 7:33).

211
Builders

Throughout history men have lived who wanted to leave a monument which they built. Match each builder with his project.

1. Bezaleel (Ex. 31:2-5)
2. Solomon and Hiram (1 Kings 6:18)
3. Uzziah (2 Chron. 26:9)
4. Jotham (2 Chron. 27:4)
5. Balak (Num. 23:13-14)
6. Judah (1 Kings 14:23)
7. David (1 Chron. 17:6)
8. Nehemiah (Neh. 4:6)
9. Rehoboam (2 Chron. 11:5)
10. Noah (Gen. 6:14)
11. A rich man (Luke 12:18)

a. Altars
b. Ark
c. Barns
d. Cities for defense
e. Castles
f. House
g. Images
h. Towers
i. Temple
j. Articles for the tabernacle
k. Wall of Jerusalem

212
Cast Lots

Casting lots was a way of making decisions in biblical days. Answer each question about casting lots.

1. What did the soldiers cast lots for when Jesus was crucified (Matt. 27:35)?
2. Who predicted that lots would be cast for Jesus' vesture (Ps. 22:18)?
3. Who cast lots to select the scapegoat (Lev. 16:8)?
4. Who cast lots to divide the land for the Israelites (Josh. 18:10)?
5. Who cast lots to see who was guilty of the sin of breaking a fast (1 Sam. 14:28-41)?
6. Who was declared guilty when the lot for guilt was cast (1 Sam. 14:42)?
7. Who did Joel say would cast lots for the Israelites (Joel 3:2-3)?
8. What did Obadiah say foreigners cast lots upon (Obad. 11)?
9. What did the mariners going to Tarshish cast lots for (Jonah 1:7)?
10. Who was declared guilty of causing the trouble when the lot was cast on the way to Tarshish (Jonah 1:7)?
11. What city had lots cast to find her honorable men (Nah. 3:10)?
12. David cast lots to decide who would perform what ministry in the Temple (1 Chron. 26:13-19)?
13. Who was elected successor to Judas by casting lots (Acts 1:26)?

213
Cities

Growing cities in our nation have frequently been in the spotlight. Match each statement with the correct city.

1. Joshua's inheritance (Josh. 19:50)
2. City where David dwelt (Isa. 29:1)
3. Location of the Temple (Ezra 1:3)
4. Named by Cain (Gen. 4:17)
5. City of refuge (Deut. 4:42-43)
6. Saul's home (1 Sam. 15:34)
7. A fenced city (Josh. 19:35)
8. Home to Naomi (Ruth 1:1)
9. City of Paul's vision (Acts 16:9)
10. Home of Simon, a tanner (Acts 9:43)
11. Jesus raised a widow's son here (Luke 7:11)
12. Elisha's special room was here (2 Kings 4:8-10)
13. Destroyed for its wickedness (2 Pet. 2:6)

a. Troas
b. Bethlehem
c. Bezer
d. Enoch
e. Gibeah
f. Hammath
g. Joppa
h. Jerusalem
i. Ariel
j. Nain
k. Sodom
l. Shunem
m. Timnath-serah

214
Coats

In many climates, coats are necessary for survival. Match each person with the proper coat.

1. Joseph (Gen. 37:3)
2. Jesus (John 19:23)
3. Aaron (Ex. 28:4)
4. Samuel (1 Sam. 2:9)
5. Goliath (1 Sam. 17:5)
6. Hushai (2 Sam. 15:32)
7. Peter (John 21:7)
8. Eve (Gen. 3:21)
9. Dorcas (Acts 9:39)
10. Job (Job 30:18)

a. Coat with collar
b. Embroidered coat
c. Coat of many colors
d. Fisher's coat
e. Handmade coats
f. Little coat
g. Coat of mail
h. Seamless coat
i. Skin coat
j. Rent coat

215
Companions

Some people in the Bible were closely associated. Match the companions below:

1. Barnabas (Acts 11:30)
2. Jonathan (1 Sam. 19:7)
3. Samuel (1 Sam. 2:11)
4. Job (Job 8:1)
5. Moses (Ex. 3:1)
6. Elijah (1 Kings 19:19-21)
7. Shadrach (Dan. 3:14)
8. Ruth (Ruth 1:16-19)
9. Mary (John 11:1-2)
10. Peter (Acts 4:13)
11. Gaius (Acts 19:29)

a. Aristarchus
b. Bildad
c. David
d. Eli
e. Elisha
f. John
g. Jethro
h. Martha
i. Meshach
j. Paul
k. Naomi

216
Complainers

People grumble and complain about a lot of things. Match the complainer and the complaint.

1. Israelites (Num. 11:5)
2. Jonah (Jonah 4:7)
3. High priest (Acts 25:7)
4. Spies (Num. 14:36)
5. Laborers (Matt. 20:10-11)
6. Scribes (Mark 14:4-5)
7. Grecians (Acts 6:1)
8. Chaldeans (Dan. 3:8-12)
9. Cain (Gen. 4:5)
10. Rachel (Gen. 30:1-2)
11. Saul (1 Sam. 18:8)

a. Childlessness
b. David's successes
c. Land
d. Jews and golden image
e. Garlic
f. Gourd
g. Ointment
h. Pennies
i. Neglect of widows
j. Offering
k. Paul

217
Construction Materials

Many different materials have been used in construction work. Fill in each blank with the material used.

1. Noah built the ark of _____ (Gen. 6:14).
2. The Tower of Babel was made of _____ and _____ (Gen. 11:3-9).
3. Solomon constructed Pharaoh's daughter a house of costly _____ (1 Kings 7:8-9).
4. David built a house of _____ (1 Chron. 17:1).
5. Jacob made a table of _____ upon which he and Laban ate to fulfill a covenant between them (Gen. 31:44-46).
6. God commanded Moses to construct an ark of _____ (Deut. 10:1).
7. The doors of the Temple were made from _____ (1 Kings 6:31-32).
8. Nehemiah used _____ to build the Jerusalem wall (Neh. 4:3).
9. Moses forged a serpent of _____ to heal serpent bites (Num. 21:9).
10. God will make gates from _____ and streets of pure _____ for the New Zion (Rev. 21:21).
11. The Israelites constructed bricks from _____ (Ex. 5:7).
12. The Ethiopians sent ambassadors in seagoing vessels made of _____ (Isa. 18:1-2).
13. The people of Tyre constructed ship boards of _____ (Ezek. 27:5).

218
Darkness

Darkness is often associated with unpleasant things. Answer each of the following questions about darkness.

1. When was Egypt in darkness for three days (Ex. 10:22)?
2. When was darkness "upon the face of the deep" (Gen. 1:2)?
3. Who saw a vision in which "an horror of great darkness fell upon him" (Gen. 15:12)?
4. When did a cloud produce darkness to one group and light to another (Ex. 14:20)?
5. When was the whole earth covered with darkness from the sixth hour to the ninth hour (Luke 23:44)?
6. When did God speak to Moses out of a thick darkness (Deut. 5:22)?
7. When will the sun be turned to darkness (Acts 2:20)?
8. When did "a mist and darkness" fall upon a man (Acts 13:8-11)?
9. Who told the spies' pursuer that the spies had left in the darkness (Josh. 2:3-5)?
10. Why did Nehemiah command the gates to be shut when darkness came (Neh. 13:19)?
11. Who came to the tomb of Jesus in the darkness of the early morning (John 20:1)?

219
Double Experience

Two of the people listed had the same experience. Circle the person who did *not* share the experience.

1. Joshua, Caleb, and Moses were told to remove their shoes, because they stood on holy ground (Josh. 5:15; Ex. 3:5).
2. Saul, Joshua, and Gideon won battles by blowing trumpets (Josh. 6:20; Judg. 7:22).
3. Moses, Joshua, and Solomon parted water for people to pass through (Ex. 14:15-16; Josh. 4:7-8).
4. Aaron, David, and Pharaoh's wise men "cast down" rods which became serpents (Ex. 7:10-12).
5. Miriam, Uzziah, and Daniel were struck with leprosy as punishment (Num. 12:10-14; 2 Chron. 26:19-21).
6. Gideon, Aaron, and Saul collected golden earrings from their people and built images with them (Ex. 32:2-4; Judg. 8:26-27).
7. Abraham, Isaac, and Zacharias were told they would each have a son in their old age (Gen. 17:19; Luke 1:17-18).
8. Korah, Dathan, and Goliath were swallowed by the earth (Num. 16:32; Deut. 11:6).
9. Samson, Moses, and Joshua drew water from unusual sources: a jawbone and a rock (Judg. 15:16-19; Ex. 17:6).
10. Caesar, Pharaoh, and Herod feared a small child (Ex. 1:22; Matt. 2:3).
11. Rebekah, Tamar, and Rachel had twins (Gen. 25:24-28; Gen. 38:24-27).
12. Jacob, Joseph, and Joshua had visions telling them to go to Egypt (Gen. 46:2-3; Matt. 2:13).

220
Double Names

Some people are called different names by different people. Match the two names for the same person in each case below.

1. Abaddon (Rev. 9:11)
2. Benjamin (Gen. 35:16-18)
3. Cephas (John 1:42)
4. Oshea (Num. 13:8-16)
5. Saul (Acts 13:9)
6. Zion (Isa. 62:1-4)
7. Simeon (Acts 13:1)
8. Naomi (Ruth 1:20)
9. Sarai (Gen. 17:15)
10. Daniel (Dan. 1:7)
11. Azariah (Dan. 1:7)
12. Hananiah (Dan. 1:7)

a. Sarah
b. Shadrach
c. Paul
d. Niger
e. Mara
f. Simon
g. Johoshua
h. Hephzibah
i. Ben-oni
j. Belteshazzar
k. Apollyon
l. Abed-nego

221
Dragons

Dragons are mentioned in the Bible infrequently. Fill in each blank with the person or object associated with a dragon.

1. Jeremiah complained because _____ had crushed him like a dragon (Jer. 51:34).
2. Ezekiel called _____ the great dragon (Ezek. 29:3).
3. _____ had a vision in which frogs came out of the dragon (Rev. 16:13).
4. _____ said, "I am a brother to dragons, and a companion to owls" (Job 30:29).
5. Jeremiah said God would make _____ a den of dragons (Jer. 9:11).
6. Jeremiah said _____ would be made a dwelling place for dragons (Jer. 51:37).
7. Isaiah said _____ the dragon would be killed in the sea (Isa. 27:1).
8. Moses said Israel's enemies' _____ is the poison of dragons (Deut. 32:33).
9. Jeremiah likened the famine to mules which snuffed up the _____ like dragons (Jer. 14:6).
10. John said the _____ received his power from the dragon (Rev. 13:2).

222
Dream Objects

Dreams can be pleasant or unpleasant experiences, depending on the objects in the dream. Match each person with the object of his dream.

1. Jacob (Gen. 31:10)
2. Joseph (Gen. 37:5-7)
3. Chief butler (Gen. 40:5-10)
4. Chief baker (Gen. 40:16-17)
5. Pharaoh (Gen. 41:25-26)
6. Nebuchadnezzar (Dan. 2:31)
7. Daniel (Dan. 7:1-2)
8. Solomon (1 Kings 3:5)
9. Midianite man (Judg. 7:13)
10. Joseph, Jesus' father (Matt. 1:20)
11. Eliphaz (Job 4:12-17)

a. Birds and baskets
b. A bright image
c. Cake of barley
d. Rams
e. Sheaves
f. Kine
g. A spirit
h. The Lord
i. Birth of God's Son
j. Vine and branches
k. Wind and beasts

223
Dreams

Answer each question with the person involved in dreaming.

1. Who "suffered many things" in a dream because of Jesus (Matt. 27:19)?
2. Who was warned in a dream not to return to Herod (Matt. 2:1-12)?
3. Who did the Lord not answer by dreams or prophets (1 Sam. 28:6)?
4. Who did God scare with dreams (Job 7:14)?
5. Who caused the people to forget God's name by their dreams (Jer. 23:25-27)?
6. Who told false dreams (Zech. 10:2)?
7. Who caused themselves to dream dreams (Jer. 29:4-8)?
8. Who did Jude call filthy dreamers (Jude 4-8)?
9. Who did Isaiah say would be "as a dream of a night vision" (Isa. 29:7-8)?
10. Who asked Joseph to interpret a dream because his interpretation of another dream was favorable (Gen. 40:16)?
11. Who was hated by his brothers because he told them his dream (Gen. 37:5)?
12. Who will cause young men to see visions and old men to dream dreams (Acts 2:17)?
13. Who did not sin because God knew his heart and revealed Sarah's identity to him in a dream (Gen 20:4-6)?

224
Elijah

Elijah was an outstanding prophet in his time. Answer each question about him.

1. How did Elijah divide the waters of the Jordan (2 Kings 2:8)?
2. How was Elijah fed when he was in hiding (1 Kings 17:3-4)?
3. How did Elijah heal a child (1 Kings 17:21)?
4. How did Elijah propose that the true God would make himself known (1 Kings 18:24)?
5. Where did Elijah find Elisha (1 Kings 19:19)?
6. Who succeeded Elijah as prophet (2 Kings 2:12)?
7. Why did Elijah flee into the wilderness (1 Kings 19:1-3)?
8. As Elijah prayed under a juniper tree, what did he pray for (1 Kings 19:4)?
9. What message did God tell Elijah to deliver to Ahab (1 Kings 21:17-19)?
10. What punishment did Elijah tell Ahaziah would be his because he sent messsengers to inquire of Baal-zebub (2 Kings 1:16-17)?
11. How many times did Elijah fill the barrels with water and pour them on the fire (1 Kings 18:33-34)?

225
Elisha

Elisha was the attendant and disciple of Elijah. Answer each question about Elisha and his ministry.

1. How did Elisha cure the spring waters (2 Kings 2:21)?
2. What did Elisha do to help the widow woman whose creditors were about to take her sons (2 Kings 4:1-7)?
3. What did the woman of Shunem do for Elisha (2 Kings 4:8-10)?
4. How did Elisha rid the pot of pottage of the poisonous wild gourd (2 Kings 4:39-41)?
5. What did Elisha tell Naaman to do to be cured of leprosy (2 Kings 5:10)?
6. How did Elisha rescue an ax head (2 Kings 6:6)?
7. How did the Lord rescue Elisha from the Syrians (2 Kings 6:18)?
8. What did Elisha use to predict the future of Joash (2 Kings 13:14-19)?
9. What did Ben-hadad ask Elisha (2 Kings 8:8)?
10. Why was the king of Syria upset with Elisha (2 Kings 6:11-12)?
11. What did Elisha tell the Shunammite woman would happen to her (2 Kings 4:15-16)?

226
Evangelism

Jesus practiced personal evangelism. Match each statement with the person to whom Jesus witnessed.

1. "My kingdom is not of this world" (John 18:31-36).
2. "This day is salvation come to this house" (Luke 19:2-9).
3. "Except a man be born again, he cannot see the kingdom of God" (John 3:1-3).
4. "Thy faith hath saved thee; go in peace" (Luke 7:38-50).
5. "Son, thy sins be forgiven thee. . . . Arise, and take up thy bed, and go thy way into thine house" (Mark 2:5,11).
6. "How hardly shall they that have riches enter into the kingdom of God!" (Luke 18:18-25).
7. "Go, wash in the pool of Siloam" (John 9:1-6).
8. "Fear not; from henceforth thou shalt catch men" (Luke 5:10).
9. "They that be whole need not a physician, but they that are sick" (Matt. 9:12).
10 "Thou art not far from the kingdom of God" (Mark 12:28,34).

a. Man with palsy
b. A scribe
c. A blind man
d. Pharisees
e. Nicodemus
f. Pilate
g. Rich young ruler
h. Simon
i. Zacchaeus
j. A woman at Simon's house

227
Family Trees

Match each child with the parent and then the grandparent.

1. Timothy (2 Tim. 1:5)
2. Joseph (Gen. 25:28; 29:28; 30:22-24)
3. Moses (Num. 26:59)
4. David (Matt. 1:5)
5. Samuel (1 Sam. 1:1,21-22)
6. Solomon (Matt. 1:6)
7. Saul (1 Sam. 9:1-2)
8. Abinadab (1 Sam. 9:1-2; 31:2)
9. Isaac (Gen. 11:27; 21:2-3)
10. Esau (Gen. 24:67; 25:21-26)

a. Abram
b. David
c. Eunice
d. Isaac
e. Kish
f. Elkanah
g. Saul
h. Jochebed
i. Rachel
j. Jesse

aa. Abiel
bb. Levi
cc. Lois
dd. Kish
ee. Sarah
ff. Terah
gg. Jeroham
hh. Jesse
ii. Isaac
jj. Obed

228
Feet

Feet were important transportation in biblical days. Fill in each blank with the person associated with the feet.

1. _____ wiped Jesus' feet with her hair (John 11:2).
2. _____ laid down at the feet of Boaz (Ruth 3:4-6).
3. _____ said she wanted to be a servant to wash the feet of David's servants (1 Sam. 25:41-42).
4. _____ had not "dressed his feet" from the day King David left for war until he returned (2 Sam. 19:24).
5. _____ had diseased feet in his old age (1 Kings 15:23).
6. _____ fell at Jesus' feet and begged for a child's healing (Luke 8:41).
7. _____ told Thomas: "behold my hands and my feet" (Luke 24:39).
8. _____ sat at Jesus' feet and "heard his word" (Luke 10:39).
9. _____ took the lame man's hand, lifted him up, and his feet received strength (Acts 3:6-7).
10. _____ said "Behold, there cometh one after me, whose shoes of his feet I am not worthy to loose" (Acts 13:25).
11. _____ took Paul's girdle and bound his own hands and feet to predict what would happen to Paul (Acts 21:10-11).

229
First People

Many people seek to be the first or best at something in life. Match these people with the first in their lives.

1. Hunter (Gen. 10:8-10)
2. Woman (Gen. 2:22-23)
3. King of Israel (1 Sam. 11:12)
4. Murdered (Gen. 4:8)
5. Grandchild (Gen. 4:17)
6. Child (Gen. 4:1)
7. Tither (Gen. 14:19-20)
8. Husband (Gen. 2:18-19)
9. Priest (Gen. 14:18)
10. Scribe (2 Sam. 8:17)

a. Abram
b. Adam
c. Cain
d. Eve
e. Seraiah
f. Melchizedek
g. Saul
h. Enoch
i. Abel
j. Nimrod

230
Forty

Fill in each blank with the person or thing associated with forty.

1. The flood of Noah's time lasted forty _____ (Gen. 7:17).
2. God told Abraham he would spare Sodom if forty _____ _____ could be found (Gen. 18:29).
3. Solomon had forty _____ in the Temple (1 Kings 7:38).
4. Moses' law stated that a wicked man could receive forty _____ for his wickedness (Deut. 25:1-3).
5. Moses stayed on Mount Sinai forty _____ (Deut. 10:10).
6. The Israelites wandered in the wilderness forty _____ (Num. 14:33).
7. Abdon had forty _____ (Judg. 12:13-14).
8. Hazael took forty _____ _____ to Elisha (2 Kings 8:9).
9. Paul received forty _____ less one five times from the Jews (2 Cor. 11:24).
10. Jonah preached that Nineveh had forty _____ to repent (Jonah 3:4).
11. David's army killed forty thousand Syrian _____ (2 Sam. 10:18).

231
Fowl

To most of us the fowl of the air add enjoyment. Underline the correct fowl in each statement.

1. Jesus said His followers should be harmless as [doves, eagles, sparrows] (Matt. 10:16).
2. Jesus told us to consider the [eagles, ravens, doves] who do not farm, yet God feeds them (Luke 12:24).
3. Jesus used the [dove, sparrow, swan] to demonstrate our value and his care for us (Luke 12:6-7).
4. Elijah was fed by [quail, ravens, stork] (1 Kings 17:6).
5. When Jesus was baptized, the Spirit of God descended upon Him like a [dove, swan, eagle] (Matt. 3:16).
6. Peter wept when the [crow, cock, hen] crowed three times (Matt. 26:75).
7. Jeremiah said the daughters of Zion became cruel like the [hawk, ostrich, cock] in the wilderness (Lam. 4:3).
8. Solomon said riches fly away like [sparrows, doves, eagles] (Prov. 23:5).
9. God told Moses to tell the Israelites, "I bare you on [eagles', owls', cocks'] wings" (Ex. 19:4).
10. Jesus overthrew the tables of the sellers of [quail, pigeons, doves] (Mark 11:15).
11. Hosea likened Ephriam to a silly [hen, dove, owl] (Hos. 7:11).
12. An Israelite not able to bring a lamb to offer to the Lord could bring two [hens, turtledoves, swans] for a sin offering and two [pigeons, quails, cormorants] for a burnt offering (Lev. 5:7).

232
God's Assurance

God gives assurance to the people He calls. Match each person with the assurance God gave.

1. Jeremiah (Jer. 1:9)
2. Paul (2 Cor. 12:9)
3. Moses (Ex. 3:17)
4. Noah (Gen. 9:9)
5. Disciples (Matt. 14:27)
6. Jacob (Gen. 31:13)
7. Mary Magdalene and Mary (Matt. 28:6)
8. Ruler of the synagogue (Mark 5:36)
9. Gideon (Judg. 6:23)
10. Hagar (Gen. 21:18)

a. "I am the God of Beth-el, where thou anointedst the pillar, and where thou vowedst a vow unto me: now arise, get thee out from this land, and return unto the land of thy kindred."

b. "Be not afraid, only believe."

c. "Arise, lift up the lad, and hold him in thine hand; for I will make him a great nation."

d. "Be of good cheer; it is I; be not afraid."

e. "My grace is sufficient for thee."

f. "He is not here: for he is risen, . . . Come, see the place where the Lord lay."

g. (When he had seen an angel) "Fear not: thou shalt not die."

h. "I have put my words in thy mouth."

i. "I establish my covenant with you."

j. "I will bring you up out of the affliction of Egypt . . . unto a land flowing with milk and honey."

233
God's Methods

God handles problems in miraculous ways. Match what God did with how He did it.

1. Parted waters of Red Sea (Ex. 14:21)
2. Moved stone at Jesus' tomb (Matt. 28:2)
3. Took Elijah to heaven (2 Kings 2:1)
4. Spoke to Moses (Ex. 3:4)
5. Fed Israelites (Ex. 16:15)
6. Changed Peter (Acts 11:5-12)
7. Created Eve (Gen. 2:12-22)
8. Created earth (Gen. 1:1-3)
9. Destroyed world (Gen. 7:23)
10. Saved Jonah physically (Jonah 1:17)
11. Destroyed Sodom and Gomorrah (Gen. 19:24)

a. Burning bush
b. Fire and brimstone
c. A flood
d. A great fish
e. Rib of a man
f. Wind
g. Sheet from heaven
h. Angel
i. His Word
j. Manna from heaven
k. Whirlwind

234
Gold

Gold has always been considered precious. Unscramble the word about a golden object in parentheses in each statement.

1. The Israelites drank "gold" (tawer) _____ (Ex. 32:19-20).
2. Pharaoh put a gold (nahic) _____ about Joseph's neck (Gen. 41:42).
3. The priest's robe had gold (lebls) _____ on the hem (Ex. 28:33).
4. The three kings presented Jesus (stifg) _____ of gold, frankincense, and myrrh (Matt. 2:11).
5. James warned about giving respect to a man wearing a gold (girn) _____ (Jas. 2:2).
6. Solomon made two-hundred (gettars) _____ of gold (1 Kings 10:16).
7. Nebuchadnezzar made an (egaim) _____ of gold for the people to worship (Dan. 3:1-5).
8. Hezekiah cut off the gold on the Temple (sodor) _____ and gave the gold to the king of Assyria (2 Kings 18:16).
9. Toi sent gold (lesessv) _____ to David to congratulate him for winning a battle (2 Sam. 8:10).
10. The king held out a gold (cesertp) _____ to Esther (Esther 5:2).
11. The Temple had ten gold (dictankelscs) _____, five on the right and five on the left before the oracle (1 Kings 7:49).
12. John saw a city which had (teretss) _____ of pure gold (Rev. 21:21).

235
Hair

To many people, hair is an important part of the body. Fill in each blank with the person associated with the statement about hair.

1. _____ had red hair (Gen. 25:25).
2. _____ was laughed at by children because he was bald (2 Kings 2:22-23).
3. _____ wiped Jesus' feet with her hair (Luke 7:37-38).
4. _____ had clothing made from camel's hair (Matt. 3:4).
5. _____ had hairs "grown like eagles' feathers" (Dan. 4:33).
6. _____ had hair that weighed two-hundred shekels (2 Sam. 14:25-26).
7. _____ lost his strength when his hair was shaven off (Judg. 16:13-20).
8. A _____ was not to cut his hair (Num. 6:2-5).
9. _____ "plucked off" the Jews' hair and made them swear not to give their daughters to heathen sons (Neh. 13:25).
10. _____ saw a spirit, and his hair stood up (Job 4:1,15).
11. _____ told His disciples the hairs of their heads were all numbered (Matt. 10:30).

236
Hangings

Perhaps one of the most-used methods of killing has been hanging. Fill in the blanks with the person involved in a hanging.

1. _____ hanged himself, because his counsel was not followed (2 Sam. 17:23).
2. _____ hanged himself on a tree while riding a mule (2 Sam. 18:10).
3. _____ hanged himself because he had betrayed Jesus (Matt. 27:3-5).
4. _____ "was hanged on a tree" for our sins (Acts 5:30-31).
5. _____ was hanged on gallows he made for another man (Esther 7:10).
6. _____ interpreted a dream to mean the butler would be released, and the baker would be hanged (Gen. 40:21-23).
7. _____ burned Ai and hanged the king (Josh. 8:28-29).
8. _____ hanged the bodies of two men over the pool in Hebron because they murdered Saul's son (2 Sam. 5:9-12).
9. _____ was spared hanging because of a covenant between Jonathan and David (2 Sam. 21:7).
10. _____ hanged the people who sacrificed to idols with Baal-peor (Num. 25:2-5).

237
Heart Quotes

The Bible has many quotes about the heart. Fill in the blanks below with the correct words about the heart.

1. "Man looketh on the _____ _____, but the Lord looketh on the heart" (1 Sam. 16:7*b*).
2. "Thou shalt love the Lord thy God with all thy heart, and with all thy _____, and with all thy _____" (Matt. 22:37).
3. "Let the words of my mouth, and the _____ of my heart, be _____ in thy sight, O Lord, my strength, and my redeemer" (Ps. 19:14).
4. "Thy _____ have I hid in mine heart, that I might not _____ against thee" (Ps. 119:11).
5. "For with the heart man _____ unto _____; and with the mouth confession is made unto _____" (Rom. 10:10).
6. "_____ in the Lord with all thine heart; and lean not unto thine own _____" (Prov. 3:5).
7. "Blessed are the _____ in heart: for they shall _____ God" (Matt. 5:8).
8. "Let not your heart be _____: ye _____ in God, believe also in me" (John 14:1).
9. "Incline thine ear unto _____, and apply thine heart to _____" (Prov. 2:2).
10. "The fool hath said in his heart, There is _____ _____" (Ps. 14:1*a*).

238
Hearts

The disposition of a person is often described by the kind of heart he has Match each person with the proper heart.

1. Absalom (2 Sam. 15:6)
2. Saul (1 Sam. 10:9)
3. Nabal (1 Sam. 25:37)
4. Solomon (1 Kings 3:9)
5. Hannah (1 Sam. 2:1)
6. Asa (1 Kings 15:14)
7. Pharaoh (Ex. 7:3)
8. Shimei (1 Kings 2:44)
9. Josiah (2 Kings 22:19)
10. Belshazzar (Dan. 5:22)
11. David (1 Kings 3:6)

a. Dead heart
b. Hard heart
c. New heart
d. Perfect heart
e. Rejoicing heart
f. Stolen hearts
g. Tender heart
h. Understanding heart
i. Unhumble heart
j. Upright heart
k. Wicked heart

239
Heat

Heat makes many foods taste better. Fill in each blank with the proper word in the statement about heat.

1. Peter said in the last days "the _____ shall melt with fervent heat, the _____ also and the works that are therein shall be burned up" (2 Pet. 3:10).
2. When Paul laid sticks on a fire, a _____ came out of the heat and fastened on his hand (Acts 28:3).
3. Jesus said the hypocrites could tell when the heat would come, but could not discern _____ _____ (Luke 12:55-56).
4. Abraham sat in the _____ _____ in the heat of the day when the angels came to visit him (Gen. 18:1).
5. Moses said that all nations one day would say, "What meaneth the heat of this great _____?" (Deut. 29:24).
6. Saul battled the Ammonites until the heat of the _____ and they were scattered "so that two of them were not left together" (1 Sam. 11:11).
7. When King David was old, they _____ him, but he got no heat (1 Kings 1:1).
8. David said the sun is like a bridegroom who goes to the end of the heaven and finds _____ hidden from the heat (Ps. 19:6).
9. The Preacher said, "If two _____ together, then they have heat: but how can one be warm alone?" (Eccl. 4:11).
10. Nebuchadnezzar commanded that the _____ be heated seven times more than normal (Dan. 3:19).

240
Hiding Places

All of us at sometime have wanted a place to hide from something or someone. Match each person with the proper hiding place.

1. Jonathan and Ahimaaz (2 Sam. 17:17-19)
2. Adam and Eve (Gen. 3:8)
3. Moses (Ex. 2:2-3)
4. Spies (Josh. 2:4-6)
5. Five kings (Josh. 10:16-17)
6. Saul (1 Sam. 10:22)
7. David (1 Sam. 20:24)
8. Joash (2 Kings 11:3)
9. Ahaziah (2 Chron. 22:9)
10. Elijah (1 Kings 17:3)

a. By the brook Cherith
b. Among the baggage
c. In a field
d. In a cave at Makkedah
e. In trees in the garden
f. In a well covered with corn
g. In a basket in a river
h. In the house of the Lord
i. In Samaria
j. In stalks of flax on a roof

241
Home

To most of us, the word *home* has a warm sound. Answer each question about a home.

1. Who was told to go home to his friends and tell them the great things the Lord had done for him (Mark 5:18-19)?
2. Why did Paul tell Corinthian church members to eat at home if they were hungry (1 Cor. 11:20-34)?
3. To whose home did Jesus send His mother (John 19:27)?
4. Why did the shepherd of one-hundred sheep call his neighbors to his home to celebrate (Luke 15:6)?
5. What problem did the centurion have at home for which he wanted Jesus' help (Matt. 8:6)?
6. What did Potiphar's wife have at home which she used to falsely accuse Joseph of adultery (Gen. 39:12-19)?
7. Why were Joseph's brothers scared when they were invited to his home to eat (Gen. 43:16-18)?
8. Who were told to bring their cattle home and why (Ex. 9:19-20)?
9. When was an Israelite to remain at home for a year (Deut. 24:5)?
10. Why did Rahab tie a scarlet thread in a window and bring her family into her home (Josh. 2:18-19)?
11. Why did Ahithophel go home, put his house in order, and hang himself (2 Sam. 17:23)?
12. Why did the man of God refuse to eat in the home of King Jeroboam (1 Kings 13:6-9)?

242
Houses

The place where we live is important to us, whether it be a house, tent, apartment, mobile home, or what. Fill in each blank with the occupant of the house.

1. _____ received Jesus into her house (Luke 10:38).
2. _____, the tanner, housed Peter (Acts 10:5-6).
3. _____, the mother of John, held a prayer meeting in her house (Acts 12:12).
4. _____ had a house next door to a synagogue (Acts 18:7).
5. _____ had a house which the Jews assaulted while looking for Paul and Silas (Acts 17:4-6).
6. _____ and company were housed by Philip on their way to Jerusalem (Acts 21:8).
7. _____ and _____ had a church in their house (Rom. 16:3-5).
8. _____ went to the house of Bethuel to find a wife (Gen. 28:1-2).
9. _____ housed the ark of the Lord three months (2 Sam. 6:11).
10. _____ built a house overlaid with gold (1 Kings 6:21-22).
11. _____ "was buried in his own house in the wilderness" (1 Kings 2:30-34).

243
Identities

Many people spend years trying to learn who they are. Who we are is important to each of us. Match each person or place with the proper identity.

1. Abaddon (Rev. 9:11)
2. Aceldama (Acts 1:19)
3. Andronicus (Rom. 16:7)
4. Nahor (Gen. 11:26)
5. Milcah (Gen. 11:29)
6. Huz and Buz (Gen. 22:20-21)
7. Bethabara (John 1:28)
8. Heli (Luke 3:23)
9. Golgotha (Matt. 27:33)
10. Herodion (Rom. 16:11)
11. Raamses (Ex. 1:11)
12. Tadmor (1 Kings 9:18)
13. Shushan (Esther 2:8)

a. Abraham's nephews
b. City built for Pharaoh
c. Sister-in-law to Abraham
d. Paul's kinsman
e. Angel of the bottomless pit
f. A palace city
g. John the Baptist baptized here
h. Field of blood
i. City Solomon built
j. Jesus' grandfather
k. Abraham's brother
l. Disciple at Rome
m. Place of a skull

244
Inscriptions

How would you like to be remembered? Match each inscription with the person or place in the statement.

1. The great river (Gen. 15:18)
2. A mighty hunter before the Lord (Gen. 10:9)
3. Most humble man on earth (Num. 12:3)
4. Generation of vipers (Matt. 3:7)
5. Foolish (Gal. 3:1)
6. Wiser than all men (1 Kings 4:29)
7. Walked with God and was not (Gen. 5:24)
8. Wicked in the sight of the Lord (Gen. 38:7)
9. His works were evil; his brother's righteous (1 John 3:12)
10. Perfect and upright, feared God and "eschewed" evil (Job 1:1)
11. A faithful man, feared God above many (Neh. 7:2)
12. An Israelite in whom there was no guile (John 1:47)

a. Cain
b. Solomon
c. Er
d. Euphrates
e. Galatians
f. Hananiah
g. Job
h. Moses
i. Enoch
j. Nathanael
k. Pharisees and Sadducees
l. Nimrod

245
Jewelry

Jewelry mentioned in the Bible includes rings, earrings, bracelets, and chains. Fill in each blank with the person who had the jewelry.

1. The servant of _____ presented Rebekah a golden earring and two bracelets when she gave him water (Gen. 24:12,20-23).
2. The family and friends of _____ each gave him a gold earring to comfort him after all the evil which had befallen him (Job 42:11-12).
3. _____ gave Joseph a ring and put a gold chain around his neck (Gen. 41:42).
4. _____ of the prodigal gave his son the finest clothes and a ring (Luke 15:22).
5. _____ made an ephod from spoils of earrings which weighed seventeen-hundred shekels (Judg. 8:24-26).
6. _____ asked Judah for his signet, bracelets, and staff as a pledge (Gen. 38:13-18).
7. The king gave _____ the royal ring to seal a bargain (Esther 3:8-10).
8. When he realized _____ could not live, a man killed him and took the bracelet from the dead man's arm and brought it to David (2 Sam. 1:10).
9. The women of Israel sang about _____ who put golden jewelry (ornaments) on their apparel (2 Sam. 1:24).
10. _____ told the men to break off their wives' earrings and bring them to him to make a golden calf (Ex. 32:2).

246
Light

Though we take light for granted, it is very important to us. Match each person with the proper statement about light.

1. Jesus
2. Wise men
3. Foolish virgins
4. Evil doers
5. Peter
6. Israelites
7. Wicked
8. David
9. Keeper of prison
10. Satan

a. Led by a pillar of light (Ex. 14:20)
b. Called for a light and fell before Paul and Silas (Acts 16:29)
c. Hate light lest their "deeds should be reproved" (John 3:20)
d. Transformed into an angel of light (2 Cor. 11:14)
e. His light shall be put out (Job 18:5)
f. Said, "The Lord is my light" (Ps. 27:1)
g. Awakened by light in prison (Acts 12:7)
h. Followed the light of a star (Matt. 2:1-2)
i. Lights in lamps burned out (Matt. 25:8)
j. Light of the world (John 8:12)

247
Little-Mentioned Occupations

Some occupations are mentioned many times in the Bible; others are seldom mentioned. Match each person with his little-mentioned occupation.

1. Aholiab (Ex. 38:23)
2. Adoram (2 Sam. 20:24)
3. Nehemiah (Neh. 2:1)
4. Herod (Acts 13:1)
5. Simon (Acts 9:43)
6. Elymas (Acts 13:8)
7. Heman (1 Chron. 6:33)
8. Jehoshaphat (1 Kings 4:3)
9. Ishmael (Gen. 21:20)
10. Demetrius (Acts 19:24)
11. Philip (Acts 21:8)

a. Archer
b. Cupbearer
c. Embroiderer
d. Recorder
e. Singer
f. Silversmith
g. Sorcerer
h. Tanner
i. Tribute
j. Tetrarch
k. Evangelist

248
Mothers and
Daughters

Few mothers and daughters are named in the Bible. Answer the following questions with the proper mother or daughter.

_____ 1. Who was the mother who instructed her daughter to ask for John the Baptist's head (Matt. 14:6-8)?

_____ 2. Who became mother to her daughter-in-law (Ruth 1:16-19)?

_____ 3. Who were the mother and daughter Paul commended for proper rearing of a son (2 Tim. 1:5)?

_____ 4. Who was the daughter who watched her baby brother in a basket boat made by her mother (Ex. 2:3-4;15:20)?

_____ 5. Who was the daughter of Leah and Jacob (Gen. 30:21)?

_____ 6. Who was the prophetess whose mother was unknown (Judg. 4:4)?

_____ 7. Who was the mother, later memorialized in salt, who fled with her two daughters (Gen. 19:15)?

_____ 8. Who was the daughter-in-law picked by a servant (Gen. 24:1-4,15)?

_____ 9. Who was the mother who left her daughters many times for other lovers and was forgiven by her husband each time (Hos. 1:3; 2:1-5)?

_____10. Who was the mother who chose her daughter-in-law (Gen. 21:17-21)?

249
Needlework

Fill in the blanks with the thing associated with needlework.

1. Sisera received _____ of many colors of needlework (Judg. 5:30).
2. The tabernacle curtain had needlework of blue, purple, and scarlet on _____ (Ex. 36:37).
3. Aaron and his sons had coats with _____ of needlework (Ex. 28:39).
4. The prophet said, "Woe to the women that _____ pillows to all armholes" (Ezek. 13:18).
5. Abram told the king of Sodom, "I will not take from a _____ even to a shoelatchet, . . . lest thou shouldest say, 'I have made Abram rich'" (Gen. 14:23).
6. Jesus said it was easier for a camel to go through the eye of a _____ than it was for a rich man to get into heaven (Matt. 19:24).
7. The Israelite women _____ goat's hair as an offering for the tabernacle (Ex. 35:25-26).
8. Goliath had a spear like a weaver's _____ (1 Sam. 17:7).
9. Adam and Eve sewed clothes of _____ (Gen. 3:7).
10. The _____ shows God's handiwork wrote the psalmist (Ps. 19:1).

250
New Testament
Books

Knowing the correct order of the books of the Bible helps the student find passages much more quickly. Place the correct number of their order in the Bible before each book of the New Testament.

1. _____ Galatians
2. _____ 2 Timothy
3. _____ James
4. _____ 3 John
5. _____ Revelation
6. _____ 1 John
7. _____ 2 Corinthians
8. _____ Mark
9. _____ Jude
10. _____ 2 Peter
11. _____ 2 John
12. _____ Acts
13. _____ Titus
14. _____ Ephesians

15. _____ John
16. _____ Colossians
17. _____ Romans
18. _____ Luke
19. _____ 2 Thessalonians
20. _____ Philippians
21. _____ Hebrews
22. _____ Matthew
23. _____ 1 Timothy
24. _____ Philemon
25. _____ 1 Thessalonians
26. _____ 1 Peter
27. _____ 1 Corinthians

251
Nicknames

Often people are given names or titles by which they are called. Match the nickname with the person.

1. That fox (Luke 13:31-32)
2. Boanerges (Mark 3:17)
3. Didymus (John 20:24)
4. Beloved disciple (John 19:26)
5. Friend of God (Jas. 2:23)
6. That wicked woman (2 Chron. 24:7)
7. Satan (Isa. 14:12)
8. Voice in the wilderness (John 1:23)
9. Israel (Gen. 35:10)
10. Beloved physician (Col. 4:14)
11. Wonderful Counsellor (Isa. 9:6)

a. Abraham
b. Athaliah
c. Herod
d. James and John
e. Jesus
f. John
g. Jacob
h. John the Baptist
i. Luke
j. Lucifer
k. Thomas

252
Old Testament Books

Knowing the books of the Bible aids Bible study. How many of the Old Testament books can you locate without an index? Arrange the books of the Old Testament in chronological order by placing the proper number of their location in front of each book.

1. ___ 2 Samuel	14. ___ Deuteronomy	27. ___ Psalms
2. ___ Job	15. ___ Nehemiah	28. ___ Isaiah
3. ___ Ecclesiastes	16. ___ 2 Kings	29. ___ Exodus
4. ___ Hosea	17. ___ Song of Solomon	30. ___ Esther
5. ___ 2 Chronicles	18. ___ Malachi	31. ___ Ezekiel
6. ___ Jonah	19. ___ Daniel	32. ___ 1 Samuel
7. ___ Joel	20. ___ Genesis	33. ___ Micah
8. ___ Nahum	21. ___ Zechariah	34. ___ Judges
9. ___ Numbers	22. ___ Obadiah	35. ___ Habakkuk
10. ___ Proverbs	23. ___ Zephaniah	36. ___ Jeremiah
11. ___ Amos	24. ___ 1 Chronicles	37. ___ Ezra
12. ___ Haggai	25. ___ Lamentations	38. ___ 1 Kings
13. ___ Ruth	26. ___ Joshua	39. ___ Leviticus

253
One to Eleven

Match each number with the proper number of items.

1. One (Gen. 27:38)
2. Two (Ex. 34:4)
3. Three (Acts 20:3)
4. Four (1 Kings 18:33)
5. Five (Matt. 14:17)
6. Six (Num. 35:6)
7. Seven (Acts 6:3)
8. Eight (2 Kings 8:17)
9. Nine (Luke 17:17)
10. Ten (Matt. 25:1)
11. Eleven (Gen. 37:9)

a. Barrels Elijah filled with water
b. Cities of refuge
c. Lepers who did not thank Jesus
d. Loaves a lad had
e. Men of honest report chosen to serve tables
f. Months Paul lived in Greece
g. Stars in Joseph's dream
h. Virgins in a parable
i. Years Jehoram reigned
j. Tablets of the law
k. Isaac's blessing

254
Owners

Many of us enjoy owning things. Possessions may seem to bring security. Fill in each blank with the thing possessed.

1. Omri bought and owned the _____ of Samaria (1 Kings 16:23-24).
2. Esau was given ownership of Mount _____ (Gen. 36:8).
3. Ahab possessed the _____ of Naboth because Jezebel had the owner killed (1 Kings 21:15-16).
4. Isaac owned _____ and herds (Gen. 26:14).
5. The Israelites were promised ownership of _____ by God (Lev. 14:34).
6. Lot's children owned _____ (Deut. 2:9).
7. Paul owned a _____ which he left in Troas and asked Timothy to bring it to him (2 Tim. 4:13).
8. A widow woman owned two _____ which she cast into the Temple treasury (Mark 12:41-42).
9. A widow woman and her son owned only a handful of _____ and a little oil in a cruse (1 Kings 17:12).
10. Paul warned the owners of a _____ of damage to their possession (Acts 27:11).
11. Jesus told the disciples to untie a _____ for him to ride, and the owner would give consent (Luke 19:33).
12. Hadad owned a _____ which Pharaoh gave to him (1 Kings 11:18).

255
Pairs

Some people are mentioned together until you think of the other person when one name is mentioned. Match each pair with their identification.

1. Huz and Buz (Gen. 22:20-21)
2. Mahlon and Chilion (Ruth 1:2-5)
3. Cain and Abel (Gen. 4:1-2)
4. Adam and Eve (Gen. 3:20)
5. Ruth and Orpah (Ruth 1:3-4)
6. Mary and Martha (John 11:5)
7. Moses and Elijah (Matt. 17:2-3)
8. Gershom and Eliezer (Ex. 18:2-4)
9. Manasseh and Ephraim
   (Gen. 41:51-52)
10. Moses and Aaron (Num. 26:50)
11. Adah and Zillah (Gen. 4:19)
12. Hophni and Phinehas
    (1 Sam. 4:11)
13. Hannah and Peninnah
    (1 Sam. 1:1-2)

a. Daughters-in-law of Naomi
b. Appeared in transfiguration
c. Nephews of Abraham
d. Sons of Adam and Eve
e. Brothers of Miriam
f. Sons of Eli
g. Sons of Joseph
h. Wives of Elkanah
i. Sons of Zipporah
j. Sisters of Lazarus
k. Sons of Naomi
l. First inhabitants of earth
m. Wives of Lamech

256
Parts of the Body

Different parts of the body were used to teach biblical truths. Fill in each blank with the proper part of the body.

1. "The _____ is deceitful above all things, and desperately wicked: who can know it?" (Jer. 17:9).
2. "If thy right _____ offend thee, pluck it out, and cast it from thee: for it is profitable for thee that one of thy members should perish, and not that thy whole body should be cast into hell" (Matt. 5:29).
3. "But the _____ can no man tame; it is an unruly evil, full of deadly poison" (Jas. 3:8).
4. "Out of the same _____ proceedeth blessing and cursing. My brethren, these things ought not so to be" (Jas. 3:10).
5. "For my _____ shall speak truth; and wickedness is an abomination to my _____" (Prov. 8:7).
6. "A wicked man hardeneth his _____: but as for the upright, he directeth his way" (Prov. 21:29).
7. "Confidence in an unfaithful man in time of trouble is like a broken _____, and a _____ out of joint" (Prov. 25:19).
8. "He becometh poor that dealeth with a slack _____: but the _____ of the diligent maketh rich" (Prov. 10:4).
9. "A wicked doer giveth heed to false _____; and a liar giveth _____ to a naughty _____" (Prov. 17:4).
10. "A fool's _____ is his destruction and his _____ are the snare of his soul" (Prov. 18:7).

257
Person, Place, or Thing?

Names of objects are important in communication. Circle the proper identity of each of the following:

1. Huzzab (Nah. 2:7)   person, place, thing
2. Hadadezer (2 Sam. 8:7)   person, place, thing
3. Sarepta (Luke 4:26)   person, place, thing
4. Rehum (Ezra 2:2)   person, place, thing
5. Nisan (Neh. 2:1)   person, place, thing
6. Thyatira (Acts 16:14)   person, place, thing
7. Zobebah (1 Chron. 4:8)   person, place, thing
8. Dodo (2 Sam. 23:24)   person, place, thing
9. Perizzite (Gen. 13:7)   person, place, thing
10. Uzziah (Isa. 6:1)   person, place, thing
11. Shittah (Isa. 41:19)   person, place, thing

258
Physical Characteristics

Physical characteristics help us to recognize people. Match each characteristic with the correct person.

1. The giant (1 Sam. 17:4)
2. Ruddy and beautiful (1 Sam. 16:12-13)
3. Without a blemish (2 Sam. 14:25)
4. Little of stature (Luke 19:2-3)
5. Hands covered with hair (Gen. 27:23)
6. Very fat (Judg. 3:17)
7. Blind (Mark 10:46)
8. Lame (2 Sam. 4:4)
9. Fair and beautiful (Esther 2:7)
10. Had twelve fingers and twelve toes (2 Sam. 21:20-22)
11. Very strong (Judg. 16:5-6)

a. Absalom
b. Bartimaeus
c. David
d. Eglon
e. Esther
f. Esau
g. Goliath
h. Mephibosheth
i. Son of Goliath
j. Samson
k. Zacchaeus

259
Pits

Pits are common items in biblical days. Fill in each blank with the person involved with a pit.

1. _____ was thrown into a pit by his brothers (Gen. 37:20-23).
2. _____ and all his men fell into a pit when God opened the earth (Num. 16:32-33).
3. During the Battle of the Kings, the kings of _____ and _____ fell into slimepits (Gen. 14:10).
4. _____ hid in pits when the Philistines came to fight them (1 Sam. 13:6).
5. _____ was buried in a pit (2 Sam. 18:17).
6. _____ slew a lion in a pit on a snowy day (2 Sam. 23:20).
7. _____ killed Gedaliah and his warriors and cast them into a pit (Jer. 41:6-7).
8. _____ asked what man would not rescue a sheep when it fell into a pit on the sabbath day (Matt. 12:11).
9. _____ will be cast into the bottomless pit where he can deceive people no more (Rev. 20:2-3).
10. _____ went to the pit to rescue Joseph, but Joseph was gone (Gen. 37:29).
11. _____ said, "A strange woman is a narrow pit" (Prov. 23:27).

260
Places

Where things happen often become special places to individuals. Match the event with the place where it happened.

1. Ruth's new home (Ruth 1:19)   a. Athens
2. Ten Commandments given (Ex. 19:18,20)   b. Antioch
3. Solomon's Temple (2 Chron. 3:1)   c. Bethlehem
4. Man called for help (Acts 16:9)   d. Damascus Road
5. First called Christians (Acts 11:26)   e. Egypt
6. John's exile (Rev. 1:9)   f. Jerusalem
7. Saul struck blind (Acts 9:1-3)   g. Macedonia
8. Gabriel sent to Mary (Luke 1:26)   h. Nazareth
9. Israelites' captivity (Josh. 24:6)   i. Philistia
10. The altar to the unknown God (Acts 17:22-23)   j. Sinai
11. Home of Goliath (1 Sam. 21:9)   k. Patmos

261
Plagues

Arrange the ten plagues in order by matching each plague with its proper number of occurrence.

1. The first plague (Ex. 7:14-24)
2. The second plague (Ex. 7:25 to 8:15)
3. The third plague (Ex. 8:16-19)
4. The fourth plague (Ex. 8:20-32)
5. The fifth plague (Ex. 9:1-7)
6. The sixth plague (Ex. 9:8-12)
7. The seventh plague (Ex. 9:13-35)
8. The eighth plague (Ex. 10:1-20)
9. The ninth plague (Ex. 10:21-29)
10. The tenth plague (Ex. 11:1-10; 12:29-42)

a. Boils
b. Cattle
c. Darkness
d. Death
e. Frogs
f. Flies
g. Lice
h. Hail
i. Locusts
j. Pollution of the Nile

262
Power

In our day, power is sought after by many people. Fill in each missing word in these statements about prayer.

1. Jesus promised _____ power after the Holy Spirit was come upon them (Acts 1:8).
2. God has "not given us the spirit of _____; but of power, and of love, and of a sound mind" (2 Tim. 1:7).
3. Paul said, "I am not ashamed of the _____: for it is the power of God unto _____ to every one that believeth" (Rom. 1:16).
4. _____ said God had brought the Israelites out of Egypt "with his mighty power" (Deut. 4:37).
5. _____ said, "All power is given unto me in heaven and in earth" (Matt. 28:18).
6. "But thou shalt remember the Lord thy God: for it is he that giveth thee power to get _____" (Deut. 8:18).
7. David asked, "Who knoweth the power of thine _____" (Ps. 90:11).
8. "He giveth power to the _____; and to them that have no might he increaseth strength" (Isa. 40:29).
9. "He hath made the _____ by his power" (Jer. 10:12).
10. God delivered _____ from the power of the lions (Dan. 6:27).
11. The devil promised Jesus power of all the kingdoms if He would _____ _____ (Luke 4:6-7).
12. Simon wanted to buy the power of _____ (Acts 8:18).

263
Promises

No one is better than the ability to keep one's promises. Fill in each blank with the proper person associated with the promise.

1. _____ promised his daughter Achsah to the man who captured Kirjath-sepher (Josh. 15:16-17).
2. _____ promised God a tenth of all God gave him in exchange for God's protection (Gen. 28:20-22).
3. _____ promised the Israelites they would not go out of Egypt empty-handed (Ex. 3:15-21).
4. _____ promised Merab to David if he would fight for Saul (1 Sam. 18:17).
5. _____ promised Ephron money for a burial ground (Gen. 23:12-13).
6. _____ promised his birthright to Jacob for a bowl of pottage (Gen. 25:33-34).
7. _____ promised the spies safety in exchange for her life (Josh. 2:3,14).
8. _____ promised to work for Laban seven years in exchange for Rachel (Gen. 29:20).
9. _____promised great riches and a wife to the man who killed the Philistine giant (1 Sam. 17:25).
10. _____ promised a Comforter when He went away (John 14:16).
11. _____ promised Jesus power and glory in exchange for reverence (Luke 4:6-7).

264
Prophets

Match each prophet with the title which more nearly describes him.

1. Jeremiah (Jer. 9:1)
2. Hosea (Hos. 3:1)
3. Elijah (2 Kings 1:8)
4. John the Baptist (Matt. 3:3-4)
5. Jesus (Luke 24:6-9)
6. Jonah (Jonah 1:3)
7. Daniel (Dan. 1:1,3-6)
8. Isaiah (Isa. 9:6-7)
9. Bar-jesus (Acts 13:6)
10. Amos (Amos 7:14)
11. Haggai (Hag. 1:13)

a. Cried in the wilderness
b. Dresser of sycamores
c. Rebellious prophet
d. False prophet
e. The Lord's messenger
f. Weeping prophet
g. Mighty prophet
h. Hairy prophet
i. Messianic prophet
j. Prophet of love
k. Prophet in captivity

265
Punishment

Sin bears its own punishment. Match each person with the correct punishment.

1. Gibeonites (Josh. 9:3-23)
2. Anathoth (Jer. 11:22-23)
3. Moses (Num. 20:7-12)
4. Ananias (Acts 5:5)
5. Miriam (Num. 12:10)
6. Achan (Josh. 7:24-25)
7. Abihu (Lev. 10:1-2)
8. Haman (Esther 7:10)
9. Zacharias (Luke 1:18-20)
10. Syrians (2 Kings 6:8,18)
11. Saul (1 Sam. 16:1)

a. Became blind
b. Stoned and burned
c. Dropped dead
d. Struck dumb
e. Hanged on gallows
f. Leprosy
g. Rejected by God
h. Death by sword
i. Not allowed to enter Promised Land
j. Served as wood cutters and water carriers
k. Devoured by fire

266
Quotes About Houses

Each of the following statements about houses was made by a biblical character. Fill in each blank with the person who made the statement.

1. _____ "As for me and my house, we will serve the Lord (Josh. 24:14-15).
2. _____ "I pray thee therefore, father, that thou wouldest send him [Lazarus] to my father's house" (Luke 16:27).
3. _____ "In my Father's house are many mansions: if it were not so, I would have told you. I go to prepare a place for you" (John 14:2).
4. _____ "Who am I, O Lord God? and what is my house, that thou has brought me hitherto?" (2 Sam. 7:18).
5. _____ "Foxes have holes, and birds of the air have nests; but the Son of man hath not where to lay his head" (Luke 9:58).
6. _____ "Lord, I will follow thee; but let me first go bid them farewell, which are at home at my house" (Luke 9:61)
7. _____ "Therefore whosoever heareth these sayings of mine, and doeth them, I will liken him unto a wise man, which built his house upon a rock" (Matt. 7:24).
8. _____ to Hezekiah, "Set thine house in order; for thou shalt die, and not live" (2 Kings 20:1).
9. _____ "Zacchaeus, make haste, and come down; for to-day I must abide at thy house" (Luke 19:5).

267
Red

Match each person with the correct statement about red in his life.

1. Zechariah (Zech. 1:8)
2. Moabites (2 Kings 3:21-22)
3. Jacob (Gen. 25:30)
4. Judah (Gen. 49:12)
5. Pharisees and Sadducees (Matt. 16:1-3)
6. John (Rev. 12:3)
7. Esau (Gen. 25:25)
8. Israelites (Ex. 25:2-5)
9. Eleazar (Num. 19:2-3)
10. Ahasuerus (Esther 1:1-6)

a. Commanded to slay red heifer
b. Fed brother red pottage
c. Gave offering of red rams' skins
d. Born red all over
e. Vision of red horses
f. Saw water as red as blood
g. Shall have eyes red with wine
h. Had red marble pavement
i. Predicted weather by red sky
j. Vision of red dragon with seven heads

268
Relatives

The family has always been a very important unit in society. Match the persons mentioned with how they are related.

1. Elisabeth to Mary (Luke 1:34-36)
2. Elkanah to Hannah (1 Sam. 1:8)
3. Orpah to Naomi (Ruth 1:11-14)
4. Herodias to Herod (Mark 6:17)
5. Esau to Abraham (Gen. 27:1; 26:1)
6. Dinah to Leah (Gen. 34:1)
7. Ishmael to Abram (Gen. 16:16)
8. Jezebel to Ahab (1 Kings 21:25)
9. Mary to Martha (Luke 10:39)
10. Benjamin to Joseph (Gen. 35:24)
11. Kish to Saul (1 Sam. 9:3)

a. Brother
b. Father
c. Cousin
d. Daughter-in-law
e. Daughter
f. Grandson
g. Sister
h. Son
i. Sister-in-law
j. Husband
k. Wife

269
Rocks

Rocks provide stability to soil. They also provide enjoyment for people who collect them. Answer each question about rocks.

1. Who died and the rocks broke (Matt. 27:51)?
2. Who sought David and his men upon the rocks of the wild goats (1 Sam. 24:2)?
3. What fell among the rocks in one of Jesus' parables (Luke 8:5-6)?
4. Who was told to speak to a rock (Num. 20:7-8)?
5. Who was told by an angel to lay unleavened cakes on a rock and pour broth over it (Judg. 6:19-20)?
6. Who found himself between two sharp rocks (1 Sam. 14:4)?
7. Who "graveth an habitation for himself in a rock" (Isa. 22:15-16)?
8. Who was told to hide his girdle in the hole of a rock (Jer. 13:3-4)?
9. Whose word is like a hammer that breaks the rocks in pieces (Jer. 23:29)?
10. To whom did Jesus say, "Upon this rock I will build my church" (Matt. 16:18)?
11. Who owned the sepulcher hewn out of a rock in which Jesus was buried (Mark 15:46)?
12. Who carried ten thousand people to the top of a rock and pushed them down (2 Chron. 25:11-12)?

270
Royalty

The Israelites thought establishing royalty was more important than God did. However, God gave them a king because they kept asking for one. Answer each question with the royalty mentioned.

1. Which king had no sons to succeed him (2 Kings 1:17-18)?
2. Which king provoked God more than any other king (1 Kings 16:3-34)?
3. Which king made a speech and as a result was eaten by worms (Acts 12:21-23)?
4. Which king ordered three men thrown into a fiery furnace (Dan. 3:19-23)?
5. Which son of a king plotted to kill his brother (2 Sam. 13:27-29)?
6. Which king had eighteen wives, sixty concubines, twenty-eight sons, and sixty daughters (2 Chron. 11:21)?
7. Which king fasted while his son was sick and worshiped when the child died (2 Sam. 12:20)?
8. Which queen heard of Solomon's wisdom and came with hard questions to test his wisdom (1 Kings 10:1)?
9. Which queen did the Ethiopian eunuch serve (Acts 8:27)?
10. Which queen was dethroned because she refused to go to the king when he commanded her to (Esther 1:19)?
11. Which queen wanted to kill John, but her husband feared him (Mark 6:19)?
12. Which king was told by a prophet that prophets would be sacrificed upon an altar to a golden calf, the altar would crash, and the ashes pour out (1 Kings 13:2-3)?

271
Salt

Salt is a much-used seasoning today just as it was in biblical days. Choose the correct answer in each statement about salt.

1. The wife of (Moses, Lot, Abraham) was turned into a pillar of salt when she looked back at the city she was fleeing (Gen. 19:23-26).
2. (Moses, David, Aaron) instructed the Israelites to put salt on the meat offerings (Lev. 2:13).
3. (Solomon, Saul, David) was assured the gift of the kingdom of Israel through a covenant of salt (2 Chron. 13:5).
4. The people of (Israel, Moab, Horeb) were told their land would become brimstone, salt, and burning if they walked in the imagination of their own hearts (Deut. 29:19-23).
5. (Ephraim, Manasseh, Judah) received the city of Salt as an inheritance (Josh. 15:62-63).
6. (Zebul, Abimelech, Gaal) defeated the city of Shechem and sowed it with salt (Judg. 9:45).
7. (Saul, David, Solomon) defeated the Syrians in the valley of salt (2 Sam. 8:13).
8. (Elisha, Elijah, Joshua) asked for a new cruise with salt to be brought to him, so he could cure the bitter spring water (2 Kings 2:19-21).
9. (Nebuchadnezzar, Uzziah, Darius) decreed that wheat, salt, wine, and oil be given to the priests in Jerusalem every day (Ezra 6:1,9).
10. The (priests, scribes, ministers) were to put salt on the bullock without blemish presented as an offering (Ezek. 43:24).
11. Our (lives, speech, knowledge) should be seasoned with salt according to Paul (Col. 4:6).

272
Senior Years

In biblical days some people lived incredibly long, full lives. Each of the following people did something at 60, 62, 80, 83, 85, 98, 100, 110, 120, 123, 127, 137, 187, 500, 969 years of age. Answer each question with the correct number of years picked from above.

1. How old was Abraham when Isaac was born (Gen. 21:5)?
2. How old was Methuselah when he died (Gen. 5:27)?
3. How old was Caleb when he inherited the land of Hebron (Josh. 14:10-14)?
4. How old was Ishmael when he died (Gen. 25:17)?
5. How old was Noah when his three sons were born (Gen. 5:32)?
6. How old was Methuselah when Lamech was born (Gen. 5:26)?
7. How old was Sarah when she died (Gen. 23:1)?
8. How many years did Joseph live (Gen. 50:26)?
9. How old was Aaron when he went with Moses to speak to Pharaoh (Ex. 7:7)?
10. How old was Aaron when he died (Num. 33:39)?
11. How old was Eli when the ark was captured and his sons killed (1 Sam. 4:11-15)?
12. How old was Moses when he retired (Deut. 31:1-2)?
13. How old was Barzillai when he was honored by the king (2 Sam. 19:32)?
14. How old was Hezron when he married (1 Chron. 2:21)?
15. How old was Darius when he took over Belshazzar's kingdom (Dan. 5:31)?

273
Shoes

Shoes are very important to some people; they collect many. Match each person with the proper statement about shoes.

1. Moses (Ex. 3:5)
2. Israelites (Deut. 29:5)
3. Boaz (Ruth 4:7)
4. Isaiah (Isa. 20:2)
5. Gibeonites (Josh. 9:1-5)
6. Joab (2 Kings 2:5)
7. Ezekiel (Ezek. 24:16-23)
8. Amos (Amos 2:6)
9. Disciples (Matt. 10:5-10)
10. Father of the prodigal (Luke 15:22)
11. John the Baptist (Mark 1:7)

a. Commanded servants to put shoes on his son
b. Instructed not to take extra shoes on mission
c. Filled his shoes with blood
d. God told him to remove his shoes
e. Put shoes on and did not weep for the dead
f. Put on old shoes in a plot to deceive Joshua
g. Removed his shoe to seal a bargain
h. Said Israel sold the needy for a pair of shoes
i. Said he was not worthy to untie Jesus' shoes
j. Walked without shoes or clothing for three years
k. Wore the same shoes forty years

274
Silver and Gold

Two precious metals often mentioned together are silver and gold. Match each name with the proper statement about silver and gold.

1. Abram (Gen. 13:2)
2. Peter (Acts 3:6)
3. Israelite women (Ex. 3:22)
4. Bezaleel (Ex. 31:1-4)
5. Moses (Deut. 7:25)
6. Disciples (Matt. 10:9)
7. Paul (Acts 20:33)
8. Asa (1 Kings 15:18-19)
9. Solomon (2 Chron. 1:14-15)
10. Jehoash (2 Kings 14:13-14)
11. Hezekiah (2 Kings 20:12-17)

a. Called to work with silver and gold
b. Coveted no man's silver and gold
c. Commanded Israelites to burn gold and silver
d. Had no silver and gold to give away
e. Made silver and gold as common as stones
f. Commanded to borrow gold and silver jewelry
g. Rich in gold and silver
h. Told not to carry silver and gold on a mission
i. Showed his silver and gold to men who later seized it
j. Plundered silver and gold from the Temple
k. Sent gold and silver to Ben-hadad

275
Songs

Singing has played a vital role in human life. People sing upon every occasion and about everything imaginable. Fill in each blank with the person connected with songs.

1. _____ asked Jacob, "Wherefore didst thou flee away secretely, . . . I might have sent thee away with . . . songs" (Gen. 31:26-27).
2. _____ sang his song of deliverance from his enemies: "The Lord is my rock" (2 Sam. 22:2).
3. _____ wrote 1,005 songs (1 Kings 4:32).
4. _____ had 288 singers "instructed in the songs of the Lord" (1 Chron. 25:7).
5. _____ said, "Where is God my maker, who giveth songs in the night?" (Job 35:10).
6. _____ wrote, "Thou art my hiding place; . . . thou shalt compass me about with songs of deliverance" (Ps. 32:7).
7. _____ said, "As he that taketh away a garment in cold weather, . . . so is he that singeth songs to an heavy heart" (Prov. 25:20).
8. _____ said, "The Lord was ready to save me: therefore we will sing my songs to the stringed instruments all the day of our life" (Isa. 38:20).
9. God told _____, "And I will cause the noise of thy songs to cease; and the sound of thy harps shall be no more heard" (Ezek. 26:13).
10. _____ predicted, "The songs of the Temple shall be howlings in that day" (Amos 8:3).

276
Sons

In biblical days, the father considered sons a blessing from God. Match each son with his father.

1. John the Baptist	a. Aaron (Ex. 6:25)
2. Moses	b. Abraham (Gen. 17:18-19)
3. Isaac	c. Adam (Gen. 4:1)
4. Samuel	d. Amram (1 Chron. 6:3)
5. Joseph	e. David (2 Sam. 3:3)
6. Eleazar	f. Elkanah (1 Sam. 1:19-20)
7. Cain	g. Isaac (Gen. 25:26-28)
8. Jacob	h. Jacob (Gen. 30:24-25)
9. James	i. Zebedee (Matt. 4:21)
10. Absalom	j. Zacharias (Luke 1:59-63)

277
Spies

Today we are constantly shocked by news about spies. Spying is not new. It goes back to the beginnings of the world. Fill in each blank with the proper person concerned with spies.

1. _____ sent spies to the Promised Land (Num. 13:17).
2. _____ and _____ were the two spies who brought back good reports of the Promised Land's capture (Num. 14:6-9).
3. The king of Syria sent a spy to find _____ (2 Kings 6:12-13).
4. _____ hid the two spies Joshua sent to Jericho (Josh. 2:1-4).
5. The Danites sent spies to Laish, who lodged in the house of _____ where they found graven images (Judg. 18:2-14).
6. _____ _____ were accused of being spies when David sent his condolences to Hanun after Hanun's father died (2 Sam. 10:1-3).
7. _____ accused his brothers of being spies when they came to Egypt to get grain (Gen. 42:9-10).
8. _____ sent spies throughout Israel to say that when the trumpet sounded, "Absalom reigneth" (2 Sam. 15:10).
9. The chief _____ and _____ sent spies to accuse Jesus by His words (Luke 20:19-20).
10. _____ wanted the Wise Men to serve as spies to bring him word about where Jesus was (Matt. 2:7-8).
11. _____ spied for the Philistines to find out the source of Samson's strength (Judg. 16:5-6).

278
Strippings

Things other than clothing are stripped. Fill in each blank with the proper person associated with the thing stripped.

1. _____ was stripped of his priestly garments in preparation for his death (Num. 20:26).
2. _____ was called a stripling by Saul (1 Sam. 17:55-56).
3. _____ was stripped of his colorful coat and placed in a pit (Gen. 37:23-24).
4. _____ told the Israelites to strip themselves of their ornaments and wait for God's judgment (Ex. 33:5-6).
5. _____ stripped off his robe and gave it to David, because of their friendship (1 Sam. 18:4).
6. _____ stripped off his clothing and prophesied before Samuel (1 Sam. 19:24).
7. _____ was stripped of his "armour" by the Philistines who put the "armour in the house of Ashtaroth" (1 Sam. 31:8-10).
8. _____ stripped off the jewels of the dead inhabitants of Seir (2 Chron. 20:23-25).
9. _____ was stripped of his glory and said he was destroyed "on every side" (Job 19:9-10).
10. _____ said, "I will go stripped and naked: I will make a wailing like the dragons, and mourning as the owls" (Mic. 1:8).
11. _____ was stripped of His clothing and given a scarlet robe to wear at His trial (Matt. 27:28).
12. _____ _____ _____ stopped to help a man who fell among thieves who stripped him of his raiment and wounded him (Luke 10:30-33).

279
Strong Things

When we purchase items, we want them to last a long time. Match each name with the strong thing associated with the name.

1. Caleb (Josh. 14:10-11)
2. Issachar (Gen. 49:14)
3. Joseph (Gen. 49:22-24)
4. Edom (Num. 20:20)
5. Ammon (Num. 21:24)
6. Kenites (Num. 24:21)
7. Thebez (Judg. 9:50-51)
8. Samson's riddle (Judg. 14:18)
9. Saul (1 Sam. 14:52)
10. Abraham (Rom. 4:16-20)
11. John's vision (Rev. 5:2)

a. Strong angel
b. Strong border
c. Strong as an ass
d. Strong "dwellingplace"
e. As strong as he was at forty
f. Strong faith
g. Strong hand
h. Arms made strong by God
i. Strong lion
j. Strong men
k. Strong tower

280
Teachers and Pupils

Every successful teacher has pupils. Match each teacher and pupi

1. Gamaliel (Acts 22:3)		a. Ahaziah
2. Elijah (1 Kings 19:19-21)		b. Balac
3. Jesus (Luke 19:8-9)		c. The Ethiopian
4. Eli (1 Sam. 1:20-28)		d. Elisha
5. Jehoiada (2 Kings 12:2)		e. Jehoash
6. Philip (Acts 8:27-31)		f. Joshua
7. Balaam (Rev. 2:14)		g. Moses
8. David (2 Chron. 3:1-3)		h. Paul
9. Jethro (Ex. 18:15-19)		i. Zacchaeus
10. Moses (Num. 27:18-20)		j. Solomon
11. Athaliah (2 Chron. 22:2-3)		k. Samuel

281
Tears

Fill in each blank with the person or thing connected with the statement about tears.

1. _____ was healed because God saw his tears and heard his prayers (2 Kings 20:5).
2. _____ said his friends scorned him, but his eyes poured out tears to God (Job 16:20).
3. _____ said he watered his couch with his tears (Ps. 6:6).
4. _____ said his meat was his tears day and night (Ps. 42:3).
5. "They that _____ in tears shall reap in joy" (Ps. 126:5).
6. _____ wished his eyes were a fountain of tears (Jer. 9:1).
7. _____ said his eyes failed with tears for Jerusalem (Lam. 2:11).
8. _____ had his desire to cry removed by God, and no tears ran down (Ezek. 24:16).
9. _____ covered the altar of the Lord with tears, weeping, and crying because God regarded not the offering (Mal. 2:11-13).
10. The _____ of the child with a dumb spirit cried out with tears, "Lord, I believe; help thou mine unbelief" (Mark 9:24).
11. _____ served the Lord with all humility of mind and with many tears (Acts 20:16-19).
12. _____ sought repentance carefully with tears but did not find it (Heb. 12:16-17).

282
Temptations

Facing temptations is common to all people. What action we take determines our character. Match the tempters with the proper target.

1. Devil (Luke 4:12-13)
2. Ananias and Sapphira (Acts 5:1-9)
3. Potiphar's wife (Gen. 39:7-8)
4. God (Gen. 22:1-2)
5. Delilah (Judg. 16:5)
6. Prophets with lying spirit (2 Chron. 18:19-22)
7. Peninnah (1 Sam. 1:2-6)
8. Judas (Matt. 26:14-15)
9. Eve (Gen. 3:6-7)
10. Serpent (Gen. 3:4-6)
11. Princes of Babylon (2 Chron. 32:30-31)
12. Wives (1 Kings 11:4)

a. Abraham
b. Adam
c. Chief Priests
d. Eve
e. Hezekiah
f. Holy Spirit

g. King Ahab
h. Jesus
i. Joseph
j. Samson
k. Solomon

l. Hannah

283
Tents

Tents were often used for housing in biblical days. Fill in each blank with the person associated with a tent.

1. _____ was uncovered in his tent, and Ham made fun of him (Gen. 9:20-21).
2. _____ took a nail from a tent and killed Sisera with it (Judg. 4:21-22).
3. _____ pitched his tent in Sodom among the wicked (Gen. 13:12-13).
4. _____ brought his bride to his mother's tent (Gen. 24:67).
5. _____ hid her father's images in her tent (Gen. 31:34).
6. _____ received his father-in-law in his tent (Ex. 18:7).
7. _____ was told a dream about barley bread tearing a tent down (Judg.7:13).
8. _____ brought the head of the giant and put Goliath's "armour" in his tent (1 Sam. 17:54).
9. _____ had a vision of Israel abiding in tents (Num. 24:2).
10. _____ pitched a tent upon a housetop and publically sinned (2 Sam. 16:22).
11. _____ and his men made war with the Hagarites and dwelt in their tents (1 Chron. 5:8-10).
12. _____ was in her tent when angels told her husband she would have a son in her old age (Gen. 18:9-12).

284
Three People and Places

Match each statement about three persons or things with the proper three persons.

1. Sons of Saul (1 Sam. 31:2)
2. Friends of Job (Job 2:11)
3. Righteous men (Ezek. 14:14)
4. Men in a fiery furnace (Dan. 3:22)
5. Cities of refuge (Deut. 4:42-43)
6. Sons of Anak (Josh. 15:14)
7. Mighty men of David (2 Sam. 23:8-11)
8. Friends of Jesus (John 11:1)
9. Daughters of Job (Job 42:14)
10. Leaders of Israelites (Mic. 6:4)
11. People in transfiguration (Mark 9:4)
12. People Paul baptized (1 Cor. 1:14-16)
13. Sons of Noah (Gen. 5:32)

a. Adino, Eleazar, Shammah
b. Elias, Moses, Jesus
c. Eliphaz, Bildad, Zophar
d. Bezer, Ramoth, Golan
e. Moses, Miriam, Aaron
f. Jonathan, Abinadab, Melchi-shua
g. Martha, Mary, Lazarus
h. Noah, Daniel, Job
i. Shadrach, Meshach, Abed-nego
j. Jemima, Kezia, Keren-happuch
k. Sheshai, Ahiman, Talmai
l. Shem, Ham, Japheth
m. Crispus, Gaius, Stephanas

285
Three Things

Match each person with the three things associated with him.

1. Jonathan (1 Sam. 20:18-20)
2. Daniel (Dan. 6:2)
3. Amos (Amos 1:3)
4. Zechariah (Zech. 11:8)
5. Peter, James, and John (Luke 9:28-33)
6. John (Rev. 6:6)
7. Jehoahaz (2 Kings 23:31)
8. Isaiah (Isa. 20:3)
9. Hannah (1 Sam. 1:22-24)
10. Bezaleel (Ex. 37:1,19)
11. Gideon (Judg. 7:20)

a. 3 transgressions
b. 3 tabernacles
c. 3 shepherds
d. 3 presidents
e. 3 months' reign
f. 3 measures of barley
g. 3 gifts
h. 3 companies
i. 3 years barefooted
j. 3 bowls
k. 3 arrows

286
Transportation

In our modern world, transportation is a necessity—not a luxury. Match each person with a way he or she traveled.

1. David (2 Sam. 19:18)
2. Zebedee (Matt. 4:21)
3. Ben-hadad (1 Kings 20:20)
4. Solomon (1 Kings 1:33)
5. Jesus (Matt. 21:7)
6. Jacob (Gen. 45:18-19)
7. Rebekah (Gen. 24:64)
8. Ahab (1 Kings 18:44)
9. Abner (2 Sam. 2:29)
10. Hiram's servants (1 Kings 5:8-9)
11. Paul's sailing companions (Acts 27:43-44)
12. Noah (Gen. 6:18-22)
13. Elijah (2 Kings 2:11)

a. On boards of the ship
b. Camel
c. Chariot
d. Colt
e. Ark
f. Ferry
g. Horse
h. Log floats
i. Whirlwind
j. Mule
k. Ship
l. Wagons
m. On foot

287
Trivia

Some pieces of information are not really important; they are interesting. Answer each trivia statement true or false.

1. It took 70,000 laborers, 80,000 stone cutters, and 3,600 overseers to build the Temple (2 Chron. 2:1-2).
2. Nehemiah discovered that the Israelites had been withholding the tithe (Neh. 13:10-12).
3. Naaman was the only man to be healed of leprosy according to the New Testament (Luke 4:27).
4. Absalom's hair weighed 200 shekels and he cut it once a year (2 Sam. 14:25-26).
5. Delilah was Samson's first wife (Judg. 15:6; 16:4).
6. Miriam and Aaron spoke against Moses because he had married an Ethiopian woman (Num. 12:1).
7. Moses was the oldest child in his family (Ex. 2:4).
8. Ahab and Obadiah hunted grass to save horses (1 Kings 18:5).
9. New believers in Ephesus burned their books worth 50,000 pieces of silver (Acts 19:19).
10. Sergius Paulus was struck dead because he interfered with the conversion of a man (Acts 13:7-11).
11. John saw two rainbows: one around the throne and one upon an angel's head (Rev. 4:3; 10:1).
12. Abimelech killed seventy half brothers in order to be made king (Judg. 9:3-5).

288
Twelve to Twenty-Two

Numbers are fascinating to many people. Match each number with the correct statement.

1. Twelve (Matt. 10:2)
2. Thirteen (1 Kings 7:1)
3. Fourteen (Gen. 46:19-22)
4. Fifteen (Gen. 7:20)
5. Sixteen (Gen. 46:16-18)
6. Seventeen (Gen. 37:2)
7. Eighteen (2 Chron. 11:21)
8. Nineteen (2 Sam. 2:30)
9. Twenty (Gen. 37:28)
10. Twenty-one (Dan. 10:3)
11. Twenty-two (1 Chron. 12:28)

a. Age of Joseph when sold into slavery
b. Number of days Daniel did not eat
c. Number of captains Zadok's father had
d. Number of apostles Jesus had
e. Number of David's unnamed servants killed in battle with Abner
f. Number of pieces of silver Joseph was sold for
g. Years Solomon spent building his house
h. Number of wives Rehoboam had
i. Number of sons and grandsons Jacob and Rachel had
j. Number of sons and grandsons Zilpah and Jacob had
k. Number of cubits the water rose during the flood

289
Twelve Tribes

The names of the twelve tribes of Israel are found in Numbers 1:5-15. Unscramble each of the following letters to spell the name of a tribe.

1. Adujh   — — — — —
2. Achassir   — — — — — — — —
3. Bulenuz   — — — — — — —
4. Beenur   — — — — — —
5. Dag   — — —
6. Mesoni   — — — — — —
7. Paerimh   — — — — — — —
8. Saemahns   — — — — — — — —
9. Jeanmibn   — — — — — — — —
10. And   — — —
11. Raesh   — — — — —
12. Taaliphn   — — — — — — — —

290
Two Things

Unscramble the word in parentheses in each statement about two things.

1. The Good Samaritan gave two (cenep) _____ to care for the man beaten by robbers (Luke 10:25).
2. The poor widow gave two (tiesm) _____, and Jesus commended her generous gift (Mark 12:42-43).
3. Jesus said if we had two (toacs) _____, we should give one to the poor (Luke 3:11).
4. Rehoboam made two (lavesc) _____ of gold for the Israelites to worship (1 Kings 12:27-28).
5. The Israelites gathered two (serom) _____ of bread on the sixth day (Ex. 16:22).
6. The Israelites who were unable to bring a lamb or a goat for a sin offering were to bring two (derttelosuv) _____ (Lev. 5:6-7).
7. God commanded Moses to make two (pursmett) _____ to call the assembly together (Num. 10:2).
8. David measured Moab with two (niles) _____: one for death and one for life (2 Sam. 8:2).
9. Paul told the Galatians two (vontansec) _____ existed (Gal. 4:23-24).
10. Elisha saw two (eabrs) _____ destroy forty-two children (2 Kings 2:24).
11. The widow, Elisha's friend, gathered two (skicst) _____ to make a fire to prepare all the food she had (1 Kings 17:12).
12. Zechariah saw two (vileo erets) _____ (Zech. 4:3).

291
Unashamed

People find causes and actions to devote themselves to of which they are proud. Fill in each blank with the person or persons in the statement about not being ashamed.

1. _____ was not ashamed of the cause of Jesus Christ (2 Tim. 1:12).
2. _____ were not ashamed of their nakedness before they sinned (Gen. 2:23-25).
3. _____ was not ashamed that he reproached Job ten times (Job 19:1-3).
4. _____ was not ashamed of Paul's chains (2 Tim. 1:16).
5. _____ is not ashamed to call the sanctified His brothers (Heb. 2:11-13).
6. _____ is not ashamed to be called the God of those for whom he prepared a city (Heb. 11:16-18).
7. _____ should not be ashamed at Jesus' coming according to John (1 John 2:28).
8. _____ said Christians should not be ashamed when they suffer as a Christian (1 Pet. 4:16).
9. _____ need not be ashamed when they rightly divide the word of truth (2 Tim. 2:15).
10. _____ said he should not be ashamed of the authority given him for edification (2 Cor. 10:8).
11. _____ said that they who wait for the Lord should "not be ashamed" (Isa. 49:23).

292
Unique Bible Statements

Some statements in the Bible are different from statements we make today. Fill in the blanks with the proper words which make the statements unique.

1. "An _____ is a vain thing for safety" (Ps. 33:17).
2. "At the last it [_____] biteth like a serpent, and stingeth like an adder" (Prov. 23:31-32).
3. "Beware of false prophets, which come to you in _____ clothing" (Matt. 7:15).
4. "For where your _____ is, there will your heart be also" (Matt. 6:21).
5. "Be not deceived: evil communications corrupt good _____" (1 Cor. 15:33).
6. "Neither cast ye your _____ before swine, lest they trample them under their feet, and turn again and rend you" (Matt. 7:6).
7. "He that shutteth his lips is esteemed a man of _____" (Prov. 17:28).
8. "Love not _____, lest thou come to poverty" (Prov. 20:13).
9. "Sufficient unto the _____ is the evil thereof" (Matt. 6:34 *b*).
10. "For what shall it profit a man, if he shall gain the whole world, and lose his own _____?" (Mark 8:36).
11. "A soft _____ turneth away wrath: but grievous words stir up anger" (Prov. 15:1).

293
Unusual Feats

Some people work for years trying to do the most unusual feats; other persons do them without such apparent effort. Fill in each blank with the person who did the unusual feat mentioned.

1. _____ slew six-hundred Philistines with an ox goad (Judg. 3:31).
2. _____ had seven-hundred left-handed soldiers (Judg. 20:15-16).
3. _____ cast his rod on the ground and it became a serpent (Ex. 4:2-4).
4. _____ pulled a building down with his own might (Judg. 16:30).
5. _____ chose soldiers by the way they drank water (Judg. 7:4).
6. _____ cured a boil with a lump of figs (2 Kings 20:7).
7. _____ caused a fig tree to wither by speaking to it (Matt. 21:16-19).
8. _____ lived in a big fish (Jonah 2:1).
9. _____ was released from prison by an angel (Acts 12:6-9).
10. _____ had a rod that budded and bloomed (Num. 17:8).
11. _____ _____ _____ produced boils on people with handfuls of ashes from a furnace (Ex. 9:8-9).
12. _____ fed one-hundred men with twenty loaves of barley and corn (2 Kings 4:42-44).

294
Valleys

Valleys are mentioned many times in the Bible. Match each valley with what happened there.

1. Siddim (Gen. 14:10)
2. Eschol (Num. 13:23; 32:5-9)
3. Achor (Josh. 7:24)
4. Elah (1 Sam. 17:19,49)
5. Jezreel (1 Kings 21:1)
6. Jehoshaphat (Joel 3:2)
7. Megiddo (2 Chron. 35:22-23)
8. Sorek (Judg. 16:4)
9. Salt or Joktheel (2 Kings 14:7)
10. Berachah (2 Chron. 20:25-26)
11. Hinnon (2 Chron. 28:1-3)

a. Ahaz offered his children to Baalim
b. Amaziah killed ten thousand people of Edom
c. Home of Delilah
d. Jehoshaphat blessed the Lord
e. Josiah slain
f. Naboth's vineyard
g. Place of the gathering of all nations
h. Place of Achan's punishment
i. Land of plenty
j. Where David killed Goliath
k. Place of "slimepits"

295
Visions

Solomon said, "Where there is no vision, the people perish" (Prov. 29:18). Match each person with his vision.

1. Peter (Acts 11:5)
2. Isaiah (Isa. 6:1)
3. Paul (Acts 16:9)
4. Daniel (Dan. 8:1-3)
5. Ezekiel (Ezek. 37:1-2)
6. John (Rev. 9:17)
7. Samuel (1 Sam. 3:1-12)
8. Nathan (2 Sam. 7:12-17)
9. Obadiah (Obad. 1-2)
10. Peter, James, and John (Matt. 17:9)
11. Cornelius (Acts 10:3)

a. Angel of God coming to him
b. David was not to build the Temple
c. Destruction of Edom
d. A great sheet
e. Horses with lion's heads
f. Lord upon his throne
g. Ram with two horns
h. Removal of Eli's family from priesthood
i. Transfiguration
j. A man calling for help
k. Valley of dry bones

296
Voices

Fill in each blank with the name of the proper person or animal.

1. _____ heard God's voice in the garden and was afraid (Gen. 3:9-10).
2. _____ heard Abel's voice from the ground (Gen. 4:10).
3. _____ could not hear the voices of singers (2 Sam. 19:34-35).
4. _____ hear the voice of their shepherd and follow him (John 10:3).
5. _____ heard the voices of the lepers and healed them (Luke 17:12-14).
6. _____ heard a voice in a vision about unclean things (Acts 10:13).
7. _____ recognized Peter's voice, but did not open the door for gladness (Acts 12:13-14).
8. _____ heard the voice of God calling him to come to the top of the mountain to receive the law (Ex. 19:20).
9. _____ heard a voice telling him his life was spared, and he recognized the voice as David's (1 Sam. 24:12-16).
10. _____ cried to God and God heard his voice (Ps. 77:1).
11. _____ wept for her children and her voice was heard in Ramah (Jer. 31:15).

297
Weapons

Any object can become a weapon when it is used as one. Circle the correct person associated with the weapon below.

1. (Sisera, David, Absalom) had weapons of nine hundred chariots of iron (Judg. 4:2-3).
2. (Jael, Deborah, Miriam) killed Sisera using a nail and hammer (Judg. 4:21).
3. (Moses, Caleb, Joshua) defeated Jericho with weapons of trumpets and shouts (Josh. 6:20).
4. (Joshua, Moses, Elijah) had only a weapon of water which he used to defeat the Egyptians (Ex. 14:21).
5. (Phinehas, Eleazar, Aaron) killed a man and woman with a javelin because the man had disobeyed God (Num. 25:7-8).
6. (Daniel, David, Goliath) killed a giant with a sling and a stone (1 Sam. 17:50).
7. (Abner, Absalom, Saul) killed Asahel with a spear (2 Sam. 2:23).
8. (Thomas, Peter, John) cut off a servant's ear with a sword at Jesus' arrest (John 18:10-11).
9. A (Levite, Ephraimite, Philistine) of Mount Ephriam cut his dead wife into twelve pieces and sent the pieces into the coasts of Israel (Judg. 19:1,29).
10. (Peter, Paul, John) was stoned at Lystra, dragged from the city, and left for dead (Acts 14:19).
11. (Elisha, Jezebel, Jehu) killed Jehoram with a bow and arrow (2 Kings 9:24).

298
Weather

Perhaps the subject most talked about is the weather. Fill in each blank with the proper weather word.

1. Gideon sought to know God's will through _____ on a fleece (Judg. 6:37).
2. Moses stretched forth his rod and God sent _____ and _____ upon Egypt (Ex. 9:23).
3. Ezekiel had a vision of a bright fire which produced _____ (Ezek. 1:13).
4. Jesus spoke and the _____ stopped (Matt. 14:32).
5. God spoke to Job out of a _____ (Job 38:1).
6. Noah received a promise through a _____ (Gen. 9:13).
7. Jacob recalled a time when the _____ consumed him by day and the _____ by night (Gen. 31:40).
8. Uzziah reigned during a terrible _____ (Zech. 14:5).
9. The Amorites died in a _____ (Josh. 10:11).
10. Job asked, "Who giveth _____ upon the earth? (Job 5:10).
11. Benaiah slew a lion in the time of _____ (2 Sam. 23:20).

299
Which Is It?

Each of the following words is a city, island, mountain, or river. Circle the proper identity of each word.

1. Abana (2 Kings 5:12)	city, island, mountain, river
2. Arimathaea (Luke 23:51)	city, island, mountain, river
3. Tyrus (Ezek. 27:32)	city, island, mountain, river
4. Ebal (Deut. 27:13)	city, island, mountain, river
5. Melita (Acts 28:1)	city, island, mountain, river
6. Shushan (Esther 3:15)	city, island, mountain, river
7. Ramah (1 Sam. 28:3)	city, island, mountain, river
8. Hor (Num. 20:22)	city, island, mountain, river
9. Gilead (Hos. 6:8)	city, island, mountain, river
10. Clauda (Acts 27:16)	city, island, mountain, river
11. Horeb (1 Kings 19:8)	city, island, mountain, river
12. Arba (Josh. 15:13)	city, island, mountain, river
13. Patmos (Rev. 1:9)	city, island, mountain, river

300
Who?

People are often known for something they did. Match each person or persons with what they did.

1. The Ephraimites (Judg. 12:5-6)
2. Jehoiakim (Jer. 36:22-28)
3. Joshua (Josh. 1:1-2)
4. Elisha (2 Kings 5:9-10)
5. Beelzebub (Matt. 12:24)
6. Malchus (John 18:10)
7. Abimelech (Judg. 9:48-49)
8. Sheba (2 Sam. 20:20-22)
9. Isaiah (2 Kings 20:11)
10. Obadiah (1 Kings 18:4)
11. Samson (Judg. 14:12)

a. Built a fire under a tower and killed about a thousand people
b. Brought the shadow of the sun backward ten degrees
c. Cut Jeremiah's scroll in pieces with a penknife and burned it
d. Could not pronounce Shibboleth and died because of it
e. Had an ear cut off by Peter
f. Had his head cut off and thrown to Joab over the wall
g. Hid a hundred prophets from Jezebel
h. Succeeded Moses
i. Offered thirty men, thirty sheets and thirty changes of clothing for the answer to a riddle
j. Told Naaman the cure for his leprosy
k. Also called the prince of the devils

301
Wind

Match each person or persons with the statement about the wind and its association.

1. Jesus (Luke 8:24)
2. Euroclydon (Acts 27:14)
3. Holy Spirit (Acts 2:1-4)
4. Job (Job 1:19)
5. Israelites (Num. 11:31-32)
6. Elijah (1 Kings 18:41-45)
7. Elisha (2 Kings 3:13-17)
8. Ezekiel (Ezek. 1:4)
9. David (2 Sam. 22:7-11)
10. Solomon (Prov. 10:25)

a. Ate quail brought in by the wind
b. Saw God upon the wings of the wind
c. Lost his children because of a "great wind"
d. Made sound as of a "mighty wind"
e. Name for a tempestuous wind
f. Predicted ditches filled with water but not by rain and wind
g. Rebuked the wind and it stopped
h. Saw a vision of a whirlwind
i. Said destruction comes as a whirlwind
j. Watched clouds for wind and rain

302
Windows

Unscramble the letters to spell the person who had an experience with a window.

1. (cehstyuu) _____ fell from a window while listening to Paul preach (Acts 20:9).
2. (aabhr) _____ let the spies down by a cord through the window (Josh. 2:17-21).
3. (oanh) _____ sent a raven and a dove from a window to see if the flood waters were gone (Gen. 8:6).
4. (beeejlz) _____ painted her face and looked out a window (2 Kings 9:30-31).
5. (ahjos) _____ was told by Elisha to open a window and shoot an arrow eastward (2 Kings 13:14-17).
6. (mliheebac) _____ looked out a window and saw Isaac and Rebekah together, so he knew they had lied about being brother and sister (Gen. 26:7-8).
7. (aeissr) _____'s mother looked out a window and cried for her son who was late coming from battle (Judg. 5:28).
8. (acihlm) _____ saw from a window that David rejoiced over the ark being brought to Jerusalem, and she hated him (2 Sam. 6:16).
9. (aeildn) _____ prayed to God before open windows (Dan. 6:10).
10. (dog) _____ will open the windows of heaven to bless the faithful giver (Mal. 3:10).
11. (evenihn) _____ "shall sing in the windows" (Zeph. 2:13-14).

303
Writers

Think of what we would miss today if there were no writers! Match each writer with the correct writing:

1. God (Ex. 34:1)
2. Pilate (John 19:19-22)
3. Paul (Philem. 10-18)
4. Jesus (John 8:6)
5. John (3 John 9)
6. Samuel (1 Sam. 10:25)
7. David (2 Sam. 11:14-15)
8. A hand (Dan. 5:5)
9. Moses (Mark 10:4-5)
10. Ezekiel (Ezek. 37:16-17)
11. Isaiah (2 Chron. 26:22)

a. Acts of Uzziah
b. Book about the kingdom
c. Death warrant for Uriah
d. Decree of divorcement
e. Labels on sticks
f. Message in sand defending a woman
g. Letter in behalf of a slave
h. Message on a wall to a king
i. Letter to a church
j. Ten Commandments
k. Title for Jesus' cross

ANSWERS

Answers

1 1-d; 2-g; 3-e; 4-i; 5-h; 6-a; 7-k; 8-j; 9-f; 10-c; 11-b

2 1-h; 2-j; 3-i; 4-f; 5-d; 6-a; 7-e; 8-c; 9-g; 10-b

3 1-e; 2-b; 3-a; 4-d; 5-f; 6-c; 7-h; 8-i; 9-g;

4 1-d; 2-g; 3-i; 4-h; 5-a; 6-e; 7-k; 8-c; 9-j; 10-f; 11-b

5 1-b; 2-c; 3-a; 4-e; 5-d; 6-f; 7-i; 8-j; 9-h; 10-g

6 1-c; 2-e; 3-d; 4-b; 5-a; 6-f; 7-j; 8-g; 9-h; 10-i

7 1-h; 2-j; 3-k; 4-i; 5-c; 6-g; 7-d; 8-f; 9-a; 10-e; 11-b

8 1. Ishmael; 2. Saul; 3. Jonathan; 4. The king of Israel (Ahab); 5. Josiah; 6. Job; 7. Elisha; 8. Isaiah; 9. David; 10. Isaac; 11. Joshua

9 1. Esaias (Isaiah); 2. Israelites; 3. Elijah; 4. Joshua; 5. Joseph; 6. Philistines; 7. Sisera; 8. Zimri; 9. Sennacherib; 10. Naaman; 11. David

10 1-e; 2-j; 3-f; 4-i; 5-g; 6-h; 7-a; 8-b; 9-d; 10-c

11 1. Peter; 2. Ananias; 3. Philip; 4. The apostles; 5. Stephen; 6. Esaias (Isaiah); 7. Barnabas; 8. The Spirit of the Lord; 9. Saul; 10. Simon

12 1. Nazareth; 2. Gabriel; 3. Bethlehem; 4. Manger; 5. The babe; 6. Mary; 7. A star; 8. A house; 9. God; 10. An angel

13 1. swine; 2. ant; 3. ostrich; 4. sparrows; 5. hen; 6. eagles; 7. cattle; 8. horse; 9. sheep; 10. lion

14 1-f; 2-k; 3-e; 4-i; 5-g; 6-h; 7-j; 8-b; 9-c; 10-d; 11-a

15 1. Moses, Numbers 11:15; 2. Jonah, Jonah 4:3; 3. Elijah, 1 Kings 19:4; 4. Isaiah, Isaiah 6:5; 5. Saul, 1 Samuel 28:15; 6. Mordecai, Esther 4:1; 7. Mary Magdalene, John 20:13

16 1-e; 2-d; 3-g; 4-j; 5-i; 6-k; 7-b; 8-f; 9-c; 10-h; 11-a

17 1. Philip and Nathaniel; 2. Matthew; 3. Peter, Andrew, James, and John; 4. Judas Iscariot; 5. James; 6. Thaddaeus; 7. Thomas; 8. the Canaanite; 9. Matthias

18 1. Noah; 2. an olive branch; 3. It did not return; 4. to fly away to rest; 5. Hezekiah; 6. inhabitants of Moab; 7. Ezekiel; 8. Ephraim; 9. Jesus; 10. the twelve

19 1-f; 2-d; 3-g; 4-j; 5-a; 6-e; 7-c; 8-i; 9-b; 10-h

20 1-k; 2-f; 3-e; 4-g; 5-a; 6-d; 7-h; 8-j; 9-b; 10-i; 11-c

21 1. pulse (vegetables) and water; 2. locust and wild honey; 3. wheat and oil; 4. manna; 5. bread and flesh; 6. loaves and fish; 7. crumbs; 8. swine's food; 9. corn (wheat); 10. meal and oil

22 1. Andrew; 2. James; 3. Peter; 4. Jesus; 5. Noah; 6. Zebedee; 7. Thomas and Nathaniel

23 1-c; 2-g; 3-i; 4-d; 5-j; 6-f; 7-a; 8-b; 9-e; 10-h

24 1. Peter, James, and John; 2. Mary; 3. Lazarus; 4. Martha; 5. Nicodemus; 6. Joseph of Arimathea; 7. John the Baptist; 8. Zacchaeus; 9. Mary Magdalene; 10. Simon the leper

25 1-e; 2-g; 3-f; 4-a; 5-b; 6-h; 7-d; 8-c; 9-j; 10-i

26 1. couch; 2. table; 3. chest; 4. table, bed, and stool; 5. bed; 6. ovens; 7. spindle; 8. bed; 9. tables; 10. candle (lamp)

27 1-i; 2-d; 3-f; 4-e; 5-c; 6-h; 7-a; 8-b; 9-j; 10-g

28 1-e; 2-g; 3-f; 4-d; 5-j; 6-a; 7-h; 8-c; 9-i; 10-b;

29 1-d; 2-e; 3-j; 4-a; 5-g; 6-f; 7-k; 8-b; 9-h; 10-i; 11-c

30 1-h; 2-e; 3-g; 4-a; 5-j; 6-d; 7-b; 8-c; 9-k; 10-f; 11-i

31 1. Nicodemus; 2. Philip; 3. Peter; 4. disciples; 5. Judas Iscariot; 6. officer at trial; 7. people at Sermon on Mount; 8. Bartimaeus; 9. scribes; 10. two blind men; 11. sick man at a pool

32 1-c; 2-e; 3-i; 4-f; 5-j; 6-h; 7-a; 8-d; 9-b; 10-g

33 1. lightning; 2. thief; 3. patience; 4. commandment; 5. Satan's; 6. the dead in Christ; 7. our bodies; 8. judge them; 9. death; 10. a place; 11. a cloud; 12. a shepherd; 13. the Father

34 1. a walking stick (staff); 2. shake the dust off of their feet; 3. preach the kingdom of God and heal the sick; 4. the Lord's Prayer; 5. "Whatsoever ye would that men should do to you, do ye even so to them"; 6. salt and light; 7. vine and branches; 8. a little child; 9. his peace; 10. bread; 11. keep his commandments

35 1-e; 2-a; 3-k; 4-b; 5-f; 6-h; 7-g; 8-j; 9-d; 10-i; 11-c

36 1. land; 2. gold, frankincense, and myrrh; 3. binding; 4. all she had; 5. cross; 6. ointment; 7. mother-in-law; 8. eat at his table; 9. by a cord; 10. robe, sword, bow, and girdle; 11. coats, garments

37 1-e; 2-i; 3-c; 4-j; 5-f; 6-a; 7-g; 8-k; 9-b; 10-d; 11-h

38 1-c; 2-h; 3-e; 4-a; 5-b; 6-f; 7-j; 8-k; 9-g; 10-i; 11-d

39 1-d; 2-g; 3-i; 4-c; 5-j; 6-h; 7-a; 8-k; 9-e; 10-b; 11-f

40 1-i; 2-h; 3-e; 4-g; 5-d; 6-j; 7-a; 8-f; 9-c; 10-b

41 1-f; 2-e; 3-g; 4-d; 5-h; 6-c; 7-i; 8-b; 9-j; 10-a; 11-k

42 1-e; 2-j; 3-g; 4-f; 5-d; 6-a; 7-h; 8-i; 9-b; 10-c

43 1. Micah, Micah 5:2; 2. Isaiah, Isaiah 7:14; 3. Hosea, Hosea 11:1; 4. Moses, Deuteronomy 18:18-19; 5. David, Psalm 22:16, 6. Isaiah, Isaiah 53:3; 7. Zechariah, Zechariah 9:9; 8. Isaiah, Isaiah 53:10; 9. David, Psalm 22:18; 10. Zechariah, Zechariah 11:12-13; 11. Isaiah, Isaiah 53:7

44 1-f; 2-g; 3-e; 4-h; 5-d; 6-i; 7-c; 8-j; 9-a; 10-k; 11-b

45 1-d; 2-g; 3-h; 4-a; 5-f; 6-e; 7-i; 8-b; 9-j; 10-c

46 1-c; 2-e; 3-g; 4-i; 5-k; 6-a; 7-j; 8-h; 9-f; 10-d; 11-b

47 1-C-a; 2-D-h; 3-I-b; 4-E-f; 5-A-g; 6-H-c; 7-F-e; 8-G-i; 9-B-d; 10-J-j

48 1-f; 2-h; 3-g; 4-i; 5-a; 6-e; 7-b; 8-d; 9-c

49 1-c; 2-e; 3-a; 4-b; 5-h; 6-i; 7-j; 8-f; 9-d; 10-g

50 1. the foolish virgins; 2. a Samaritan man; 3. Elisha; 4. Asher; 5. Simon; 6. Jacob; 7. Joab; 8. Solomon; 9. Hiram; 10. Elijah

51 1-a; 2-e; 3-d; 4-b; 5-f; 6-c; 7-i; 8-g; 9-j; 10-h

52 1-f; 2-k; 3-h; 4-a; 5-i; 6-c; 7-j; 8-b; 9-e; 10-g; 11-d

53 1-e; 2-i; 3-f; 4-c; 5-j; 6-d; 7-h; 8-a; 9-g; 10-b

54 1-b; 2-d; 3-i; 4-c; 5-g; 6-f; 7-h; 8-e; 9-j; 10-a

55 1-d; 2-j; 3-g; 4-h; 5-b; 6-e; 7-a; 8-f; 9-i; 10-k; 11-c

56 1. Genesis 3:15; 2. Genesis 22:18; 3. Hosea 11:1; 4. Isaiah 53:5; 5. Isaiah 53:4-5; 6. Psalm 34:20; 7. Jeremiah 31:31-34; 8. Hosea 1:10; 9. Psalm 118:22-23; 10. Psalm 2:1-2

57 1-i; 2-j; 3-g; 4-a; 5-f; 6-b; 7-d; 8-c; 9-e; 10-h

58 1-g; 2-i; 3-e; 4-k; 5-d; 6-j; 7-a; 8-f; 9-b; 10-h; 11-c

59 1-f; 2-k; 3-a; 4-j; 5-b; 6-d; 7-i; 8-g; 9-c; 10-h; 11-e

60 1-g; 2-i; 3-k; 4-a; 5-e; 6-c; 7-d; 8-f; 9-j; 10-b; 11-h

61 1-e; 2-h; 3-i; 4-f; 5-b; 6-j; 7-d; 8-a; 9-g; 10-c

62 1-j; 2-b; 3-e; 4-h; 5-g; 6-i; 7-c; 8-f; 9-a; 10-d

63 1. David, Psalm 23:1; 2. Isaiah, Isaiah 6:8; 3. Jesus, John 3:3; 4. Paul and Silas, Acts 16:31; 5. Paul, 1 Corinthians 13:13; 6. Jesus, John 14:1; 7. David, Psalm 51:10; 8. Joshua, Joshua 24:1,15; 9. John the Baptist, John 1:29; 10. Peter, Acts 3:6

64 1. Paul; 2. Jonah; 3. James and John; 4. the disciples; 5. Peter; 6. Peter, Thomas, Nathaniel, James, and John; 7. Noah; 8. Paul; 9. Solomon

65 1-a; 2-b; 3-c; 4-b; 5-b; 6-a; 7-b; 8-c; 9-c; 10-b

66 1-d; 2-j; 3-f; 4-g; 5-c; 6-e; 7-a; 8-h; 9-b; 10-i

67 1. David; 2. Isaiah; 3. Jesus; 4. An angel; 5. Abel; 6. Solomon; 7. Asa; 8. Jacob; 9. Priests; 10. Mesha

68 1. Philip; 2. Saul; 3. Peter; 4. Isaiah; 5. Simeon; 6. Stephen; 7. David; 8. Elisha; 9. Cornelius; 10. Belshazzar

69 1-e; 2-g; 3-i; 4-c; 5-f; 6-h; 7-a; 8-j; 9-b; 10-d

70 1. Onesimus; 2. Naaman; 3. Pharaoh; 4. Joseph; 5. Moses; 6. Abraham; 7. Ziba; 8. Gehazi; 9. Peter; 10. Elijah; 11. Job

71 1-i; 2-e; 3-h; 4-j; 5-a; 6-c; 7-b; 8-d; 9-g; 10-f

72 1-c; 2-e; 3-j; 4-f; 5-i; 6-b; 7-d; 8-k; 9-a; 10-g; 11-h; 12-l

73 1-e; 2-g; 3-d; 4-c; 5-a; 6-h; 7-i; 8-b; 9-f

74 1-g; 2-d; 3-k; 4-a; 5-i; 6-e; 7-c; 8-f; 9-h; 10-j; 11-b

75 1-F-d; 2-C-e; 3-I-g; 4-H-h; 5-A-f; 6-B-i; 7-G-b; 8-E-c; 9-D-a

76 1-d; 2-h; 3-j; 4-e; 5-k; 6-a; 7-f; 8-i; 9-c; 10-g; 11-b

77 1-f; 2-i; 3-g; 4-a; 5-e; 6-c; 7-k; 8-b; 9-h; 10-j; 11-d

78 1. false, we are not told; 2. true; 3. false, cattle are not mentioned; 4. false, the Wise Men were told to follow the star; 5. false, an angel not angels; 6. false, no number is given; 7. true; 8. true; 9. false, we are not told; 10. false, Herod wanted to kill him; 11. true

79 1-e; 2-g; 3-h; 4-i; 5-a; 6-f; 7-b; 8-d; 9-c

80 1-c; 2-g; 3-f; 4-e; 5-h; 6-i; 7-b; 8-j; 9-a; 10-d;

81 1-c; 2-h; 3-a; 4-k; 5-g; 6-b; 7-f; 8-j; 9-d; 10-1; 11-i; 12-e

82 1-e; 2-h; 3-i; 4-a; 5-j; 6-d; 7-k; 8-b; 9-g; 10-f; 11-c

83 1-i; 2-d; 3-h; 4-e; 5-f; 6-a; 7-b; 8-j; 9-g; 10-k; 11-c

84 1-c; 2-e; 3-i; 4-j; 5-a; 6-f; 7-h; 8-b; 9-g; 10-d

85 1-c; 2-i; 3-e; 4-h; 5-f; 6-b; 7-g; 8-a; 9-d; 10-j

86 1. Moses and Aaron; 2. John (the Baptist); 3. The Spirit of God; 4. Amos (God); 5. An Ethiopian eunuch; 6. Jesus; 7. Moses; 8. A sick man; 9. Elijah; 10. Noah

87 1-c; 2-j; 3-d; 4-e; 5-i; 6-f; 7-h; 8-b; 9-g; 10-a

88 1-j; 2-i; 3-a; 4-h; 5-b; 6-g; 7-c; 8-f; 9-d; 10-e

89 1-e; 2-i; 3-g; 4-b; 5-d; 6-h; 7-a; 8-f; 9-j; 10-c

90 1. Egyptians, Exodus 14:25; 2. Sisera's mother, Judges 5:28; 3. Ezekiel, Ezekiel 1:16; 4. Daniel, Daniel 7:1,9; 5. the enemies of God, Psalm 83:2,13; 6. Jeremiah, Jeremiah 18:3-6; 7. Solomon, 1 Kings 7:1,27-30; 8. Ezekiel, Ezekiel 10:6; 9. Nebuchadrezzar, Ezekiel 26:7-10; 10. Nineveh, Nahum 3:2,7

91 1. Exodus and Deuteronomy; 2. Psalms; 3. Proverbs; 4. Jonah; 5. Acts; 6. Joshua; 7. Esther; 8. Daniel; 9. Matthew; 10. Genesis; 11. Philemon

92 1. mountain; 2. Gethsemane; 3. desert; 4. tomb; 5. baptized; 6. Calvary; 7. teaching; 8. house; 9. upper room; 10. Judea

93 1-d; 2-h; 3-k; 4-a; 5-j; 6-b; 7-i; 8-f; 9-c; 10-g; 11-e

94 1. John the Baptist; 2. Jesus; 3. Joshua; 4. Job; 5. Solomon; 6. Peter; 7. Esther; 8. Samuel; 9. Samaritan woman; 10. Martha

95 1. Tamar; 2. Naomi; 3. Zeruah; 4. Anna; 5. She gave all she had; 6. Ruth; 7. He raised her dead son; 8. wise woman of Tekoah; 9. seven men were chosen to minister to the people; 10. Orpah

96 1. Philip; 2. Paul and Silas; 3. Stephen; 4. Paul; 5. Daniel; 6. Dorcas; 7. Andrew; 8. John the Baptist; 9. Matthias and Barsabas; 10. Peter; 11. Philip; 12. Barnabas and Saul; 23. Priscilla and Aquila

97 1. Abigail's; 2. Sarah; 3. Dinah; 4. Julia; 5. queen of Sheba; 6. Huldah; 7. Herodias; 8. Mary; 9. Elisabeth; 10. Rahab's; 11. Esther

98 1-d; 2-f; 3-e; 4-j; 5-i; 6-c; 7-b; 8-g; 9-h; 10-a

99 1. shittim; 2. cedar; 3. cedar; 4. olive; 5. fir; 6. fir, cedar; 7. oak; 8. fir; 9. olive, pine, myrtle, palm; 10. shittim; 11. gopher; 12. cedar

100 1-7; 2-12; 3-40; 4-969; 5-100; 6-18; 7-90; 8-12; 9-10; 10-40; 11-3½ ; 12-2; 13-500

101 1-e, 2-h, 3-f, 4-k, 5-g, 6-i, 7-j, 8-l, 9-c, 10-a, 11-d, 12-b

102 1-d, 2-e, 3-f, 4-i, 5-l, 6-j, 7-h, 8-g, 9-k, 10-a, 11-b, 12-c

103 1-Jonah's, 2-Moses', 3-Cain's, 4-Jacob's, 5-Balaam's, 6-Balak's, 7-Herodias's, 8-Samson's, 9-Saul's, 10-David's, 11-Jezebel's

104 1-priests, 2-sanctify, 3-holy, 4-Boaz, 5-king, 6-fast, 7-"to the burying," 8-death, 9-see, 10-Holy Ghost [Spirit], 11-healing

105 1-God, 2-kings, 3-God, 4-Nebuchadnezzar, 5-Christ, 6-wives, 7-God, 8-public officials (magistrates), 9-servants, 10-younger people, 11-Children, 12-ordinance of man

106 1-e, 2-k, 3-f, 4-j, 5-c, 6-h, 7-d, 8-b, 9-g, 10-a, 11-i

107 Absalom, Boaz, Cornelius, Delilah, Eli, Felix, Gabriel, Hannah, Iscariot, Joseph, Kish, Lazarus, Matthias, Nathan, Onesimus, Peter, Quartus, Rahab, Samson, Timothy, Uriah, Vashti, Wise Men, X-none, young maidens, Zacchaeus

108 1-sparrow, 2-pelican, 3-eagles, 4-hen, 5-peacocks, 6-quails, 7-ostrich, 8-owl, 9-stork, 10-hawk, 11-turtledoves or pigeons, 12-raven, 13-swallow

109 1-Bartimaeus, 2-Elisha, 3-two angels, 4-Elymas, 5-Job, 6-Moses, 7-Jesus, 8-Jesus, 9-Pharisees, 10-Samson, 11-Saul

110 1-d, 2-j, 3-f, 4-b, 5-g, 6-k, 7-a, 8-e, 9-i, 10-c, 11-h

111 1-e, 2-j, 3-f, 4-l, 5-k, 6-c, 7-h, 8-d, 9-i, 10-a, 11-m, 12-g, 13-b

112 1-f, 2-g, 3-i, 4-c, 5-j, 6-k, 7-a, 8-h, 9-d, 10-e, 11-b

113 1-ministering, 2-meek, quiet, 3-dumb, 4-faithful, 5-foul, 6-good, 7-humble, 8-new, 9-perverse

114 1-pulpit, 2-musicians, 3-hymn, 4-altar, 5-prayer, 6-The word of God, 7-preacher, 8-offering, 9-worship, 10-singers, 11-message

115 1-m, 2-i, 3-j, 4-f, 5-d, 6-a, 7-c, 8-l, 9-b, 10-h, 11-e, 12-k, 13-g

116 1-Judah, 2-Israelites, 3-Jesus', 4-Israelites, 5-Mary, 6-Legion, 7-Jesus, 8-Lazarus, 9-Jesus, 10-Saul, 11-Mordecai

117 1-k, 2-g, 3-a, 4-h, 5-b, 6-j, 7-d, 8-c, 9-f, 10-e, 11-i

118 1-d, 2-f, 3-k, 4-b, 5-j, 6-h, 7-a, 8-i, 9-g, 10-c, 11-e

119 1-i, 2-e, 3-d, 4-h, 5-c, 6-j, 7-k, 8-b, 9-g, 10-a, 11-f

120 1-c, 2-f, 3-i, 4-j, 5-b, 6-k, 7-g, 8-d, 9-a, 10-e, 11-h

121 1-light, 2-firmament; 3-fruit trees, grass, seas; 4-moon, sun, stars; 5-fish, fowl; 6-beast, cattle, male and female, 7-God rested

122 1-c, 2-f, 3-k, 4-h, 5-i, 6-g, 7-j, 8-a, 9-d, 10-b, 11-e

123 1-d, 2-i, 3-e, 4-l, 5-k, 6-j, 7-m, 8-b, 9-f, 10-n, 11-a, 12-h, 13-c, 14-g

124 1-Abner, 2-Laban, 3-Ananias, 4-Herod, 5-Michal, 6-Saul, 7-Eliphaz, 8-Christ, 9-Shechem, 10-Pharaoh, 11-Jacob

125 1-f, 2-j, 3-g, 4-c, 5-b, 6-i, 7-a, 8-e, 9-d, 10-k, 11-h

126 1-g, 2-c, 3-k, 4-h, 5-b, 6-e, 7-f, 8-j, 9-a, 10-i, 11-d

127 1-i, 2-e, 3-b, 4-a, 5-c, 6-j, 7-d, 8-h, 9-g, 10-k, 11-f

128 1-Jeremiah, 2-damsel, 3-Simon, 4-Elymas, 5-Pharaoh, 6-Nebuchadnezzar, 7-king of Babylon, 8-Moses, 9-Saul, 10-Belshazzar, 11-Manasseh

129 1-Gideon, 2-Lazarus, 3-Jezebel, 4-Jesus, 5-Ahab, 6-Jesus, 7-God, 8-Goliath, 9-Ishbosheth, 10-Mephibosheth, 11-Hazael

130 1-Noah, 2-Ham, 3-Shem, 4-Lot, 5-David, 6-Peter, 7-Elah, 8-Hannah, 9-Nabal, 10-Paul, 11-Moses

131 1-Mary Magdalene, Mary, and Salome; 2-the angel of the Lord; 3-Jesus; 4-Soldiers; 5-Mary Magdalene; 6-Peter; 7-John; 8-Mary Magdalene; 9-Cleopas; 10-disciples; 11-Thomas

132 1-ravens, 2-a widow, 3-meal and oil, 4-three, 5-twelve, 6-three, 7-prayed, 8-let him die, 9-a still small voice, 10-fire, 11-mantle, 12-wilderness, 13-whirlwind, 14-rise and eat, 15-7,000

133 1-d, 2-g, 3-k, 4-e, 5-h, 6-j, 7-a, 8-i, 9-f, 10-b, 11-c

134 1-salt, 2-Elijah, 3-raising, 4-Gehazi, 5-Naaman, 6-iron axe head, 7-lepers, 8-chariot, 9-bow and arrows, 10-horses, 11-wash, 12-multiplying her oil, 13-valley full of ditches

135 1-Nahash, 2-Jonathan, 3-Ahijah, 4-Elisha, 5-Zedekiah, 6-Jesus, 7-Daniel, 8-Peter, 9-Saul, 10-Moses, 11-Elisha

136 1-Timothy, Eunice, Lois; 2-Mary, Martha, Lazarus; 3-Adam, Eve, Cain, Abel; 4-Joseph; 5-Jacob, Esau, Isaac, Rebekah; 6-Samuel, Eli; 7-Mary, Joseph; 8-James, John, Zebedee; 9-Miriam, Moses, Aaron; 10-John the Baptist, Zacharias, Elisabeth; 11-Hosea, Gomer, Jezreel, Lo-ruhamah, Loammi

137 1-k, 2-h, 3-j, 4-g, 5-i, 6-e, 7-f, 8-c, 9-d, 10-a, 11-b

138 1-Eli, 2-Elkanah, 3-Jephthah, 4-Abraham, 5-Isaac, 6-David, 7-Mordecai, 8-Kish, 9-Job, 10-Alphaeus, 11-Noah, 12-Enoch

139 1-Thou shalt have no other gods before me, 2-God, 3-fruits of the land, 4-Eliphaz, 5-Darius, 6-Gomer, 7-kingdom of God, 8-remove the beam from our eye, 9-bury his father, 10-fish, 11-Mary Magdalene, 12-Simon, 13-Mary

140 1-e, 2-h, 3-j, 4-k, 5-a, 6-i, 7-c, 8-g, 9-d, 10-f, 11-b

141 1-g, 2-k, 3-i, 4-e, 5-b, 6-h, 7-a, 8-c, 9-f, 10-j, 11-d

142 1-Judah, 2-Jonah, 3-Darius, 4-Abel, 5-Caesar, 6-Shem, 7-Noah, 8-Elias, 9-Issachar, 10-Agrippa, 11-Joseph

143 1-shepherd, 2-thief and a robber, 3-porter, 4-shepherd, 5-stranger, 6-Jesus, 7-Thieves and robbers, 8-man, 9-thief, 10-shepherd, 11-hireling, 12-shepherd, 13-sheep

144 1-e, 2-f, 3-b, 4-j, 5-i, 6-c, 7-a, 8-g, 9-h, 10-k, 11-d

145 1-Esau, 2-Jesus, 3-The Israelites, 4-Ebedmelech, 5-The prodigal son, 6-enemy, 7-Pharisee, 8-Jesus, 9-David, 10-Peter, 11-Jesus

146 1-e, 2-m, 3-g, 4-j, 5-a, 6-k, 7-i, 8-f, 9-b, 10-h, 11-c, 12-d, 13-l

147 1-i, 2-d, 3-e, 4-j, 5-c, 6-g, 7-f, 8-h, 9-a, 10-k, 11-b
148 1-d, 2-g, 3-h, 4-j, 5-i, 6-k,7-a, 8-c, 9-f, 10-e, 11-b
149 1-g, 2-h, 3-k, 4-d, 5-a, 6-j, 7-e, 8-b, 9-f, 10-i, 11-c
150 1-c, 2-h, 3-a, 4-j, 5-i, 6-b, 7-k, 8-d, 9-e, 10-g, 11-f
151 1-colt, 2-drove them out, 3-two mites, 4-an upper room, 5-pitcher of water, 6-pray, 7-thirty, 8-Barabbas, 9-Simon of Cyrene, 10-forgiveness, 11-wine mingled with myrrh, 12-King of the Jews, 13-Joseph of Arimathea
152 1-eleven, 2-coat, 3-dreams, 4-twenty, 5-ruler, 6-dreams, 7-food, 8-spying, 9-bread, 10-life, 11-wagons
153 1-e, 2-i, 3-j, 4-h, 5-a, 6-k, 7-c, 8-g, 9-d, 10-f, 11-b
154 1-Absalom, 2-God, 3-widow, 4-Jesus, 5-Gallio, 6-Moses, 7-Deborah, 8-congregation, 9-king, 10-Solomon, 11-Pharisees
155 1-Jairus's house; 2-Sarah; 3-those who weep; 4-Sennacherib; 5-Sanballat, Tobiah, Geshem; 6-Abraham; 7-Psalmist; 8-wisdom; 9-the wicked; 10-sorrow
156 1-stones, 2-fiery, 3-clothes, 4-scribe, 5-field, 6-praying, 7-priests, 8-fulfill, 9-jot, 10-love the Lord, 11-doers
157 1-e, 2-j, 3-a, 4-f, 5-i, 6-k, 7-d, 8-h, 9-b, 10-g, 11-c
158 1-f, 2-h, 3-a, 4-j, 5-c, 6-i, 7-b, 8-k, 9-e, 10-d, 11-g
159 1-c, 2-g, 3-i, 4-j, 5-b, 6-d, 7-f, 8-k, 9-e, 10-h, 11-a
160 1-killed an Egyptian; 2-burning bush; 3-ten; 4-Passover; 5-a pillar of cloud and pillar of fire; 6-manna; 7-Ten Commandments; 8-smite a rock; 9-choose, train, and use other men; 10-one hundred and twenty; 11-God
161 1-d, 2-k, 3-e, 4-j, 5-f, 6-i, 7-a, 8-h, 9-b, 10-g, 11-c
162 1-i, 2-h, 3-b, 4-g, 5-a, 6-j, 7-f, 8-k, 9-d, 10-e, 11-c
163 1-h, 2-d, 3-c, 4-g, 5-i, 6-b, 7-a, 8-f, 9-j, 10-e
164 1-c, 2-g, 3-f, 4-d, 5-i, 6-j, 7-k, 8-b, 9-h, 10-e, 11-a
165 1-lilies, 2-thorns and thistles, 3-grass, 4-mustard, 5-barley, 6-gourd, 7-coriander, 8-flax, 9-vine, 10-bulrushes, 11-rose
166 1-be done unto you, 2-the desires of thine heart, 3-according to his purpose, 4-out of all their troubles, 5-hear my voice, 6-be opened unto you, 7-thou knowest not, 8-shall be opened, 9-will answer him, 10-we receive of him, 11-believing ye shall receive
167 1-Moses, Moses; 2-Simon, 3-Samuel, 4-Peter, 5-Job, 6-Jesus, 7-Nehemiah, 8-Paul, 9-Paul, 10-Jesus
168 1-c, 2-f, 3-h, 4-a, 5-j, 6-b, 7-k, 8-g, 9-e, 10-i, 11-d
169 1-h, 2-k, 3-d, 4-j, 5-c, 6-i, 7-a, 8-f, 9-b, 10-g, 11-e
170 1-Noah, 2-Elijah, 3-God, 4-Jesus, 5-Paul, 6-Jeremiah, 7-Isaiah, 8-God, 9-Moses, 10-the Israelites, 11-Sodom
171 1-h, 2-g, 3-d, 4-i, 5-f, 6-a, 7-e, 8-j, 9-k, 10-b, 11-c
172 1-Felix, 2-Deborah, 3-Ahaz, 4-Rhoda, 5-Matthew, 6-Hagar, 7-Naaman, 8-Sapphira, 9-Isaiah, 10-Noah, 11-Eli
173 1-Jesus, 2-Jeremiah, 3-seraphim, 4-Jesus, 5-Jesus, 6-Jesus, 7-the psalmist, 8-David, 9-Jesus, 10-Jesus, 11-Elisha
174 1-j, 2-i, 3-b, 4-h, 5-k, 6-a, 7-c, 8-d, 9-f, 10-g, 11-e
175 1-Lois (2 Tim. 1:5), 2-Lot (Gen. 11:27), 3-Rachel (Gen. 29:12), 4-Ruth (Ruth 1:4), 5-Thomas (Matt. 10:3), 6-Abel (Gen. 4:4), 7-Mark (Acts 12:12), 8-Noah (Gen. 5:29), 9-Esther (Esther 2:7), 10-Eli (1 Sam. 1:25), 11-Bathsheba (2 Sam. 11:3)

176 1-f, 2-g, 3-e, 4-h, 5-d, 6-i, 7-c, 8-j, 9-a, 10-k, 11-b

177 1-beds, 2-anointing, 3-markets, 4-anoint, 5-feet, 6-Israelites, 7-The priests, 8-Abimelech, 9-Paul, 10-Jesus, 11-Israel (Jacob)

178 1-Joseph, 2-David, 3-Jesus, 4-David, 5-Isaiah, 6-Nebuchadrezzar, 7-Moses, 8-an angel, 9-Abel, 10-Rachel, 11-Jesus

179 1-ants, 2-conies, 3-spider's web, 4-locusts, 5-bees, 6-fly and bee, 7-gnat, 8-hornets, 9-flea, 10-mice, 11-lice

180 1-f, 2-k, 3-j, 4-a, 5-g, 6-b, 7-i, 8-c, 9-e, 10-h, 11-d

181 1-raiment, 2-fire, 3-garments, 4-water, 5-wine, 6-perfume, 7-perfume, 8-battle, 9-ointment of spikenard, 10-gifts, 11-grapes

182 1-Peter, 2-Paul, 3-Eutychus, 4-Joab, 5-Solomon, 6-Job, 7-the Psalmist, 8-Solomon, 9-Jesus, 10-Paul

183 1-e, 2-h, 3-f, 4-k, 5-a, 6-b, 7-g, 8-i, 9-d, 10-c, 11-j

184 1-k, 2-i, 3-e, 4-a, 5-c, 6-d, 7-j, 8-g, 9-h, 10-b, 11-f

185 1-i, 2-d, 3-k, 4-c, 5-j, 6-f, 7-b, 8-g, 9-e, 10-a, 11-h

186 1-Tubal-cain, 2-God, 3-image, 4-Jesus, 5-Jews, 6-Barnabas and Simeon, 7-women, 8-Jesus, 9-Peter, 10-John, 11-Comforter

187 1-one-third of a shekel; 2-casting lots; 3-burn upon the altar; 4-vegetables, fruits, herbs, flocks, and dough; 5-the son of Aaron; 6-fled to their fields; 7-they did not receive their portions; 8-gathered the people; 9-testified against them; 10-shut the gates; 11-Solomon

188 1-g, 2-i, 3-h, 4-k, 5-b, 6-a, 7-c, 8-e, 9-f, 10-j, 11-d

189 1-j, 2-k, 3-d, 4-i, 5-c, 6-f, 7-h, 8-g, 9-a, 10-e, 11-b

190 1-Paul and Silas; 2-the disciples; 3-Moses and the Israelites; 4-those victorious over the beast; 5-the Israelites; 6-Deborah and Barak; 7-Saul and David; 8-Hezekiah; 9-David and Asaph; 10-Jezrahiah; 11-God

191 1-Ishmael, 2-Israelites, 3-Enemies, 4-Jesus, 5-Samaritan, 6-Sisera, 7-the psalmist, 8-Paul, 9-The rich man, 10-Abraham's, 11-Samson, 12-David

192 1-f, 2-l, 3-n, 4-c, 5-j, 6-m, 7-g, 8-b, 9-k, 10-e, 11-i, 12-d, 13-h, 14-a

193 1-lying, 2-wholesome, 3-naughty, 4-backbiting, 5-stammering, 6-false, 7-froward, 8-deceitful, 9-soft, 10-slow, 11-perverse

194 1-g, 2-k, 3-j, 4-c, 5-i, 6-b, 7-e, 8-h, 9-a, 10-f, 11-d

195 1-cup and platter, 2-bowl, 3-pot, 4-basin, 5-pitcher, 6-pans, 7-candlestick, 8-cruse, 9-vial, 10-kneadingtroughs, 11-baskets, 12-spoons

196 1-k, 2-e, 3-g, 4-h, 5-a, 6-j, 7-d, 8-i, 9-b, 10-f, 11-c

197 1-Jericho, 2-Tyrus, 3-Jerusalem, 4-Jerusalem, 5-Babylon, 6-house, 7-Jerusalem, 8-Judah, 9-water, 10-vineyard, 11-Beth-shan, 12-Aphek, 13-Jezreel

198 1-d, 2-j, 3-i, 4-e, 5-h, 6-b, 7-k, 8-c, 9-f, 10-g, 11-a

199 1-d, 2-e, 3-j, 4-k, 5-a, 6-i, 7-c, 8-g, 9-b, 10-h, 11-f

200 1-ground, 2-sticks, 3-stone, 4-plaster, 5-finger, 6-heart, 7-forehead, 8-posts and gates, 9-roll and pen, 10-rod, 11-table

201 1-k, 2-e, 3-h, 4-f, 5-a, 6-i, 7-j, 8-c, 9-g, 10-b, 11-d

202 1-f, 2-k, 3-g, 4-b, 5-j, 6-a, 7-e, 8-i, 9-c, 10-h, 11-d

203 1-j, 2-e, 3-g, 4-d, 5-b, 6-k, 7-c, 8-h, 9-i, 10-f, 11-a

204 1-Ezra, 2-Zophar, 3-Israel, 4-A steward, 5-Paul, 6-Moab, 7-Jerusalem, 8-The prophets, 9-Paul, 10-David

205 1-Build three tabernacles; 2-Went back to sleep and dreamed again; 3-His hair was cut, and God had left him; 4-Gave burnt offerings and made a feast; 5-They were afraid of

dying; 6-The child was dead; 7-Cry aloud; 8-Erected an altar; 9-They thought Lazarus was merely asleep; 10-Kill himself

206 1-He was blind; 2-Jericho; 3-Timaeus; 4-"Jesus, thou son of David, have mercy on me"; 5-Be quiet (hold his peace); 6-Cried louder; 7-Cast off his outer garment, got up, and went to Jesus; 8-Restore his sight; 9-Gave him sight; 10-Go your way; your faith has healed you; 11-Followed Jesus

207 1-i, 2-g, 3-h, 4-f, 5-a, 6-j, 7-d, 8-b, 9-e, 10-c

208 1-Joseph's, 2-Moses, 3-David, 4-Shimei, 5-Baal's prophets, 6-The Moabites, 7-Peter, 8-The chief priests, 9-Jesus, 10-The high priest, 11-Pilate

209 1-Hilkiah, 2-Shaphan, 3-Josiah, 4-Ezekiel, 5-Moses, 6-Ezra, 7-Ahasuerus, 8-Baruch, 9-Ezekiel, 10-Isaiah, 11-Moses, 12-John

210 1-Melchizedek, 2-Hagar, 3-The Egyptians, 4-Joseph, 5-God, 6-Jesse, 7-David, 8-Obadiah, 9-Elisha, 10-Nehemiah, 11-The disciples, 12-John the Baptist

211 1-j, 2-i, 3-h, 4-e, 5-a, 6-g, 7-f, 8-k, 9-d, 10-b, 11-c

212 1-His garments, 2-Psalmist, 3-Aaron, 4-Joshua, 5-Saul, 6-Jonathan, 7-Their enemies, 8-Jerusalem, 9-To see who was causing the storm, 10-Jonah, 11-Nineveh, 12-Gatekeepers, 13-Matthias

213 1-m, 2-i, 3-h, 4-d, 5-c, 6-e, 7-f, 8-b, 9-a, 10-g, 11-j, 12-l, 13-k

214 1-c, 2-h, 3-b, 4-f, 5-g, 6-j, 7-d, 8-i, 9-e, 10-a

215 1-j, 2-c, 3-d, 4-b, 5-g, 6-e, 7-i, 8-k, 9-h, 10-f, 11-a

216 1-e, 2-f, 3-k, 4-c, 5-h, 6-g, 7-i, 8-d, 9-j, 10-a, 11-b

217 1-Gopher, 2-Brick and slime, 3-Stones, 4-Cedars, 5-Stones, 6-Wood, 7-Olive trees, 8-Stone, 9-Brass, 10-Pearls and gold, 11-Straw, 12-Bulrushes, 13-Fir trees

218 1-During the plague of darkness, 2-Before God created light, 3-Abraham, 4-When the Israelites were fleeing from the Egyptians, 5-At Jesus' crucifixion, 6-At the giving of the Ten Commandments, 7-In the last days, 8-When Elymas tried to turn a man away from the faith, 9-Rahab, 10-So no one could bring in merchandise on the sabbath, 11-Mary Magdalene

219 1-Caleb, 2-Saul, 3-Solomon, 4-David, 5-Daniel, 6-Saul, 7-Isaac, 8-Goliath, 9-Joshua, 10-Caesar, 11-Rachel, 12-Joshua

220 1-k, 2-i, 3-f, 4-g, 5-c, 6-h, 7-d, 8-e, 9-a, 10-j, 11-l, 12-b

221 1-Nebuchadrezzar, 2-Pharaoh, 3-John, 4-Job, 5-Jerusalem, 6-Babylon, 7-Leviathan, 8-Wine, 9-Wind, 10-Beast

222 1-d, 2-e, 3-j, 4-a, 5-f, 6-b, 7-k, 8-h, 9-c, 10-i, 11-g

223 1-Pilate's wife, 2-Wise Men, 3-Saul, 4-Job, 5-False prophets, 6-False prophets, 7-Nebuchadnezzar's captives from Babylon, 8-Ungodly men, 9-Nations that fight against Mount Zion, 10-Pharaoh's chief baker, 11-Joseph, 12-God, 13-Abimelech

224 1-With his mantel, 2-Ravens, 3-Stretched himself upon the child three times and prayed, 4-He would burn the sacrifice on the altar, 5-In a field plowing, 6-Elisha, 7-Jezebel wanted to kill him, 8-To die, 9-The same dogs which licked the blood of Naboth would lick Ahab's blood, 10-He would not get off his sick bed but would die, 11-Three

225 1-With salt, 2-Multiplied her oil supply, 3-Built and furnished a room for him, 4-Added meal to it, 5-Go wash in the River Jordan seven times, 6-Cast a stick into the water, and the axe head floated, 7-Caused him to be blind, 8-Bow and arrows, 9-Will I recover from my disease?, 10-Elisha was telling the king of Israel what the Syrians were saying, 11-She would have a son

226 1-f, 2-j, 3-e, 4-k, 5-a, 6-g, 7-c, 8-h, 9-d, 10-b

227 1-c, cc; 2-i, ii; 3-h, bb; 4-j, jj, 5-f, gg; 6-b, hh; 7-e, aa; 8-g, dd; 9-a, ff; 10-d, ee

228 1-Mary, 2-Ruth, 3-Abigail, 4-Mephibosheth, 5-Asa, 6-Jairus, 7-Jesus, 8-Mary, 9-Peter, 10-John the Baptist, 11-Agabus

229 1-k, 2-d, 3-g, 4-i, 5-h, 6-c, 7-a, 8-b, 9-f, 10-e

230 1-Days, 2-Righteous men, 3-Baths, 4-Stripes, 5-Days, 6-Years, 7-Sons, 8-Camels' burdens, 9-Stripes, 10-Days, 11-Horsemen

231 1-Doves, 2-Ravens, 3-Sparrow, 4-Ravens, 5-Dove, 6-Cock, 7-Ostrich, 8-Eagles, 9-Eagles', 10-Doves, 11-Dove, 12-Turtledoves and pigeons

232 1-h, 2-e, 3-j, 4-i, 5-d, 6-a, 7-f, 8-b, 9-g, 10-c

233 1-f, 2-h, 3-k, 4-a, 5-j, 6-g, 7-e, 8-i, 9-c, 10-d, 11-b

234 1-Water, 2-Chain, 3-Bells, 4-Gifts, 5-Ring, 6-Targets, 7-Image, 8-Doors, 9-Vessels, 10-Sceptre, 11-Candlesticks, 12-Streets

235 1-Esau, 2-Elisha, 3-Sinful woman, 4-John the Baptist, 5-Nebuchadnezzar, 6-Absalom, 7-Samson, 8-Nazarite, 9-Nehemiah, 10-Eliphaz, 11-Jesus

236 1-Ahithophel, 2-Absalom, 3-Judas, 4-Jesus, 5-Haman, 6-Joseph, 7-Joshua, 8-David, 9-Mephibosheth, 10-Moses

237 1-Outward appearance; 2-Soul, mind; 3-Meditation, Acceptable; 4-Word, sin; 5-Believeth, righteousness, salvation; 6-Trust, understanding; 7-Pure, see; 8-Troubled, believe; 9-Wisdom, understanding; 10-No God

238 1-f, 2-c, 3-a, 4-h, 5-e, 6-d, 7-b, 8-k, 9-g, 10-i, 11-j

239 1-Elements, Earth, 2-Viper; 3-This time; 4-Tent door; 5-Anger; 6-Day; 7-Covered; 8-Nothing; 9-Lie; 10-Furnace

240 1-f, 2-e, 3-g, 4-j, 5-d, 6-b, 7-c, 8-h, 9-i, 10-a

241 1-Demon-possessed man, 2-They were not sharing their own food, 3-John, 4-A lost sheep was found, 5-A sick servant, 6-His outer garment, 7-They felt Joseph thought they had stolen money, 8-The Egyptians because hail was coming, 9-When he married, 10-To fulfill a covenant, 11-His counsel was not followed, 12-God had charged him not to

242 1-Martha, 2-Simon, 3-Mary, 4-Justus, 5-Jason, 6-Paul, 7-Priscilla and Aquilla, 8-Jacob, 9-Obed-edom, 10-Solomon, 11-Joab

243 1-e, 2-h, 3-l, 4-k, 5-c, 6-a, 7-g, 8-j, 9-m, 10-d, 11-b, 12-i, 13-f

244 1-d, 2-l, 3-h, 4-k, 5-e, 6-b, 7-i, 8-c, 9-a, 10-g, 11-f, 12-j

245 1-Abraham, 2-Job, 3-Pharaoh, 4-The father, 5-Gideon, 6-Tamar, 7-Haman, 8-Saul, 9-Saul, 10-Aaron

246 1-j, 2-h, 3-i, 4-c, 5-g, 6-a, 7-e, 8-f, 9-b, 10-d

247 1-c, 2-i, 3-b, 4-j, 5-h, 6-g, 7-e, 8-d, 9-a, 10-f, 11-k

248 1-Herodias, 2-Naomi, 3-Eunice and Lois, 4-Miriam, 5-Dinah, 6-Deborah, 7-Lot's wife, 8-Rebekah, 9-Gomer, 10-Hagar

249 1-Spoils, 2-Linen, 3-Girdles, 4-Sew, 5-Thread, 6-Needle, 7-Spun, 8-Beam, 9-Fig leaves, 10-Firmament

250 1-9, 2-16, 3-20, 4-25, 5-27, 6-23, 7-8, 8-2, 9-26, 10-22, 11-24, 12-5, 13-17, 14-10, 15-4, 16-12, 17-6, 18-3, 19-14, 20-11, 21-19, 22-1, 23-15, 24-18, 25-13, 26-21, 27-7

251 1-c, 2-d, 3-k, 4-f, 5-a, 6-b, 7-j, 8-h, 9-g, 10-i, 11-e

252 1-10, 2-18, 3-21, 4-28, 5-14, 6-32, 7-29, 8-34, 9-4, 10-20, 11-30, 12-37, 13-8, 14-5, 15-16, 16-12, 17-22, 18-39, 19-27, 20-1, 21-38, 22-31, 23-36, 24-13, 25-25, 26-6, 27-19, 28-23, 29-2, 30-17, 31-26, 32-9, 33-33, 34-7, 35-35, 36-24, 37-15, 38-11, 39-3

253 1-k, 2-j, 3-f, 4-a, 5-d, 6-b, 7-e, 8-i, 9-c, 10-h, 11-g

254 1-Hill, 2-Seir, 3-Vineyard, 4-Flocks, 5-Canaan, 6-Ar, 7-Cloak, 8-Mites, 9-Meal, 10-Ship, 11-Colt, 12-House

255 1-c, 2-k, 3-d, 4-l, 5-a, 6-j, 7-b, 8-i, 9-g, 10-e, 11-m, 12-f, 13-h

256 1-Heart; 2-Eye; 3-Tongue; 4-Mouth; 5-Mouth, lips; 6-Face; 7-Tooth, foot; 8-Hand, hand; 9-Lips, ear, tongue; 10-Mouth, lips

257 1-Place, 2-Person, 3-Place, 4-Person, 5-Thing (month), 6-Place, 7-Person, 8-Person, 9-Person, 10-Person, 11-Thing (tree)

258 1-g, 2-c, 3-a, 4-k, 5-f, 6-d, 7-b, 8-h, 9-e, 10-i, 11-j

259 1-Joseph, 2-Korah, 3-Sodom and Gomorrah, 4-The Israelites, 5-Absalom, 6-Benaiah, 7-Ishmael, 8-Jesus, 9-Satan, 10-Reuben, 11-Solomon

260 1-c, 2-j, 3-f, 4-g, 5-b, 6-k, 7-d, 8-h, 9-e, 10-a, 11-i

261 1-j, 2-e, 3-g, 4-f, 5-b, 6-a, 7-h, 8-i, 9-c, 10-d

262 1-His disciples, 2-Fear, 3-Gospel of Christ, salvation, 4-Moses, 5-Jesus, 6-Wealth, 7-Anger, 8-Faint, 9-Earth, 10-Daniel, 11-Worship him, 12-The Holy Spirit

263 1-Caleb, 2-Jacob, 3-God, 4-Saul, 5-Abraham, 6-Esau, 7-Rahab, 8-Jacob, 9-Saul, 10-Jesus, 11-The devil

264 1-f, 2-j, 3-h, 4-a, 5-g, 6-c, 7-k, 8-i, 9-d, 10-b, 11-e

265 1-j, 2-h, 3-i, 4-c, 5-f, 6-b, 7-k, 8-e, 9-d, 10-a, 11-g

266 1-Joshua, 2-The rich man, 3-Jesus, 4-David, 5-Jesus, 6-A would-be follower of Jesus, 7-Jesus, 8-Isaiah, 9-Jesus

267 1-e, 2-f, 3-b, 4-g, 5-i, 6-j, 7-d, 8-c, 9-a, 10-h

268 1-c, 2-j, 3-d, 4-i, 5-f, 6-e, 7-h, 8-k, 9-g, 10-a, 11-b

269 1-Jesus, 2-Saul, 3-Some seed, 4-Moses, 5-Gideon, 6-Jonathan, 7-Shebna, 8-Jeremiah, 9-The Lord's, 10-Peter, 11-Joseph of Arimathaea, 12-Amaziah

270 1-Ahaziah, 2-Ahab, 3-Herod, 4-Nebuchadnezzar, 5-Absalom, 6-Rehoboam, 7-David, 8-Queen of Sheba, 9-Candace, 10-Vashti, 11-Herodias, 12-Jeroboam

271 1-Lot, 2-Moses, 3-David, 4-Israel, 5-Judah, 6-Abimelech, 7-David, 8-Elisha, 9-Darius, 10-Priests, 11-Speech

272 1-100, 2-969, 3-85, 4-137, 5-500, 6-187, 7-127, 8-110, 9-83, 10-123, 11-98, 12-120, 13-80, 14-60, 15-62

273 1-d, 2-k, 3-g, 4-j, 5-f, 6-c, 7-e, 8-h, 9-b, 10-a, 11-i

274 1-g, 2-d, 3-f, 4-a, 5-c, 6-h, 7-b, 8-k, 9-e, 10-j, 11-i

275 1-Laban, 2-David, 3-Solomon, 4-David, 5-Elihu, 6-David, 7-Solomon, 8-Hezekiah, 9-Tyre, 10-Amos

276 1-j, 2-d, 3-b, 4-f, 5-h, 6-a, 7-c, 8-g, 9-i, 10-e

277 1-Moses, 2-Joshua and Caleb, 3-Elisha, 4-Rahab, 5-Micah, 6-David's servants, 7-Joseph, 8-Absalom, 9-priests and scribes, 10-Herod, 11-Delilah

278 1-Aaron, 2-David, 3-Joseph, 4-Moses, 5-Jonathan, 6-Saul, 7-Saul, 8-Jehoshaphat, 9-Job, 10-Micah, 11-Jesus, 12-The good Samaritan

279 1-e, 2-c, 3-h, 4-g, 5-b, 6-d, 7-k, 8-i, 9-j, 10-f, 11-a

280 1-h, 2-d, 3-i, 4-k, 5-e, 6-c, 7-b, 8-j, 9-g, 10-f, 11-a

281 1-Hezekiah, 2-Job, 3-David, 4-David, 5-Sow, 6-Jeremiah, 7-Jeremiah, 8-Ezekiel, 9-Judah, 10-Father, 11-Paul, 12-Esau

282 1-h, 2-f, 3-i, 4-a, 5-j, 6-g, 7-l, 8-c, 9-b, 10-d, 11-e, 12-k

283 1-Noah, 2-Jael, 3-Lot, 4-Isaac, 5-Rachel, 6-Moses, 7-Gideon, 8-David, 9-Balaam, 10-Absalom, 11-Bela, 12-Sarah

284 1-f, 2-c, 3-h, 4-i, 5-d, 6-k, 7-a, 8-g, 9-j, 10-e, 11-b, 12-m, 13-l

285 1-k, 2-d, 3-a, 4-c, 5-b, 6-f, 7-e, 8-i, 9-g, 10-j, 11-h

286 1-f, 2-k, 3-g, 4-j, 5-d, 6-l, 7-b, 8-c, 9-m, 10-h, 11-a, 12-e, 13-i

287 1-T, 2-T, 3-F, 4-T, 5-F, 6-T, 7-F, 8-T, 9-T, 10-F, 11-T, 12-T

288 1-d, 2-g, 3-i, 4-k, 5-j, 6-a, 7-h, 8-e, 9-f, 10-b, 11-c

289 1-Judah, 2-Issachar, 3-Zebulun, 4-Reuben, 5-Gad, 6-Simeon, 7-Ephraim, 8-Manasseh, 9-Benjamin, 10-Dan, 11-Asher, 12-Naphtali

290 1-Pence, 2-Mites, 3-Coats, 4-Calves, 5-Omers, 6-Turtledoves, 7-Trumpets, 8-Lines, 9-Covenants, 10-Bears, 11-Sticks, 12-Olive Trees

291 1-Paul, 2-Adam and Eve, 3-Bildad, 4-Onesiphorus, 5-Jesus, 6-God, 7-Believers (Little children), 8-Peter, 9-Workers, 10-Paul, 11-Isaiah

292 1-Horse, 2-Wine, 3-Sheep's, 4-Treasure, 5-Manners, 6-Pearls, 7-Understanding, 8-Sleep, 9-Day, 10-Soul, 11-Answer

293 1-Shamgar, 2-Gibeah, 3-Moses, 4-Samson, 5-Gideon, 6-Isaiah, 7-Jesus, 8-Jonah, 9-Peter, 10-Aaron, 11-Moses and Aaron, 12-Elisha

294 1-k, 2-i, 3-h, 4-j, 5-f, 6-g, 7-e, 8-c, 9-b, 10-d, 11-a

295 1-d, 2-f, 3-j, 4-g, 5-k, 6-e, 7-h, 8-b, 9-c, 10-i, 11-a

296 1-Adam, 2-God, 3-Barzillai, 4-Sheep, 5-Jesus, 6-Peter, 7-Rhoda, 8-Moses, 9-Saul, 10-Asaph, 11-Rachel

297 1-Sisera, 2-Jael, 3-Joshua, 4-Moses, 5-Phinehas, 6-David, 7-Abner, 8-Peter, 9-Levite, 10-Paul, 11-Jehu

298 1-Dew, 2-Thunder and hail, 3-Lightning, 4-Wind, 5-Whirlwind, 6-Rainbow, 7-Drought and frost, 8-Earthquake, 9-Hailstorm, 10-Rain, 11-Snow

299 1-River, 2-City, 3-City, 4-Mountain, 5-Island, 6-City, 7-City, 8-Mountain, 9-City, 10-Island, 11-Mountain, 12-City, 13-Island

300 1-d, 2-c, 3-h, 4-j, 5-k, 6-e, 7-a, 8-f, 9-b, 10-g, 11-i

301 1-g, 2-e, 3-d, 4-c, 5-a, 6-j, 7-f, 8-h, 9-b, 10-i

302 1-Eutychus, 2-Rahab, 3-Noah, 4-Jezebel, 5-Joash, 6-Abimelech, 7-Sisera, 8-Michal, 9-Daniel, 10-God, 11-Nineveh

303 1-j, 2-k, 3-g, 4-f, 5-i, 6-b, 7-c, 8-h, 9-d, 10-e, 11-a